Historical studies in international corporate business

Historical studies in international corporate business

Edited by

ALICE TEICHOVA

Emeritus Professor of Economic History, University of East Anglia

MAURICE LÉVY-LEBOYER

Professor of Economic History, Université de Paris-Nanterre

and

HELGA NUSSBAUM

Emeritus Professor of Economic History
Akademie der Wissenschaften der DDR

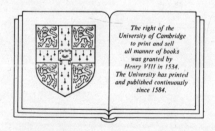

The right of the
University of Cambridge
to print and sell
all manner of books
was granted by
Henry VIII in 1534.
The University has printed
and published continuously
since 1584.

CAMBRIDGE UNIVERSITY PRESS

Cambridge New York New Rochelle Melbourne Sydney

& ÉDITIONS DE LA MAISON DES SCIENCES DE
L'HOMME

Paris

Published by the Press Syndicate of the University of Cambridge
The Pitt Building, Trumpington Street, Cambridge CB2 1RP
32 East 57th Street, New York, NY 10022, USA
10 Stamford Road, Oakleigh, Melbourne 3166, Australia

First published 1989

Printed in Great Britain by The University Press, Cambridge

British Library cataloguing in publication data
Historical studies in international corporate business.
   1. Multinational companies, to 1985
   I. Teichova, Alice   II. Lévy-Leboyer, Maurice, *1920–*   III. Nussbaum, Helga
   338·8′8′09

Library of Congress cataloguing in publication data
Historical studies in international corporate business / edited by Alice Teichova,
Maurice Lévy-Leboyer, and Helga Nussbaum.
      p. cm.
      "Papers submitted to the section 'Debates and controversies' at the Ninth
International Economic History Congress, which was held in Berne, Switzerland,
in August 1986"–Pref.
      Includes index.
      ISBN 0 521 35600 8
      1. International business enterprises–Congresses.
   2. International business enterprises–Finance–Congresses.
   I. Teichova, Alice.   II. Lévy-Leboyer, Maurice.   III. Nussbaum, Helga.
   IV. International Congress on Economic History (9th: 1986: Berne, Switzerland)
   HD2755.5.H56   1988
   338.8′8–dc19   88–16927

ISBN 0 521 35600 8

UP

Contents

Preface

The editors have great pleasure in presenting the second volume of papers submitted to the section 'Debates and controversies' at the Ninth International Economic History Congress which was held in Berne, Switzerland, in August 1986 on the theme 'Multinational enterprise: international finance, markets and governments in the twentieth century'. It complements the first volume, *Multinational enterprise in historical perspective* (Cambridge, 1986), by raising further theoretical questions, by inquiring into aspects of international corporate business such as research and development, financial operations, common and diverging policies of business and governments, by comparing multinational activities in different industries (e.g. mass-produced consumer goods) and by extending the geographical area to China, Japan and Latin America.

The editors wish to thank all authors of contributions and the many discussants who took part in the meetings at Berne. The assistance of Valerie Striker of the University of East Anglia in assembling the papers is gratefully acknowledged. Warm thanks are due to William Davies and his staff at the Cambridge University Press for getting the first volume out in time for the Congress and for supporting the preparation of this volume for publication. It is hoped that the present book will prove to engender the same wide interest which the first volume enjoyed.

1 Introduction: multinational enterprise

BARRY SUPPLE

So much work has already gone into this theme, and so many accomplished experts have contributed papers on the general and theoretical, as well as on the detailed and empirical question of multinational enterprises, that there hardly appears much scope for a further contribution. And yet the sheer volume and variety of submissions – evidence of the pervasive significance of the topic as well as of the persistence of the organisers of this session – mean that some search for main issues might be useful. Looking through the contributions on multinational enterprises produced for this Congress, it is not difficult to detect a small number of themes which recur, and are worth emphasising.

I

The initial point is perhaps an obvious one. It concerns the role of historical research. The problem of multinational firms actually existed in the contemporaneous world of economic observation and political anxiety before it became a fully-fledged and explicit topic of historical inquiry. As with other questions in applied economics (inflation, for example, or economic development), it soon became clear that not only did multinationals have a history, they also only *exist* in history. The historian's task, then, became the essential one of empirical elucidation: to examine the origins of multinational enterprise and investment, to produce a typology of such activities, and to suggest (through case-studies and comparative work) answers to such questions as: Why do multinational enterprises evolve? What explains the varying forms they take? What have been the determinants of their success and failure? What economic and political repercussions have they had on their 'host' countries?

Before turning to some of these specific issues, it is worth drawing attention to the almost inevitable methodological consequences of recruiting History to such a task.

First, historians discovered (or, rather, reminded themselves) that

1

multinationals were by no means a new phenomenon in the 1960s – or even in the twentieth century. Examples of firms whose investments and activities transcended national boundaries could, indeed, be identified in very early times. However, in terms of the issues which are most relevant to the question in the later twentieth century, the effective origins of modern multinationals lay in the second half of the nineteenth century. For it was then that the growth of large-scale corporations (especially manufacturing firms) coincided with the emergence of an international economy. And it was this coincidence which stimulated the diffused extension of international activity beyond the contractual structures of the market or the authoritarian boundaries of state activity.

The second result of exploring the historical dimension was a reminder of the cosmopolitan nature of the subject. The point which was emphasised and has since been extensively elaborated was that multinational activity was decidedly not devised by American companies in the 1960s. Rather, West Europe generally and Britain in particular have figured very prominently in the century or more of modern history in which multinationals have flourished. This fact, in turn, had two broad implications.

On the one hand, the development of multinational enterprise, although still a relatively late phase in the long evolution of capitalism, has not been *distinct* from the trends which have characterised modern industrialism since the mid-nineteenth century. Instead, it has been intimately bound up with the emergence of the modern firm and the modern international economy. On the other hand, the suspicion of American economic 'imperialism', or anxieties about the monopolistic tendency in mature capitalism, which played such an important role in the conceptual identification of the multinational company in the 1960s, may well have been misplaced. For the phenomenon has, in a sense, been omnipresent. In itself, then, it does not represent a higher (perhaps even the final) stage of capitalism. At the same time, however, it might still be possible to argue (as I shall suggest in a moment) that, even though the multinational enterprise has been an integral part of international economic growth for over 100 years, its more *recent* flowering indicates a new phase. Yet the fact remains that, unless we are to believe that the modern state never had an independent existence, there has clearly been no *linear* trend towards political control or the erosion of sovereignty by multinational companies. Instead, their history has been one of variety and of oscillation between dependence and assertion, autarky and internationalism, free markets and managed economies.

The third consequence of the particular historiography of multinationals is a rather more methodological one, and is well illustrated in the abundance and diversity of papers submitted for this theme. Given the ingenuity of historians and the empirical abundance of the past, the 'lesson' of history appears to be that the reality of things is much more complicated than 'theory', or attempts at theorising, would lead us to expect. Useful and systematic generalisation seems almost impossible. Yet this is hardly surprising: in the 'real world' which history attempts to describe, simple categorisations rarely exist; everything *does* seem connected with everything else; dense variety seems universal. As so often happens, the outcome of historical research is the paradoxical conclusion that while the past is a seamless web, individual institutions are also distinctive. On both scores – the obstacles to conceptualisation and the uniqueness of phenomena – history (as always) undermines the drive towards theory. And in the case of multinational enterprises, it blurs the distinctions and characteristics, the causal chains and explanations, which the desire for conceptual clarity presupposes.

II

Against this rather general background, it is also possible to distinguish a number of more specific issues relating to the question of multinational enterprise as it emerges from the literature presented to the Congress held in Bern in August 1986.

The first, and most fundamental, point is of course the definitional one. What, exactly, are we talking about when we refer to multinational enterprise? And even if we can adequately specify an institutional form, is it *sufficiently* different from other modes of behaviour to justify close conceptual analysis?

This issue is in many respects similar to the debate about the conceptual distinctiveness of international economic theory. Indeed, even more strikingly than in the case of international as against national markets and trading, the question arises as to whether *explanations* of the growth of international firms are conceptually very different from explanations of the growth of the firm in general. It is, after all, striking that concepts such as market internalisation, the control of transaction costs, and the harbouring of returns from technical and managerial advantages, can all be used indifferently to explain the growth of firms (and of internalised and non-contractual relationships) *within* a national economy as well as across national boundaries. In fact, and as with theories of international trade, the essential difference – the consideration which might justify the separate treatment of multinational enterprises – is, precisely, the existence of contrasting *national* economic arrangements, and of political boundaries with the concomitant assertion of economic control, or of devices to avoid its consequences.

Multinational firms are therefore worth studying at a different level from intra-national firms because their activities bridge markets which are more *obviously* separated from each other (by distinctive currencies, laws, controls, capital and labour supplies, and institutions) than are the markets *within* particular countries.

The fact that multinational firms encompass transactions which were formerly mediated by more purely market institutions raises two related points of considerable significance for historians. First, to what extent do they represent a distinctive stage of economic evolution? Second, what are the implications of the growth of multinational enterprises for the political economy of the modern state?

As economists and contemporary historians remind us, modern multi-nationals now tend to predominate in technology-intensive industries, providing closely integrated packages of scarce technology, capital and associated managerial skills. It was not always so, and until 1914 – perhaps until the 1960s – resource-based international firms, or multinational enterprises with an effective command of mobile investment funds, tended to be much more important. This is not to deny that some 'core' characteristics have remained more or less unchanged (the management of international capital or technology flows, for example). But both the relative importance and the orientation of multinationals have obviously changed in the last quarter of a century – and with them has changed the nature of economic decision-making in the *developed* world.

There is, of course, a question as to whether the resulting internalisation of markets may have had outcomes as 'rational' as those produced by 'external' and more competitive markets. From the perspective of the 'host' countries, however, once multinationals attain a large size, there is an apparently greater volatility of economic processes, an easier circumvention of local market and institutional conditions, more abrupt changes in the flow of investment and economic activity. At one level it might be argued that all this represents an artificial and deleterious influence, since the operation of multinationals, by transcending national boundaries, has 'distorting' effects on patterns of employment, investment and industrial location. The overt business policies of individual firms, and above all of firms with an international base, is now a much more critical consideration in the performance of industrialised economies.

On the other hand, and assuming that multinational firms are primarily influenced by costs, prices, and profit-motives, the internalisation of markets may indeed make for a more 'rational' or *effective international* allocation of resources and economic activities than would have obtained if production and trade had been managed solely by contractual relationships. This is because such contractual relationships would have to encounter the imperfections of transnational markets for factors of production, goods and services. They would be impeded by tariffs and laws, controls and national institutions. In this sense the enormous growth in multinational enterprise may therefore well have shaped what Dr Cantwell calls a 'global capitalism'. In other words, the unusually rapid growth of multinational networks may be tipping the balance to a new, *and much more cosmopolitan*, pattern of decision-taking. And although the outcome for individual national economies may be a greater vulnerability to economic fluctuations and structural changes, the overall result may (paradoxically) be a closer approximation to the theoretical world of market economics and mobile resources.

This also has implications for the 'remoter' history of multinationals in the nineteenth century. For example, to what extent did they contribute to the overcoming of barriers to the cosmopolitan operation of the emerging world economy? Is it possible that the creation of an international economy in the late nineteenth century was as much dependent on the growth of multinational firms (in service as well as primary and secondary industries) as on the easing of market contracts and transactions? Were markets extended through the expansion of the firm *across frontiers* rather than the proliferation of individual firms, contracts and competition?

A good deal of historical research, like economic theorising, has gone into explaining the origins and processes by which multinational firms have grown over the last century or so. And this is an undoubtedly important issue. But it is at least equally important to explore the varying consequences of the *existence* of such firms, as distinct from the prolongation of markets, contracts and institutional distinctions between different economies.

All this primarily concerns the multinational enterprise as a market phenomenon. But, as is widely accepted, it is misleading – even unreal – to concentrate on economic relationships alone. A good deal of the historical contribution to the discussion of multinationals makes it clear that intermingled with the 'internationalism' which characterised their activities were the national anxieties and resentments at 'foreignisation' of economic activity. Operating across national boundaries and in varying institutional settings is, after all, a political as much as an economic process; and its apparent 'economic' consequences can have predominantly 'political' effects in terms of local reactions to the concentration of decision-taking and specific patterns of investment, employment, production, and trade. Alternatively, the sheer scale and scope of multinational enterprises operating within relatively less well developed societies, has frequently given such firms a disproportionate political and social role.

I end these comments, therefore, on an obvious but I hope useful note. Multinational enterprise may, after all, be a matter for political economy rather than economic theory. Hence the fact that, conceptually speaking, multinationals and foreign direct investment may not be easily distinguishable from 'ordinary' firms and 'normal' capital accumulation and investment is not necessarily significant. Given the new-found concern of economists with institutional analysis, and the enduring interest of historians in the interlocking of economic, social and political considerations, we may well be able to accept without intellectual guilt that the central features of multinational enterprise have, in the last resort, been their political and institutional implications.

2 History, the social sciences and economic 'theory', with special reference to multinational enterprise

EDITH PENROSE

The foreign (or international) firm, the multinational (or transnational) corporation, the multinational enterprise, are among the many names applied to the same complex economic organisation – an organisation which is neither a firm nor a corporation in the normal economic or legal sense, which may be incorporated domestically and only partly foreign-owned, which nevertheless is not international since it normally has a single nationality (although there are the few rare cases where its parentage is indeed multinational). It is not entirely within the jurisdiction of any single government. To the extent that the multinational enterprise dominates major international industries it has its roots in the industrialised developed world and thus early came to express in many ways in its own being both the pervasive interdependence of countries and their drive for independence, the positive and negative aspects of economic imperialism, a beacon for economic development and a siren call to a false path.

To describe it or to attempt 'to penetrate its nature' while looking at it from the point of view of any one of the social sciences, including economic history, is an exercise reminiscent of that of the proverbial blind men describing the elephant some part of which each touches: the observations are all valid but even when all are taken together the 'nature' of 'the' elephant is still not understood.

I include economic history among the crowd of blind men despite the fact that of all the sciences it takes (or rather its practitioners are in principle qualified to take) the broadest view of social phenomena. But at the same time, economic historians can only ask relevant questions of the past with the help of other social sciences, just as other social sciences cannot generally answer interesting questions about the present without the help of history, or at the very least an implicit, perhaps unconscious, sense of past experience.

Joseph Schumpeter in his great *History of economic analysis* listed the four 'techniques' employed by a 'scientific' economist: history, statistics, theory, and economic sociology, of which he considered history by far the most important and the one he would most choose to study if he had to choose among them. He gave three grounds for his choice:

7

First the subject matter of economics is essentially a unique process in historic time... Second, the historical report cannot be purely economic but must inevitably reflect also 'institutional' facts that are not purely economic: therefore it affords the best method for understanding how economic and non-economic facts *are* related to one another and how the various social sciences *should* be related to one another. Third,... most of the fundamental errors currently committed in economic analysis are due to lack of historical experience more often than to any other shortcoming of the economist's equipment.[1]

But the scope of an analysis of the multinational enterprise is defined, as in all analytical study, by the questions we ask and want to answer. And it is largely in this respect that economic historians depend on other social sciences. The historian's art extends beyond the attempt to establish the facts of the past; like other social scientists the historian recognises that facts are interesting only in relation to each other. They must be portrayed on a meaningful canvas. It is true that for economists, economic historians sometimes seem to depart from an interesting path in order to collect 'facts', blade of grass by blade of grass, with no particular purpose in mind other than to count grasses for the fun of it (and who are we to deprive them of their fun? After all, many economists often seem to be engaged primarily in an exercise designed to establish how many angels can remain in equilibrium on the point of a pin). At the same time, however, even in these activities both believe themselves to be providing essential details for a broader, more accurate or more profound picture on a larger canvas (and who are we to gainsay them?)

But we must now change the metaphor. Our picture is a moving one and the camera must so select the facts it puts together as to depict the undepictable: the causal, unobservable, relationships between facts. This is exactly what social science in general is usually fundamentally concerned to uncover, and the field in which its practitioners in their several areas are most qualified to dig. In terms of *function*, not of individuals, social scientists ask questions of the present or the past which are based on assumptions they think are likely to be applicable to those aspects of the societies that they want to analyse. With the aid of these assumptions they attempt to formulate hypotheses and to produce coherent explanations. In 'explaining' history, that is to say, in making the past intelligible, historians have to use the same type of assumptions, although perhaps not in an equally rigorous form. Thus historians borrow heavily from all the social sciences just as the latter borrow from historians; they live on each other to an extent greater than is realised by either. This symbiotic relationship is to a considerable extent responsible for the need both continually to re-write history and continually to re-consider the 'models' of the social sciences.

After the Second World War economists seem to have 'discovered' the multinational enterprise as an economic institution worthy of attention in its own right, and were quickly joined by political scientists, economic historians and other social scientists. There had, of course, earlier been the occasional economist's article as well as important histories of large enterprises with international activities. I have the impression, however, (admittedly not properly researched) that the attention devoted to multinational enterprises by economic historians was largely provoked by the growing literature from economists. The attention of economists had in turn been attracted by the growing political significance of this international institution in an era of declining political imperialism and growing political nationalism following the rapid post-war decolonisation and growth in the numbers of independent states.

This process, however, was not accompanied by declining economic imperialism, of which the multinational enterprise seemed the obvious instrument: one found frequent references to the (irrelevant) fact that the gross turnover of many multinationals was several times the national income of many countries, or to the (relevant) fact that those who ran the multinationals formed an international economic 'élite' who often made alliances with domestic political 'élites' of their host countries to exploit the people. For some time, the term 'transfer pricing' was almost synonymous with economic exploitation.

Such observations provide the very stuff of controversy, and social scientists of all ideological persuasions joined in the investigations. The list of academic 'disciplines' that are represented is impressive and instructive: organisation theorists and social psychologists, students of business strategy, management and inter-cultural administration, financial analysts, international trade theorists, development economists, industrial organisation theorists, political scientists, game theorists, econometricians, statisticians in all fields, 'pure' economic theorists, economic historians....

It is useless, indeed frivolous, to quibble about whether these and other types of specialisations that could have been added, are appropriately classed as separate disciplines of social science. The point is that practitioners from each specialisation approach the analysis of the nature, purpose, function, effect, or whatever, of multinational enterprises from different points of view, with different tools of analysis, different value weights, in effect, asking different questions which spring from their different theories about the world they see. All are relevant for an understanding of the phenomenon of the multinational enterprise. Economic historians need not distinguish among them but when they investigate and document the historical evidence, they are implicitly or explicitly 'testing' the hypotheses put forward by writers from other disciplines, or, at a very minimum, providing the material for others to do so.

Earlier I stated that in referring to economic historians I was referring to their function – their role as producers of history – and not to them as individuals. I did this because I recognise that individual historians do in fact have many 'subsidiary' skills in, for example, economics, political science, sociology or the analysis of business strategies. In the production of history some such skills are often, if not always, combined with their training as historians, with the emphasis, presumably, on economic affairs in the broad spirit of the opening paragraph of Alfred Marshall's *Principles*: '...[economics] examines that part of individual and social action which is most closely connected with the attainment and with the use of the material requisites of wellbeing'.[2]

Today, economists prefer a much tighter and more precise definition, for Marshall's definition would admit too many 'technically' untrained people into a profession jealous of its standing in the pecking order of the social sciences. One of the reasons for the pre-eminent standing of economics in this pecking order, is the rigorous quality of its 'theory' together with the availability of the statistics and of the techniques, both mathematical and statistical, with which to refine and to 'test' theories. The pecking order produced by these qualities is mirrored in the economics profession itself where those producing the 'purest' and most abstruse theory and those able to use the most advanced mathematics and econometrics have nowadays the highest prestige. There are good reasons for this, although many have argued that it has resulted in the seduction of many of the best brains in economics, and therefore of much of economics itself, into the arms of the elegant and beautiful away from the useful and homely (in both the English and American senses of that word).

Economic historians, along with many economists, suspect that the present fashions in 'pure' theory (whatever that is) are likely to lead to a dead end from their point of view, but they should not allow this suspicion to encourage them to accept a distinction, far too commonly made, between a 'real' world of history and a world of theory. It is impossible for economic historians to select and make sense of the 'facts' of history without the aid of the theories developed by students of economic affairs defined in the broader sense. Some of the 'theory' may be little more than dressed-up common-sense deductions from common observations and therefore not even recognised as such, but much of it has a deeper significance. Without theoretical analysis of cause and consequence one has no standard against which to appraise the significance of any given set of observations, for this significance is a question of what difference the observations make to what might otherwise have been the historical interpretation.

With reference to multinational enterprises, it seems to me that these points are illustrated very well by Barry Supple's chapter in which he asks exactly the types of question that are asked by economists and which can only be asked if there are theories in the questioner's mind the usefulness or application of which only reasonably contemporary history can 'test' or illuminate. In other words, there would seem to be a genuine complementarity between theory and history, not an opposition. I was therefore puzzled to note that Professor Supple seemed to discern a tension between history and theory when he noted that ' ... the "lesson" of history appears to be that the reality of things is much more complicated than "theory", or attempts at theorising, would lead us to expect' and that '...history (as always) undermines the drive towards theory'.

There may be a genuine disagreement between Professor Supple and myself, for it seems to me that theory is needed precisely *because* reality *is* so complicated; events that are accidental to the connections we want to study often intervene in such a way that without 'theory' we cannot isolate from the seamless web the facts relevant to the questions we want to ask of history. 'Theory' is, by definition, a simplification of 'reality' but simplification is necessary in order to comprehend it at all, to make sense of 'history'. If each event, each institution, each fact, were really unique in all aspects, how could we understand, or claim to understand, anything at all about the past, or indeed the present for that matter? If, on the other hand, there are common characteristics, and if such characteristics are significant in the determination of the course of events, then it is necessary to analyse both the characteristics and their significance and 'theoretically' to isolate them for the purpose.

I am not sure that Professor Supple would disagree with the above and there may not in fact be much of a difference between us; we may simply be using the same word with a different meaning. From the context I could conclude that Professor Supple has a theory different from mine about what is meant by 'theory'! If he means by the word 'theory' a universal, comprehensive generalisation purporting to explain all aspects of economic reality in one grand model, or even a comprehensive theory of 'the' multinational enterprise designed to capture all of its characteristics and their significance in one system of abstract ideas without reference to specific questions about its nature and activities, then I agree with him in placing 'history' in opposition to 'theory'. History will almost certainly 'undermine the drive towards theory' in this sense, if for no other reason than that suggested by Schumpeter quoted above: ' ... the subject matter [of economics] is essentially a unique process in historic time', and here I do not object to the word 'unique' since it is used precisely to suggest that universal truths without reference to time and space are unlikely to characterise economic affairs.

Economists, having decided to devote considerable special attention to the multinational enterprise after economic and political developments following the Second World War brought the extent of its activities to their attention, naturally began not only to study its behaviour and structure but also and perhaps primarily to ask what difference its activities made in a variety of areas: economic growth and development, international trade and investment and the international location of industry, international finance and national balances of payments, industrial organisation, international competition and technological progress, etc. To do this they had to develop theories, not just about the multinational enterprise as such, but about its relation to other aspects of economic life. People interested in different things asked different questions and produced different theories.

The natural tendency of economic historians in these circumstances is to ask almost at once, what's new? Have economists suddenly discovered something, or simply begun to pay attention to something that has existed for a long time? They begin systematically to examine the past. Not that nothing had earlier been done, for certainly business historians, a lively and thriving group in economic history, had long been active but had devoted their attention largely to the history of individual firms or individual industries. To deal with a class of firms, however, a definition is needed of the class and herein lies a difficulty.

In the first place, of course, a definition of a firm (or enterprise) has to be accepted. Some thirty years ago in my *Theory of the growth of the firm*[3] I discussed this problem at length, pointing out that there are many different definitions and concepts of what is a firm, depending on the question being investigated. For example, the 'firm' in the theory of the firm (the term often applied to the theory of price and output for which the 'firm' is central) is a very different creature from the firm in the theory of the growth of the firm.

The same type of problem exists for the discussion of multinational firms. These are usually defined as firms operating or producing in more than one country, thus crossing national boundaries. There are many types of such firms: industrial, agricultural, financial, transportation, tourism... The differences among these different types may be much more significant than their similarities. Analysts with different interests will ask different questions. Moreover, many of the characteristics of enterprises have changed as passing time has brought changes in many aspects of the environment, for example, in technology, including the technology of administration. Of what significance in these circumstances are arguments over when and how did 'the' multinational enterprise emerge, what are 'its' characteristics, and most of the similar questions that are often posed by economists and economic historians alike?

I do not have the space here to explore further this aspect of the study of multinational enterprises but I think that the problem of generalisation – of trying to produce 'a' theory of the multinational enterprise – has its roots in the futility of making definitions without asking relevant and reasonably precise questions about why the definition is sought. But it is hard to ask questions without also knowing why you ask them – that is to say, without a theory.

I end at the point at which I entered: economic theories give economic historians of economic institutions something to bite on. The results are as important to economists as they are to historians; history is as important for the development of economic theories as theories are to the elucidation of history. The relationship is a symbiotic, ongoing one; not only is the past (and the present, if such exists,) a seamless web, but also social science itself, perhaps all science. The problem of separating what is 'real' from what 'exists' I suspect will be resolved neither by economists nor by historians.

NOTES

1 Joseph Schumpeter, *History of economic analysis* (New York, 1959), pp. 12–13.
2 Alfred Marshall, *Principles of economics*, 8th edn (London, 1920), p. 1.
3 Edith Penrose, *Theory of the growth of the firm* (Oxford–New York, 1959, 2nd ed. 1980).

3 The changing form of multinational enterprise expansion in the twentieth century

JOHN CANTWELL

Introduction

This chapter sets out with two rather ambitious objectives. The first follows from an attempt to place international economic expansion in the twentieth century in its historical context. One aspect of this expansion has been the evolution of the multinational enterprise (MNE). The aim here is to distinguish four phases in the evolution of the international firm, corresponding to four different periods which appear to have characterised an emerging international economic system since around 1600.

The chosen division between periods consequently reflects an essentially macroeconomic rather than a business history perspective. In particular, the objective is to identify the major underlying forces behind international economic growth, and how they have changed as the world economy has become more integrated. It is suggested that the components comprising the mainspring of capital accumulation in each period were at the same time shaping the typical form of expansion of the firm.

It is argued that the MNE is representative of the type of international economy that has grown up since 1945, in the sense that the rise of new technologies and products, a wider international division of labour, and the greater integration of production and services across countries have all been associated with the rapid growth of MNEs. However, this argument is seen to suggest rejection rather than support for the commonly held view (especially prevalent among economic nationalists) that MNEs behave sufficiently differently from other firms to warrant an entirely separate kind of analysis. The notion that the growth of MNEs in industry and services in the twentieth century has weakened the economic authority and influence of nation states or governments is also found to be questionable.

The second objective is a more precise description of how MNEs have responded to changes in their macroeconomic environment in the twentieth century, or how their development has been associated with certain macroeconomic trends. Here attention is focused on the growth of MNEs in

15

manufacturing industry. Particular reference is made to the effects of trends in technological innovation and changes in the trading and competitive environment on international production.[1] The emphasis is on real rather than financial factors as determinants of the pattern of international production.

The historical development of the international firm

Each stage in the development of the international firm can be related to a certain historical period of international economic expansion. Each period has been characterised by the rise of a particular type of economic activity, which has constituted the principal source of capital accumulation. The dates which separate the four historical periods are somewhat arbitrarily chosen.

The first period is that of merchant capitalism, or mercantilism, which ran from before 1600 to around 1770. This period and that immediately preceding it saw the rise of a monetary economy in Europe through the import of large quantities of precious metals, and consequently the earliest types of international firms were the Italian and German owned banking networks, whose origins date back to the fifteenth century. However, the main source of capital accumulation in the seventeenth and early eighteenth centuries was the rise of international trade. Merchants employed the capital they thereby acquired in re-organising production at home (the 'putting out' system). The kind of international firm that best characterised the mercantilist period was therefore the trading company, often reliant on a monopoly position granted by the state.

The second period, running from about 1770 to 1890, was the period of industrial capitalism, distinguished by the rise of manufacturing industry in the more economically advanced countries. This was a period of the growth of manufactories and then the factory system within national firms. At this stage international production was typically organised by individual entrepreneurs, moving abroad to exploit particular market opportunities, and by resource-based trading companies, serving a growing demand for raw materials.

The third period may be described as one of finance capitalism, between around 1890 and 1945, though some of its features still prevail today. This period is marked out by the rise of powerful banks and financial institutions, and by an increasing concentration among industrial firms within each developed country. Firms entered into national and sometimes international cartels as a means of securing monopolistic positions and raising profits, and it was financial rather than industrial capital which grew most rapidly. It was in this period of larger firms when the modern MNE began to come into its

Table 3.1. *The changing form of the international firm associated with changes in the form of capital accumulation*

Historical period:	Main source of capital accumulation:	Main type of international company associated with each period			
		International merchant bank	International trading co. serving world markets	Expatriate ventures in manufacturing & construction	Resource based trading company serving national industry
Merchant capitalism	Colonial trade	x	x		
Industrial capitalism	National industry			x	x
Finance capitalism	Finance capital	+			+
Global capitalism	International networks of production, trade and finance	+	+		

Historical period:	Main source of capital accumulation:	Main type of international company associated with each period			
		International manufacturing cartel	International import-substituting manufacturing company	Globally integrated manufacturing company	International service chains
Merchant capitalism	Colonial trade				
Industrial capitalism	National industry				
Finance capitalism	Finance capital	x	x		
Global capitalism	International networks of production, trade and finance	?	+	x	x

Note: x First appearance   + Reappearance or continuation   ? Possible future development own. The modern MNE is a firm that moves from domestic production and export to the organisation of related productive activities abroad.

The final period, from 1945 onwards, will be called the era of global capitalism. Since 1945 we have seen the rise of international production, trade and finance across the industrialised countries, in networks which have recently expanded to encompass the newly industrialising countries. Such networks are typically organised by MNEs (including multinational banks), operating in markets in which international oligopolistic competition is the general rule. Capital accumulation has proceeded most rapidly within MNEs, whose international networks have grown much faster than their domestic activity. The relationship between historical trends in capital accumulation and the form of development of international firms is summarised in table 3.1.

Merchant capitalism (c 1600–1770)

The rise of the merchant class in Europe was allied to the emergence of national states, and the centralisation of formerly independent towns and feudal regions under a system of absolute monarchy. The state helped to implant infant trade and industry through supportive regulations at home and protectionist barriers, aimed at establishing advantages for the enterprises of its own country over foreign competition. In return, the merchants provided the means for paying for a growing bureaucratic apparatus and an army. European states at various times imposed maximum wage legislation, granted specific individuals or trading companies monopoly rights over areas of trade or production, offered subsidies and tax concessions to entrepreneurs, and sought out experienced master craftsmen for them from abroad. The leadership of international trade passed from the Italian and Hanseatic cities to Spain and Portugal, and then to Holland before England.

One of the main sources of capital accumulation in Europe was the enormously profitable colonial trade.[2] Owing in part to their monopoly position, trading companies were able to buy cheap in the colonies and sell dear when re-exporting to European markets. The merchants then channelled some of the capital accumulated from international trade into industrial production for export, through their organisation and control of the non-local sales of an expanding cottage industry, and through financial centres such as those in Amsterdam and London (see Chapman, 1979). The rise of a money economy in Europe brought with it inflation, impoverishing many traditional craftsmen of the guild system, bringing them into the orbit of merchants turned buyers up come putters out, thus promoting cottage industry.

Occasionally, merchants were responsible for organising production abroad as well as at home, where it was necessary to support their international trading operations. The earliest recorded international co-ordination of production was carried out by the Italian banking families, but their impact was insignificant compared to the chartered land and trading companies of the sixteenth and seventeenth centuries. The scope of the colonial involvement of some British, Dutch and French companies incorporated some early manufacturing activities. Moreover, the transborder migration of population (sometimes as a result of persecution) was often accompanied by capital and skills, and many industries owed their origin to such migrations (Cantwell and Dunning, 1984).

Industrial capitalism (c 1770–1890)

The industrial revolution began in Britain, and then spread to what are today's industrialised countries. In this period the major source of capital accumulation was the rise of manufacturing industry, linked to the growth of railways and transport systems. This was associated with the establishment of large markets for industrial goods, and the growth of competition between industrial firms spurred by continuous innovation in emerging capital goods sectors (Rosenberg, 1976). As new industries flourished, and capital goods producers established themselves, the social or inter-industry division of labour between firms increased, as well as the extent of the organised technical division of labour within the firm through the rapid development of the factory system.

Labour productivity grew by leaps and bounds in industrial factories on the basis of the extensive application of machinery (see Landes, 1969, who discusses the emergence of technological dynamism in Europe). At this time industrial firms had as their central objective the reduction of costs through innovation, rather than the securing of a monopolistic power over resources or in their final product markets. For this reason (and because it was the foremost industrial country) free trading arguments eventually won the day in Britain, and were prevalent by the 1850s.

Many firms built up important export positions, but these were generally based on the technological advantages of producing at home, before firms and industries in later developing countries 'caught up'. Foreign activities were mainly concerned with sales rather than production (see Chapman, 1985, and Cottrell, 1980). At least until the 1870s, international production on the whole was left to individual entrepeneurs, and specialised trading companies that brought in resources, often from the colonies or dependent territories.

Finance capitalism (c *1890–1945*)

The rise of large banks in the developed countries at the turn of the century was closely linked to industrial concentration and the spread of national cartels. Profits were frequently raised by restricting competition, thereby increasing the promoter's profits earned by the banks in the establishment of new facilities in the industrial joint stock companies. Large banks required a large promoter's profit, just as large joint stock companies required the mobilisation of a large volume of bank capital (Hilferding, 1981). Industrial concentration, the rationalisation of production, and cartel movements were associated with the rise of mass production technologies and the standardisation of their products, and with improvements in transport and communications. This increased co-ordination of production is described by Chandler and Daems (1974) as the rise of managerial capitalism, and by Hannah (1976) as the rise of a corporate economy.

Allied to the greater concentration of industry (which increased profits through improved technical efficiency and economies of scale as well as the restriction of competition), financial instruments were developed as a means of appropriating profits. This is as true of the large joint stock companies, which were able to increase their share of profits through stock dilution, as it is of the large banks. Even in Britain, where these two institutions maintained a greater separation than elsewhere, financial means of accumulating capital gained in strength. Whereas capital had previously been accumulated mainly by individual merchants (merchant capital), and then by individual industrialists and entrepreneurs through the expansion of productive activity (industrial capital), it was now accumulated primarily in a financial form by huge institutions (finance capital).

The formation of international cartels was fostered by the spread of tariff barriers, initially in countries such as the US and Germany which were fast 'catching up', and then in the depression of the 1930s reaching every industrialised country. Trade barriers and the political risk of foreign ownership facilitated cartel agreements based on the geographical allocation of international markets, by combining national cartels and dominant firms that were already well established in their respective regions.

Vertical integration and the division of labour within the firm generally increased, at the expense of the co-ordination of activities between numerous independent firms through the market mechanism. Investments abroad within MNEs became significant from around the 1870s, and before 1914 these were chiefly vertically integrated investments of a resource-based kind (Dunning, 1983). These were most often located in the colonial territories, as were some early manufacturing investments, since in these countries the costs of 'psychic distance' (that is, the costs of overcoming a strange language, culture etc.) had been reduced. However, the US and Germany joined the traditional investors (Britain, the Netherlands and France) at the end of the nineteenth century, when the institutional mode of international production was dramatically affected by the emergence of finance capitalism, and its main organisational form, the joint stock company.

Although many of today's strongest manufacturing MNEs trace their roots back to this period, they typically grew up in an international environment which encouraged them to establish some co-operation with their major competitors. Moreover, at an early stage the growth of MNEs in manufacturing depended upon particular types of technological and other related skills, and it would have been difficult for them to pursue an independent strategy aimed at an international industry as a whole, rather than one segment of it. For these reasons, the period designated here as finance capitalism, while it spawned MNEs as a means by which joint stock companies could take advantage of a new range of technological developments, was essentially characterised by international cartels and agreements between firms, rather than international competition between MNEs.

The international production of most British MNEs either began in the colonies, which often provided the initial experience necessary to further international expansion, or it arose out of trading relationships. Yet although in this period the UK, the country with the largest empire, was the most important source country for MNEs, the conditions for the future growth of international production favoured US based corporations. It was the US that pioneered the technological and organisational changes on which the modern MNE was nurtured (Chandler, 1977; Williamson, 1981). Franko (1972) explains how European firms were much slower than US firms to introduce links between subsidiaries in a global network and a divisional structure, which was bound up with their operation in a generally more negotiated or cartelised environment.

Global capitalism (c 1945 onwards)

The period since 1945 has witnessed the rapid growth of international economic interdependence, such that no national economy can now be treated in isolation from the global picture. Capital accumulation has increasingly centred on international networks of production, trade and finance, based in the developed (OECD) countries, and now extending to the newly industrialising countries. Allied to this, international production and trade has expanded most rapidly in manufacturing industry, and more recently in services, displacing the previously dominant position of resource-based foreign direct investment.

The early post-war period is best known for the surge in technological development, the peak of US hegemony, the improvement in international communications and stable exchange rates. These conditions, combined with the dollar shortage which was a result of the 'technological gap' between Europe and the US, led to the beginning of a massive growth of international production mainly in West Europe, supported by the transfer of technology with US MNEs. From around 1960 onwards the MNE came of age, just as the national corporation had at the end of the previous century in the US. The most prominent feature of this development has been the growth and diversification of existing US and European MNEs, associated with the rise of intra-industry trade and production in Europe and North America. Meanwhile, the European countries on the whole improved their competitive position (with US hegemony declining), and Japan and the newly industrialising countries emerged as powerful new centres for capital accumulation, and hence as source countries for a range of new MNEs.

The rise of global capitalism has brought with it an underlying tendency towards the integration within MNEs of international networks which stretch across the industrialised world. This tendency towards 'rationalised' investments has been strongly reinforced by the slow down in the growth rates of industrial markets since the early 1970s. The common thread linking the 1950s and the 1980s has been that capital accumulation has continued to proceed most rapidly within international networks; what has changed is the more integrated way in which those networks are now organised. As this trend has developed MNEs have steadily moved away from an earlier role as financiers (except for the multinational banks, which have taken this function over), and have gradually become global organisers of economic systems. The technological advantages of manufacturing MNEs (over other firms) have increasingly been based on systems or galaxies of related innovations, rather than particular products or processes.

However, the rise of globally integrated MNEs has often also been associated with a decline in vertical integration at a national level. A renewed growth of the social division of labour between firms especially in the service sector, has crept out from under the long run historical trend towards an increasingly expansive division of labour co-ordinated within the firm. Global MNEs are more prepared to subcontract out locally repair services, legal and technical services, and segments of research activity in new technologies not central to their operations. This is partly due to the increasing pressure of trade unions, which is greater in large concentrated plants.

It follows from what has been said that the MNE is the natural extension of the type of large industrial company which came to the fore in the period of finance capitalism. It works according to similar principles as any other firm, except that it comes to organise a division of labour between countries rather than within national boundaries. The MNE has therefore proved most amenable to the same type of analysis which applies to the growth of firms in general (see, for example, Buckley and Casson, 1976).

Now it may be true that the greater international mobility of industry in the post-war period has meant that strong dynamic countries grow faster, while uncompetitive countries are quickly abandoned and stagnate (a process that is discussed further in Cantwell, 1988). However, the increasing importance of MNEs in industry and services need not imply a weakening in the economic influence of governments and nation states. On the contrary, in a highly interdependent world government policies form a crucial determinant of the pattern of international production, trade and finance. For example, the recent expansion of Japanese MNEs in Europe and North America is partly attributable to the encouragement of their own government to go abroad, and protectionist barriers (and subsidies to inward investment) erected by European and North American governments. It is, of course, clear that no government in the modern era of global capitalism can adopt an autarkic policy irrespective of its international repercussions; but this is a consequence of the strong linkages between economies in general, rather than the greater power of MNEs as such, which is simply part of the same underlying process of internationalisation of industry, commerce and finance.

The expansion of MNEs in manufacturing industry and global macroeconomic trends in the twentieth century

The sectoral distribution of international production has changed markedly during the twentieth century. Resource-based investment and colonial trade has gradually been displaced by import-substituting investment in manufacturing facilities in other developed countries, related to the increasing share of trade moving between the industrialised countries. More recently, such import-substituting activities have been linked up into global networks with the rise of rationalised investments. While MNEs have appeared in most manufacturing industries, they are especially prevalent in high technology intensive industries, in which they have developed technological advantages over other firms. Elsewhere, they often rely on advantages in marketing and distribution.

Before 1945 the spread of trade barriers was a major factor in the growth of import-substituting investment, by which a firm establishes production facilities in a market to which it has previously exported. After 1945, so called import-substituting investment was generally associated with trade expansion at a macroeconomic level, and this is explained by the greater integration of world markets, and the development of intra-industry trade and production.

We now briefly consider, in turn, how the pattern of MNE activity has been affected by trends in technological innovation and by the trading and competitive environment confronting firms.

Trends in innovation

World leadership in technological innovation passed from Britain in the nineteenth century to the US by early in the twentieth century. The total number of patents granted in the US rose from 13,441 in 1880 to 41,614 in 1914, while the share granted to foreign residents rose from 6% in 1880 to 13% in 1900, before slipping back to 11% in 1914 (OTAF, 1977). In the post-war period European firms underwent a certain revival, and innovation in Japan took off. Innovative success by the firms of each of these countries laid the foundations for them to become MNEs. The discussion that follows attempts to relate the economic fortunes of countries to the internationalisation of firms.

A strong economy (built on a platform of innovative indigenous firms) initially creates a strong export position. Although this may be partially offset by outward investment, in a basically sound world economy such a country maintains a net balance of payments surplus and hence a strong currency. As relatively backward economies begin to catch up technologically and/or begin to erect trade barriers against the surplus country, the leading firms in the strong country are inspired to increase international production. The reason is that since the relative growth of production and markets rises in countries 'catching up', while their indigenous firms become more innovative, and their local tariffs raise the cost of imports, the location advantages of producing directly within these countries rises. This is in essence the position of many British and European manufacturing firms who began producing in the US before 1914, and of US firms that began producing in Europe in the late 1950s and the 1960s.

Past a certain point, the export position of the technologically leading country may be weakened, as the indigenous capability of other countries rises. This happened to the US by the late 1960s, and the combination of trade deficits and net outward investment meant that its overall balance of payments showed a substantial deficit. Under the Bretton Woods fixed exchange rate system the US dollar was not allowed to depreciate in order to offset this deficit, and as a result the dollar was widely viewed as being overvalued. This overvaluation contributed to a yet higher outward investment, since US interests were able to buy up European firms and assets more cheaply in dollar terms, and this offered a secondary, financial explanation for rising US foreign direct investment (emphasised by Aliber, 1970).

The situation is slightly different where countries are diverging rather than converging in their technological capacities (where the technology leader is establishing its lead), and where the world operates under a flexible exchange rate system. In this case, lagging economies not only respond by building up trade barriers against the new surplus country, but they may also raise their government spending and borrowing to attempt to offset the comparatively weak rate of growth of private investment, pushing up their interest rates. In addition, as entrepreneurial expectations become more pessimistic in countries falling behind, speculative pressure may be opened up in their financial markets, forcing the price of their financial assets down and their interest rates up, as domestic firms find it more difficult to finance their expenditure.

Faced by higher interest rates abroad, the inherently strongest economy sees its outward portfolio or financial investment rise, while due to greater protectionism abroad it sees its outward direct investment rise and its exports fall off a little. This combination may mean that despite its faster productivity growth rate that the country finds that its total outward investment runs ahead of its exports. As it moves into an overall balance of payment deficit, under a flexible exchange rate system its currency depreciates. This is essentially the position of Japan, the emerging technology leader today.

The other important means of balance of payments adjustment to take into account is that real wages tend to rise fastest in countries with the strongest productivity growth rates. This facilitates the restructuring of an economy such as the Japanese towards a larger technology-intensive traded goods sector, and conversely in the case of countries where productivity growth and real wages lag behind. As Japan has upgraded its industrial structure, for firms in declining sectors the relative rise in wages has acted as an additional incentive for them to transfer production facilities abroad. Apart from the increase in the domestic costs of production, the rise in wages and national income leads to an increase in imports, though in the Japanese case this effect has been limited since the propensity to import out of income has remained low.

The US today constitutes a special case. Its favourable domestic growth rate in recent years has been sponsored by higher government spending, and higher immigration restraining the rate of increase of wages. This growth has been supported by strong inward investment, both by portfolio capital movements which help to finance faster growth, and which have been attracted by the higher interest rates occasioned by the government's deficit; and by the direct investments of European and Japanese companies as location advantages have moved back towards the US. However, faster growth has also increased imports and created a current account deficit.

This combination of heavy inward investment and trade deficits was also characteristic of the developing countries in the late 1970s, but unlike them the flow of foreign capital onto the US has outweighed the impact of its trade deficit, and sustained a buoyant currency (at least for a time). The high value of the dollar has compounded the balance of trade deficit and led to greater protectionist pressure in the US.

The US example provides a good illustration of the way in which real rather than financial factors tend ultimately to regulate the location decisions of MNEs. MNE investments in the US have been rising for some years, and continue to rise due to high profitability (partly occasioned by a fall in the share of wages), and the increasing relative importance of the US market, despite the current overvaluation of the dollar which makes US firms more expensive to acquire in foreign currency terms.

Changes in the trading and competitive environment

The form of MNE expansion in the twentieth century has been strongly influenced by changes in the overall rate of growth of the world economy, and by shifts in the relative rates of growth of different countries and regions.

The slow down of the inter-war period and since the early 1970s provided an impetus away from expansive import-substituting investments and towards rationalised investment. This essentially implies a move away from a dispersing location of industry in an increasing number of production sites, towards greater specialisation in a smaller number of production sites. However, although pressure towards the formation of integrated international industries was present as early as the inter-war period (Casson *et al.* 1986), it was overtaken by the spread of beggar-my-neighbour trade policies which encouraged firms to enter international cartels or increase import-substituting investments instead. Today, globally integrated MNEs have expanded the scope of their rationalised networks from the OECD countries to the newly industrialising countries (NICs).

This is also related, of course, to the faster relative growth of the NICs, where local enterprises have become quite innovative, especially in Southeast Asia. Some MNEs based in the industrialised countries in traditional industries (such as food products and textiles) have found their technological advantage eroded by firms from the NICs, to the extent that they have laid increasing emphasis on their processing and marketing networks, buying in from independent agents in the developing countries. Other MNEs which retain technological advantages (such as in pharmaceuticals or electronics) have established directly integrated investments in the NICs. These issues are discussed further in Cantwell and Dunning (1985).

The crucial issue in deciding on the form likely to be taken by MNE expansion in the immediate future is the extent to which protectionism takes root. A rise in protectionism would lead back towards import-substituting investments, and it might even lead towards a reconsideration of the possibility of new international cartels or negotiated agreements between MNEs.

NOTES

The author wishes to thank Mark Casson, John Dunning, Tony Corley, Steve Nicholas and Francesca Sanna Randaccio for helpful comments on an earlier draft.

1 International production is defined as production under common ownership across national borders.
2 This view is supported by extensive empirical evidence in the work of the classical economists, most notably Adam Smith and Karl Marx. In modern times it is supported by the historians of British economic growth, Deane and Cole (1967). It has recently been challenged by O'Brien (1982), although according to his estimates even in 1784–6 (well into the industrial revolution), the total profits earned from British trade with the 'periphery' were about 55% of total gross investment by British investors at home and abroad. O'Brien is particularly concerned to attack Wallerstein's (1974) 'world system' perspective, according to which European industrialisation is seen as dependent upon the exploitation of the periphery. The view taken here is rather different; namely, that a 'global system' only emerged after 1945, but that certain features of recent developments – such as the role of the international trading company serving world markets – have parallels in mercantilist times.

REFERENCES

Aliber, R. Z. (1970). 'A theory of direct foreign investment', in C. P. Kindleberger, (ed.), *The International Corporation: A Symposium* (Cambridge, Mass.).
Buckley, P. J., and Casson, M. C. (1976). *The Future of the Multinational Enterprise* (London).
Cantwell, J. A. (1988). *Technological Innovation and Multinational Corporations* (Oxford, forthcoming).
Cantwell, J. A., and Dunning, J. H. (1984). 'The emergence of multinationals in the organisation of international production', in A. Fonseca, (ed.) *Multinationals in Third World Countries: towards a code of conduct* (Rome).
(1985). 'The "new forms" of international involvement of British firms in the third world', Report submitted to the OECD, January, publication forthcoming.
Casson, M. C., et al. (1986). *Multinationals and World Trade: Vertical Integration and the Division of Labour in World Industries* (London).
Chandler, A. D. (1977). *The Visible Hand: The Managerial Revolution in American Business* (Cambridge, Mass.).
Chandler, A. D., and Daems, H. (1974). 'Introduction' in H. Daems and H. Van Der Wee (eds), *The Rise of Managerial Capitalism* (Louvain).
Chapman, S. D. (1979). 'British marketing enterprise: the changing role of merchants, manufacturers and financiers, 1700–1860', *Business History Review*, 53: 2 (Summer).
(1985). 'British-based investment groups before 1914', *The Economic History Review*, 38: 2 (May).
Cottrell, P. L. (1980). 'Commercial enterprise', in R. A. Church (ed.), *The Dynamics of Victorian Business* (London).

Deane, P., and Cole, W. A. (1967). *British Economic Growth, 1688–1959* (Cambridge).

Dunning, J. H. (1983). 'Changes in the level and structure of international production: the last one hundred years', in M. C. Casson (ed.), *The Growth of International Business* (London).

Franko, L. G. (1972). 'The growth, organisational structure and allocative efficiency of European multinational firms: some emerging hypotheses', in G. Y. Bertin, (ed.), *The Growth of the Large Multinational Corporation* (Paris).

Hannah, L. (1976). *The Rise of the Corporate Economy* (London).

Hilferding, R. (1981). *Finance Capital: A Study of the Latest Phase of Capitalist Development* (London (translation of original 1910 edition)).

Landes, D. (1969). *The Unbound Prometheus* (Cambridge).

OTAF (1977). *Technology Assessment and Forecast, Seventh Report* (Washington).

O'Brien, P. (1982). 'European economic development: the contribution of the periphery', *The Economic History Review*, 35: 1 (February).

Rosenberg, N. (1976). *Perspectives on Technology* (Cambridge).

Wallerstein, I. (1974). *The Modern World System* (New York).

Williamson, O. E. (1981). 'The modern corporation: origin, evolution, attributes', *Journal of Economic Literature*, 19: 4 (December).

4 Electrical research, standardisation and the beginnings of the corporate economy

MIKULÁŠ TEICH

While there is little disagreement among students of the history of multinational enterprise as to what Alfred Chandler seeks to argue in his chapter in *Multinational enterprise in historical perspective*, there are nevertheless a few gaps to be filled in this area. Chandler summarises his argument by stressing that 'an understanding of technological and organizational differences and changes within operating units is essential to an explanation of the beginnings and continued growth of the industrial multinational enterprise'.[1] Since about 1880 a salient feature of this development was, as its factor and product, mass production methods linked with standardisation. Here a major impetus came from electrical engineering which required internationally acceptable electrical units. A satisfactory solution of this problem was a precondition before electrification's economic and social potential could be realised.

The aim of what follows is to draw attention to this rather neglected aspect of the history of scientific and industrial relations, which is, however, relevant to the understanding of the origins and development of the corporate economy in its national and multinational context.

The late nineteenth-century 'climacteric'

The term 'multinational corporation' itself, as noted by D. K. Fieldhouse, is of recent date (1960).[2] However in his influential book *The Unbound Prometheus* (1969) David Landes does not appear to make use of it. To be sure, Landes discusses the emergence of international cartels and other monopolistic combinations during the late nineteenth century, associated with the processes of concentration and integration in industry, which he views as a 'new, commercial version of the enclosure movement'.[3] Though occurring in distinct historical periods and affecting different sectors of the economy, the case for comparing enclosures and combination of businesses is that they were expressions of the rationalisation of capitalist enterprise. It has to be remembered, however, that the rise of the amalgamation movement

29

in the closing decades of the nineteenth century extended beyond the borders of one country. 'What we have, in short,' writes Landes, 'is a shift…from one-nation to a multi-nation industrial system.' Continuing he perceives it as 'change of life' or 'climacteric' through which the world economy was passing, coinciding

with an equally fundamental technological transformation [that] only complicated what was intrinsically a difficult adjustment – so difficult, indeed, that the most determined efforts of the wisest of men did not avail to appease the resentments and enmities that grew out of the consequentially altered balance of political power. Marxist students of history have been wont to see the international rivalries that preceded the First World War as the thrashing of a system in process of decline and dissolution. *The fact is that these were the growing pains of a system in process of germination.*[4]

In view of Landes' remarks on Marxist students of history, it is of interest to recall, that there were Marxist contemporaries, such as R. Hilferding (1877–1941) and V. I. Lenin (1870–1924), who addressed themselves to the problem under review. Indeed their approach goes some way to throw light on the climacteric of the late nineteenth century, noted by Landes. Thus Lenin regarded the concentration of production, reflected in the emergence and growth of giant corporations as a qualitative change in capitalism. He interpreted their growing control of production and distribution, nationally and internationally, as 'socialisation', albeit based on the private ownership of capital.[5] Referring to this form of economic socialisation, Lenin observed particularly that 'the process of technical invention and improvement becomes socialized'.[6] He certainly perceived that a large banking concern such as Morgan was able to accelerate technical progress through means that could not possibly be compared with those of the past.[7]

Organised invention and research and the origin of the General Electric Company

In this connection it is apposite briefly to trace the origin of General Electric. The beginnings of this firm, one of the largest in the USA, have to be looked for in the period when Thomas Alva Edison (1847–1931) started to work systematically on the problem of the incandescent lamp in the late 1870s.[8] He built in Menlo Park an unprecedented place of work. It was a firm for inventions. Edison was a capitalistic entrepeneur who employed mechanics[9] as well as trained scientists. Operational costs of this unusual capitalist enterprise were by no means small. Thus the total expenses of developing incandescent lighting, from 1878 to 1886, amounted to about $650,000 out of which about 42% was spent on experimental work.[10]

Never before had such sums been employed on technical research and development, nor did Edison possess them. In 1878 the Edison Electric Light

Company was founded with the backing of J. P. Morgan and Henry Villard,[11] the leading Wall Street financiers of the time, with the objective of securing all discoveries and improvements resulting from Edison's work on electric lighting. Edison successively founded three further firms for the production of incandescent lamps, dynamos and electric conductors. In 1889 the four companies merged into the Edison General Electric Company linked to the banks Morgan and Kuhn, Loeb & Co., and through Villard also to the Deutsche Bank in Berlin. In 1892 there followed a merger of two of the three largest American electrical firms, Edison General Electric and Thomson–Houston, into the General Electric Company.

Thus, in the course of thirteen years, the world's leading electrical corporation grew out of the company originally founded for the financing and exploiting of electrical inventions and research. In 1889 Edison sold his financial interest to the General Electrical Company in order to recover personal financial independence for his inventive activity. It is true that he became a member of its board of directors but he lost interest in the technical development of the company's manufacturing branches. It is indicative of his views that he opposed the merger of Edison General Electric with Thomson–Houston on grounds he explained in writing to Villard: 'If you make the coalition, my usefulness as an inventor is gone. My services wouldn't be worth a penny. I can only invent under powerful incentive. No competition means no invention'.[12] Although Edison pioneered corporate industrial research in the United States, he bowed out of it. He concluded that within the large new company there was not room for the brand of individual capitalism he wished to be involved in – that is, to operate a free enterprise in inventive activities.

It took eight years for the General Electric Company to institutionalise research for its needs. Before the establishment of the General Electric Research Laboratory in late 1900 the corporation's interests in industrial research were limited and came essentially under two heads: engineering design and measurements of electric units. They were taken care of by the Calculating Department and Standardising Laboratory respectively at Schenectady where General Electric's central office was located. The delay in establishing the General Electric Research Laboratory was closely bound up with the doubts of the General Electric executives regarding the potential value of internally conducted industrial scientific research. According to L. S. Reich, the author of a recent study of the history of the General Electric Research Laboratory, they

believed that major technological departures generally came from individuals who did not work well in the engineering environment of large corporations. For these advances they depended on the temporary services of outside inventors and scientist – engineers; or, like their competitors, they attempted to buy patent rights to the most important new electrical inventions from all over the world.[13]

The key figure behind the change of attitude that led to the creation of the General Electric Research Laboratory was, by all accounts, the brilliant mathematical engineer Charles Proteus Steinmetz (1865–1923).[14] Steinmetz, who was in charge of the Calculating Department, emigrated from Germany in 1888 because he was liable to be arrested for socialist activities. It can hardly be doubted that his lifelong concerns over socio-political issues conditioned his interest in socialising scientific and technical activities for the needs of industry.[15]

In Europe this tendency was paralleled by setting up organisations involving – separately or jointly – the state, industrial and academic worlds. For example, in Germany it found expression in the foundation of the Physikalisch-Technische Reichsanstalt (1887) and in Britain in the creation of the National Physical Laboratory (1899–1900).

Physikalisch–Technische Reichsanstalt

The most effective backer of the Physikalisch-Technische Reichsanstalt was the electrical engineer, inventor and entrepreneur Werner Siemens (1816–1892). In 1885 he placed a site of nearly two hectares at the disposal of the Imperial Government which undertook to bear the cost of building, equipping and maintaining the new research body.[16] This was some forty years after Werner Siemens got acquainted with electric telegraphy and, indeed, devised a self-interrupting dial telegraph. This success induced him eventually to quit the Prussian army – he served as lieutenant at the Artillery Workshop in Berlin – and to turn to the manufacturing of telegraph systems. But before then, for this purpose, he founded in 1847, with the mechanic Johann Georg Halske, the firm Siemens and Halske[17] which grew so successfully that at his death it belonged to the four major world companies in the electrical field (General Electric, Westinghouse and Allgemeine Elektrizitäts-Gesellschaft being the other three).[18] Central to Werner Siemens' entrepreneurship was the recognition of the indispensable role of scientific knowledge of electricity for technical advance and consequently for commercial profit.

What interests us here is that, after identifying early the absence of a generally accepted unit of resistance as the major obstacle to the technical and commercial utilisation of electricity, he proceeded to construct one. Having experimented with mercury since 1858, he published his proposal for a reproducible unit of electrical resistance in 1860.[19] It became known as the 'Siemens unit' and was taken to be the resistance offered to the electric current by a column of mercury, at 0 °C, of a length of 1 m and a cross-section of 1 mm^2. Siemens' mercury unit did not differ much from the unit promoted by the British Association for the Advancement of Science Committee on Electrical Standards about which more is to come.

The Siemens mercury unit was widely in use until 1884. In that year an international conference took place in Paris to obtain an agreement on electrical units. As regards the unit of resistance – denoted as the 'ohm' – it was specified that it was to be the resistance to the current by a column of mercury 106 cm in length. Nine years later (1893) there was a further change when the International Electrical Congress held in Chicago resolved that the unit of resistance was the 'international ohm'. It was defined as the resistance offered to an unvarying electric current by a column of mercury at the temperature of melting ice, 14.4211 g in mass, and of a length of 106.3 cm.[20]

Fundamental measurement of electrical magnitudes involved protracted experimentation with inadequate recognition given for the services rendered. These considerations, Werner Siemens thought, explained why there was no room for this kind of scientific effort, although socially necessary, in university or private laboratories. It was an area eminently suited for governmental research. This is how Werner Siemens, in 1883, ended his plea for the founding of the Physikalisch-Technische Reichsanstalt:[21]

The technical consequences ought certainly not to be undervalued which will result from the application of electric currents of any desired strength in the most varied branches of industry. The country which first realizes them will thereby attain a great advantage over other countries. There are, therefore, important questions of political economy which depend on the state support of scientific advance in this department. It is to be added that owing to the application of electricity on a large scale the necessity has become apparent of fixing determined electrical units for trade and of permanent arrangements for the control of the units coming into use. Although these units have been brought forward and rendered practicable in the first instance in Germany, an organization was wanting to carry out the laborious scientific work to completion necessary for practical application, and there is danger that here again England and France will gain precedence of us. Already this burning question of electric units of measurement makes the quickest possible foundation of an organization for scientific experimental research with suitable buildings and apparatus of such necessity that it cannot be refused. The necessary funds for carrying this out are hardly of consideration compared with the incalculable advantage which will arise from such a well-endowed organization furnished with necessary means.

The British Association for the Advancement of Science Committee on Electrical Standards

The setting up of the National Physical Laboratory also was closely linked to the matter of measuring resistance and other electrical magnitudes. Here it is convenient to start with the work of the famed Scotsman William Thomson, later Lord Kelvin (1824–1907) in the 1850s, in particular with his theoretical and practical studies on cabling.[22]

Engaged in devising electrical measurement instruments, Thomson became only too well aware of the value of a coherent system of electrical units that tied up with the system of absolute or fundamental units of length (meter), mass (kilogram) and time (second). It was thanks to the already mentioned British Association for the Advancement of Science Committee on Electrical Standards (appointed 1861 at the suggestion of Thomson) that the subject was given complex scientific study.[23] Among the members of the Committee, which functioned in the first instance between 1861 and 1870 were several eminent British physicists of whom, in addition to Thomson, J. Clerk Maxwell (1831–79) and J. P. Joule (1818–89) were the most distinguished.

One important decision of the Committee was to accept that electrical resistance was measurable in terms of velocity, and to choose the magnitude meter per second as the absolute unit of resistance. As it was too small for practical purposes the Committee adopted as the practical unit of resistance a quantity which was 10^7 times as great as the meter per second. It became known as the 'British Association unit' or the 'B.A. unit'. The other important decision of the Committee was to initiate systematic investigations on the best form and material for the preparation of standard resistance coils, representing the B.A. unit. After approved standard coils of different alloys were deposited at the Kew Observatory in 1864, the Committee's labours came virtually to an end. The Committee felt that 'at least as far as electrical resistance was concerned, [it] made this measurement a tangible and practical operation' and that it was in no position to contribute more. Consequently, while advising comparisons of resistance of the coils from time to time, the Committee on its own recommendation was disbanded in 1870.

In 1874 the standard coils were transferred to the just opened Cavendish Laboratory in Cambridge. Four years later Clerk Maxwell, the first Cavendish Professor of Experimental Physics, asked John Ambrose Fleming (1849–1945) to establish whether their values remained constant.[24] When further re-examination by other workers showed a discrepancy in the resistance values of the B.A. unit, the Electrical Standards Committee was reappointed in 1881. Among the members of the Committee were Lord Rayleigh (1842–1919), the second Cavendish Professor, and Richard Tetley Glazebrook (1854–1935), who then held the post of demonstrator at the Cavendish Laboratory. It was largely due to their efforts that the value of the B.A. unit of resistance was redetermined and found to be about 1% smaller than the ohm, the unit of resistance adopted in Paris in 1884.

It is against this background that J. A. Fleming's paper, read to the Society of Telegraph-Engineers and Electricians in November 1885, has to be viewed.[25] In it Fleming pointed out that the practical consequences of purely scientific concerns with electrical measurements were of critical importance to public welfare. Electric energy became 'a marketable commodity as a loaf of bread' and was 'as much the subject of purchase and sale as a barrel of beer or 1,000 cubic feet of gas'. There was an overriding need for its accurate measurement with instruments conforming to recognised standards. With this in mind, Fleming suggested that the work on units of resistance by the British Association Committee on Electrical Standards should be extended to include electrical instruments in general. For this purpose, Fleming pleaded, 'a national electrical standardizing laboratory' serving both commercial and general scientific needs should be established. Fleming recommended that this matter should be taken up by the Council of the Society of Telegraph-Engineers and Electricians, in conjunction with the British Association for the Advancement of Science Committee on Electrical Standards and the Council of the Royal Society. To strengthen his case Fleming (who was to invent the thermionic diode in 1904) provided examples of the unity of electrical theory and practice, as the following quotation from the paper shows:

It is remarkable that the industrial applications of electrical science have forced into existence a standard of accuracy far greater than would ever be attained in mere laboratory work. It is a mistake to suppose that measurements in practical and commercial work are less exact than those undertaken for purely scientific purposes. It was the attempt to make submarine telegraphy a commercial success which forced and demanded an accuracy in the measurement of electrical resistance and capacity never before desired; and it is electric lighting which has developed a corresponding necessity for accuracy in the measurement of current strength and electro-motive force. And applied science has paid back with interest the demand thus made on the abstract and pure science for assistance. Owing to the exactness of the measurements thus demanded we know, for instance, more about the flow of electricity in conductors from the everyday phenomena of submarine cables than could have been obtained in half a century of study of laboratory effects. And it behoves those who have the interest of pure science at heart that tribute is exacted from the countless operations of industrial science, by making its measurements, undertaken in practical operations readily available for the uses of theoretical science. And in no way can this be done except by the earnest effort to obtain and enforce the highest possible accuracy and unity in commercial measurements, based upon and referred to known and common standards.

National Physical Laboratory

Fleming's proposal found an altogether positive response from the participants in the discussion which followed the delivery of the paper[26]. This came out most notably in the speech of R. E. Crompton (1845–1940), one of the pioneers of electrical engineering in Britain.[27] Crompton also had a precise notion of what was to be done if the government would not be willing to be involved. In that case, he suggested, it would be up to the English manufacturers themselves to work together in the task of setting up a standardising laboratory. That this was in the electrical manufacturing industries' very own interest Crompton explained as follows:[28]

We cannot go on any longer as we are now doing without independent check on our individual attempts at calibration. I have been at great pains and expense to get our own instruments correctly standardised, but the results have not been entirely satisfactory. It is almost impossible for manufacturers in what has been well named 'the heavy electrical trades', for the reasons mentioned by Dr Fleming, to arrange a satisfactory calibrating room at or near their works. Freedom from vibration and absence of disturbance of the magnetic readings is not obtainable; further than that, we none of us have sufficient leisure for carrying out these calibrations in the way they should be carried out. Therefore, for purely commercial reasons, we manufacturers are fully prepared to assist in any reasonable scheme which will give us the independent check on standardising that we require and I think that the best method of doing this will be to let this Society move in the matter.

What emerged at the end of the meeting was that the motion wishing 'the Council of the Society to consider the best means by which the standardisation of electrical apparatus can preferably be carried out into effect, as suggested in the paper communicated by Dr Fleming this evening', was passed unanimously.[29] But it took four years – in the meantime the Society became the Institution of Electrical Engineers – before it bore its first fruit. In 1889 the then President of the Board of Trade (Sir Michael Hicks-Beach) received a joint deputation of the Institution and the London Chamber of Commerce. Its plea led to the establishment of the Electrical Standardizing Laboratory of the Board of Trade for the purpose of maintaining standards of the electrical units of current, pressure (electro-motive force) and resistance.

This statutory limited character of the work of the Electrical Standardizing Laboratory came under closest scrutiny during the sittings of the Committee (1897–8), appointed by the Treasury, to consider the desirability of establishing a National Physical Laboratory.[30] Comprising no less than six Fellows of the Royal Society, the high-powered Committee of nine was chaired by Lord Rayleigh, then the Secretary of the Royal Society. It is no exaggeration to say that its conclusion that 'a public institution should be founded for standardizing and verifying instruments, for testing materials, and for the determination of physical constants' largely turned on the evidence regarding electrical matters. It was presented by experts in the field such as Major Philip Cardew, R.E., the head of the Electrical Department of the Board of Trade; R. T. Glazebrook, F.R.S., at that time Assistant Director of the Cavendish Laboratory and Secretary of the Electrical Standards Committee of the British Association; R. E. Crompton; W. E. Ayrton, F.R.S., Dean and Professor of Applied Physics at the City and Guilds of London Central Technical College and others.

On reading the minutes of the proceedings the impression produced is that Crompton's evidence was of invaluable assistance to the Committee in two ways.[31] It helped to clarify the character of the work to be carried out in the envisaged new public institution and gave an indication of the annual sum needed to keep it going. Crompton was in the position to be concrete on these points because he had operated a laboratory, quite apart from his works, 'for the last ten or twelve years'. He had it installed in two floors of his London house with a staff consisting of a head, four chief assistants and three general assistants engaged on specific investigations directly important to his business – that is, on the examination and testing of materials, and on the standardising of measurement instruments. In reply to the question of whether these investigations had proved of great value to him Crompton stated: 'We simply could not do without them.' He also explained that the progress in the distribution and utilisation of electricity in England was hampered by the fact that the domestic manufacturer was unable to supply instruments standardised to measure sub-multiples of the ohm (the hundredth, the thousandth and the ten-thousandth). Such standards were not available in the country and while a possibility existed to compare, say, a thousandth of an ohm with an ohm at the Cavendish Laboratory, it would be very laborious. As to the Board of Trade Electrical Standardizing Laboratory, it could not undertake the comparison because until recently, Crompton believed, there was no fixed scale of fees for this kind of work. According to him:

The only thing we could do was either to purchase from the Reichsanstalt, or, which is the more common thing, to send our standards over to them to compare for us, and that is costly.

In view of what has been said there obviously was a need around 1900, in the interest of electrical progress in Britain, to have a public laboratory active in fundamental electrical measurement. The Committee in its submission to the Treasury put the case for it clearly:[32]

The electrical units being based upon theoretical definitions are on a somewhat different footing from units of weights and measures. Investigations are continually being made as to the degree of accuracy with which the legal standards represent the absolute values. Furthermore, there is some uncertainty as to the permanence of the standard instruments. Investigations on both these points are carried out systematically at the Reichsanstalt, but there is no provision for such work at the Board of Trade Electrical Laboratory or at any public institution of this country. It is, however, in the highest degree desirable that the Government Department which is the custodian of the standards should undertake, or have official relations with an institution which can undertake, to carry out or to verify the results of such inquiries... The testing of instruments at the Board of Trade laboratories might be considerably extended if the staff of these laboratories were increased; but there are numerous classes of instruments which do not fall at present within the scope of their work, inasmuch as there are no legal standards whereby the instruments could be tested, and it does not appear to be necessary that such legal standards should be established. The Committee are of opinion that a public laboratory in addition to the advantage to be obtained by the scientific investigation of problems useful to industry would be of great practical use to the commercial community in testing the various forms of measuring instruments which cannot at present be tested under any legal authority.

It was from Crompton that the Committee obtained an idea of the annual cost of the upkeep of the new research institution. It cannot be an accident that the Secretary to the Treasury went on record that 'Her Majesty's Government would be prepared to ask Parliament to vote an annual sum of £4,000 for five years certain as a grant in aid of the expenses of the proposed institution'[33]. £4,000 was the figure given by Crompton regarding the laboratory expenditure, while about £3,000 were recovered in fees for investigations for outside firms.

After the Government's formal approval (1899) of the proposal to establish the National Physical Laboratory, it is worth pointing out that its first Director from 1 January 1900 was Glazebrook whose basic qualification for the job stemmed from his long-standing involvement in standardising work in the electrical field.

Very shortly after Glazebrook took up his appointment, a talk entitled 'The standardisation of electrical engineering plant' was given (8 February 1900) to a meeting of the Institution of Electrical Engineers by a member, R. P. Sellon.[34] By standardisation he meant 'the general acceptance to a far greater extent than at present obtained in this country of certain standards of output, quality, efficiency, or other characteristics of electrical engineering plant, to meet ordinary requirements of usage for light, traction, and power'[35]. That the issue was a very live one was demonstrated by the fact that more speakers wished to participate in the discussion than could be accommodated and so the meeting was adjourned to another evening (22 February 1900). In his reply Sellon concentrated on what he thought were the main questions in the discussion.

There was an overwhelming consensus that British electrical manufacturers lagged in standardisation behind their American and Continental competitors which put them at disadvantage both in the world and home markets. According to Sellon the explanation would appear to lie in the following:

According to American and Continental practice the producer determines, in a large measure, the character of the plant employed by the user; while according to British custom the buyer very generally imposes upon the manufacturer not merely a specification of the ends he wishes to attain, but the details of means by which he desires those ends to be achieved.

This is due to the fact that under the American and Continental system producers largely secure outlets through the agency of powerful financial organizations created by and allied to their interests, who are concerned simply with commercial results, and are content to leave the technical means of attaining them to the manufacturing interests with whom they co-operate. In America these organisations take the form of colossal Trusts or consolidations of competing interests; on the Continent that of Industrial Banks. In either case there is a close relation between producer and buyer.

In Great Britain, on the other hand, the demand for electrical engineering plant in recent years has issued chiefly from local authorities or from private users unconnected with any manufacturing interests; and these have very naturally had recourse to electrical engineers acting in a consulting capacity or passing permanently into their service, to guide them in the choice of plant to fulfil their requirements.

That the practical operation of this system in the past has been primarily responsible for the relative absence of standardisation in this country, with its attendant evils alike to user and producer, appears certain.[36]

The majority present, either manufacturers or consulting engineers, concurred that standardisation was desirable. There was less clarity about whether standardisation was practicable (S. Z. de Ferranti believed it was too late) and also about who was to be responsible for it, the manufacturer or the consulting engineer. Sellon himself agreed with those who inclined to blame the manufacturer for the absence of standardisation. But he opposed the opinion that the Institution should itself be concerned with standardisation:[37]

...I agree with those who take the view that it is against the spirit of Englishmen to have regulations imposed upon them if they are unwilling to receive them. Just as you cannot make people virtuous by Act of Parliament, so you cannot make people standardise by regulations which are irksome to them. I can see no hope for success in the consideration of this matter by a committee of the Institution unless it be approached with a willing mind by both the manufacturer and the consulting engineer.

As it turned out, the principle of standardisation in electrical technology in Britain took a backseat well into the 1930s.[38] Why this was so is part and parcel of the ongoing debate on Britain's industrial malaise since the 1880s or so.[39] It is commonly held that in the period under review British scientists had little concern with industrial matters. This article, short as it is, shows that it was not for want of interst of (top level) British scientists in advancing the scientific side of electrical industry that the latter fell behind the American and German competitors.

NOTES

This article arises out of my comments on Professor Chandler's contribution to the conference on the origins and development of multinational enterprise, held at the University of East Anglia (Norwich) in late March of 1985. See A. D. Chandler, Jr, 'Technological and organizational underpinnings of modern industrial multinational enterprise: the dynamics of competitive advantage' in A. Teichova, M. Lévy-Leboyer, H. Nussbaum (eds.), *Multinational enterprise in historical perspective* (Cambridge, 1986), pp. 30–54.

1 *Ibid.*, p. 52.
2 D. K. Fieldhouse, 'The multinational: A critique of a concept', in Teichova, Lévy-Leboyer, Nussbaum (eds.), *Multinational Enterprise*, p. 9.
3 D. S. Landes, *The Unbound Prometheus* (Cambridge, 1969), pp. 245–7.

4 *ibid.*, pp. 247–8. Emphasis by Landes. The word 'climacteric' was coined by E. H. Phelps-Brown in 1952, see *ibid.*, p. 235, note 1.

5 'Capitalism in its imperialist state leads directly to the most comprehensive socialization of production; it, so to speak, drags the capitalists, against their will and consciousness, into some sort of new social order, a transitional one from complete free competition to complete socialization. Production becomes social, but appropriation remains private. The social means of production remain the private property of a few' V. I. Lenin, *Imperialism the highest stage of capitalism. A popular outline*, *Selected Works in Three Volumes*, vol. 1 (Moscow, 1975), p. 649.

6 *Ibid.*

7 *Ibid.*, 665

8 Few personalities in American technological and business history have attracted more attention than Thomas Alva Edison. Wyn Wachhorst for his study *Thomas Alva Edison* (Cambridge, Mass., 1981) examined 62 books, 21 pamphlets, 326 more chapters and excerpts, 936 periodical articles, 3,218 newspaper items, 148 book reviews, 4 plays, 5 films and 4 television documentaries (p. 6). Yet there is no comprehensive critical account of his life and work. It may be that this will follow the publication of the *Thomas A. Edison Papers* by the Johns Hopkins University Press. Its editor Reese V. Jenkins examines the problems which a historian of technology faces in a thoughtful article: 'Words, images, artefacts and sound: Documents for the history of technology'. *The British Journal for the History of Science*, 20 (1987), 39–56.

9 'Edison's mechanics worked on a minimum wage and piece-work system. If the job cost more than the estimate, the mechanic received a minimum wage; if it cost less, he received in addition to his wage the difference saved.' See J. G. Crowther, *Famous American men of science*, vol. 2 (Harmondsworth, 1944), p. 77.

10 H. C. Passer, *The electrical manufacturers 1875–1900* (Cambridge, Mass., 1953), p. 87.

11 On Villard see D. G. Buss, *Henry Villard A study of transatlantic investments and interest, 1870–1895* (New York, 1978). I owe this reference to Professor Chandler.

12 See Passer, pp. 78–104; 321–2.

13 L. S. Reich, *The making of American industrial research, science and business at GE and Bell, 1876–1926* (Cambridge, 1985), p. 61.

14 G. Wise, 'A new role for professional scientists in industry: industrial research at General Electric, 1900–1916', *Technology and Culture*, 21 (1980), 4008–29 (pp. 413–14); Reich, *The making of American industrial research*, pp. 62f.

15 There is as yet no comprehensive biography of Steinmetz. This would have to pay attention to his social and political views, including his positive attitude to the plan of electrification of Russia in the early 1920s. His letter to Lenin and Lenin's reply are worth quoting here:

Febr 16, 1922

My Dear Mr Lenin,

B. W. Lassow's return to Russia gives me an opportunity to express to you my admiration of the wonderful work of social and industrial regeneration which Russia is accomplishing under such terrible difficulties.

I wish you the fullest success and have every confidence that you will succeed. Indeed, you must succeed for the great work which Russia has started must not be allowed to fail.

If in technical, and more particular in electrical engineering matters, I can assist Russia in any manner with advice, suggestion or consultation, I shall always be very pleased to do so, so far as I am able.

Fraternally yours,
Charles P. Steinmetz

Published in *Nation*, 19 July 1922, p. 78.

Moscow. April 10, 1922

Dear Mr Steinmetz,
I thank you cordially for your friendly letter of February 16, 1922. I must admit to my shame that I heard your name for the first time only a few months ago from Comrade Krzhizhanovsky, who was the Chairman of our State Commission for working out a Plan for the Electrification of Russia and now Chairman of the State General Planning Commission. He told me of the outstanding position which you have gained among the electrical engineers of the whole world.

Comrade Martens has now made me better acquainted by his accounts of you. I have seen from these accounts that your sympathies with Soviet Russia have been aroused by your social and political views. On the other hand, as a representative of electrical engineering and particularly in one of the technically advanced countries, you have become convinced of the necessity and inevitability of the replacement of capitalism by a new social order, which will establish the planned regulation of economy and ensure the welfare of the entire mass of the people on the basis of the electrification of entire countries. In all the countries of the world there is growing, more slowly than one would like, but irresistibly and unswervingly, the number of representatives of science, technology, art, who are becoming convinced of the necessity of replacing capitalism by a different socio-economic system, and whom the 'terrible difficulties' [in English] of the struggle of Soviet Russia against the entire capitalist world do not repel, do not frighten away but, on the contrary, lead to an understanding of the inevitability of the struggle and the necessity of taking what part in it they can, helping the new to overcome the old.

In particular, I want to thank you for your offer to help Russia with your advice, suggestions, etc. As the absence of official and legally recognised relations between Soviet Russia and the United States makes the practical realisation of your offer extremely difficult both for us and for you, I will allow myself to publish both your letter and my reply, in the hope that many persons who live in America, or in countries connected by commercial treaties both with the United States and with Russia, will then help you (by information, by translations from Russian into English, etc.) to give effect to your intention of helping the Soviet Republic.

With very best greetings,

Yours fraternally,
Lenin

Published in *Pravda*, 19 April 1922, see V. I. Lenin, *Collected Works*, 4th edn (Moscow, 1966), vol. 35, pp. 552–3.

16 W. von Siemens, *Inventor and entrepreneur*, 2nd edn (London–Munich, 1966), p. 268.
17 *Ibid.*, pp. 41–2, 52.
18 I. C. R. Byatt, *The British electrical industry* (Oxford, 1977), p. 166.
19 W. von Siemens, *Scientific and technical papers*, translated from the 2nd German edn, vol. 1 (London, 1892), pp. 162–80.

20 M. E. Hospitalier (ed.), *Exposition universelle internationale de 1900 Congrès internationale d'électricité Paris, 18–25 Août 1900, Rapports et procès-verbaux* (Paris, 1901), pp. 17–19. The volume reprints the decisions taken at previous International Electrical Congresses which started in Paris in 1881.

21 Siemens, *Scientific and technical papers*, vol. 2 (London, 1895), pp. 587–8. The founding of the *Physikalisch–Technische Reichsanstalt* is discussed by F. Pfetch in his article 'Scientific organization and science policy in Imperial Germany, 1871–1914; The foundation of the Imperial Institute of Physics and Technology', *Minerva*, 8 (1970), 557–80.

22 W. Thomson, *Mathematical and physical papers*, Articles LXXII to LXXXV, vol. 2 (Cambridge, 1884).

23 For details regarding the problems and progress in this field, see the invaluable reprint of *Reports of the Committee on Electrical Standards Appointed by the British Association for the Advancement of Science* (Cambridge, 1913).

24 J. A. Fleming, *Fifty years of electricity. The memories of an electrical engineer* (London, 1922), pp. 282–3.

25 J. A. Fleming, 'On the necessity for a national standardising laboratory for electrical instruments', *Journal of the Society of Telegraph-Engineers and Electricians*. 14 (1885), 488–503.

26 Discussion, *ibid.*, 503–21.

27 See his *Reminiscences* (London, 1928).

28 *Journal of the Society of Telegraph-Engineers and Electricians*, 14 (1885), 510–11.

29 *Ibid.*, 519.

30 *Report of the Committee appointed by the Treasury to consider the desirability of establishing a National Physical Laboratory*, C. 8976 (1898): *Minutes of Evidence taken before the Committee appointed by the Treasury to consider the desirability of establishing a National Physical Laboratory: with Appendices and Index*. C. 8977 (1898).

31 For Crompton's evidence, see C. 8977, pp. 50–4.

32 See C. 8976, pp. 2–3.

33 E. Pyatt, *The National Physical Laboratory A History* (Bristol, 1983), p. 20.

34 R. P. Sellon, 'The standardisation of electrical engineering plant', *Journal of the Institution of Electrical Engineers*, 29 (1899–1900), 291–314; 315–44.

35 *Ibid.*, 314.

36 *Ibid.*, 293.

37 *Ibid.*, 343.

38 L. Hannah, *Electricity before Nationalisation. A Study of the Development of the Electricity Supply Industry in Britain to 1948* (London and Basingstoke, 1979), pp. 38f.

39 For a recent stimulating substantial survey, see D. C. Coleman and Christine MacLeod, 'Attitudes to new techniques: British businessmen, 1800–1950', *Economic History Review*, 39 (1986), 588–611.

5 The nature of multinationals, 1870–1939[1]

T. A. B. CORLEY

Introduction

What kinds of multinational enterprises (MNEs) existed before 1939? When and why had they been set up? In which branches of activity and in which countries did they operate, and were there any systematic differences between the various types: those, say, established to exploit overseas raw materials (supply-orientated MNEs) and those for producing goods overseas (market-orientated MNEs)? How was head-office control exercised over the foreign branches? Precise answers to these and associated questions would be valuable, both as extensions to our historical knowledge and as empirical evidence to which present-day theories of the MNE could be applied: for instance, the types of advantage firms are held to pursue when venturing abroad. So far these theories have had to be tested with current or very recent data.[2]

To be sure, there are many case studies of pre-1939 MNEs, which have individually or jointly yielded some useful generalisations and hypotheses.[3] Also work has been, or is being, undertaken on today's top MNEs and their historical background, including – where relevant – that for the period being considered here.[4] Such work is far from complete in that it omits smaller firms which operated overseas and those which have gone out of production: these omissions could possibly have been quite significant in aggregate. Nor do these researches differentiate enough between the various MNE types.

A systematic enquiry seeking to cover all MNEs of every country would indeed prove a massive task and often encounter unbridgeable gaps in our knowledge. A small pilot study, such as the one outlined in the present note, may however show some of the benefits as well as the possible costs of attempting a broader survey than hitherto. So as to provide a framework, the remainder of the Introduction will show why 1870 to 1939 seems to form a self-contained period of research into MNEs, the next section will deploy existing overall quantitative data. Then a sample of firms will be presented for investigation. Further motives for and the financing of overseas

43

production, and the question of entrepreneurship in this context will be considered before some concluding remarks are made.

The period considered here ranges from the 1870s to 1939, since it was for the purpose of this note a reasonably uniform one. In the 1870s MNEs, as we understand them today, started to evolve. From about 1800 until that decade, by contrast, direct capital exports had mainly taken the form of expatriate investment or individual entrepreneurs' or syndicates' outlays to buy majority share interests in foreign companies.[5] Thereafter the composition of foreign direct investment (FDI) changed. A typical producing firm tended to grow by building up sales at home, and then developing export markets: for reasons to be discussed below, it might later decide to use FDI for setting up overseas branches.

Such extensions of domestic activity through foreign branches and affiliates, building up from that decade onwards, were made possible by improvements in both communications and knowledge. Fast steamships and railways, conveying people and correspondence around the world more rapidly than before, and the telegraphic cable, increased the homeward flow of information and outward head-office instructions. Personal contacts, trade magazines such as *The Grocer* and *Chemist & Druggist*, and general newspapers and journals disseminated knowledge internationally, of the host-country markets, actual or potential rivals' activities and so on.

The year 1939 heralded the end of an era because of the new developments that followed the Second World War. In the post-1945 era notably different patterns of FDI emerged, with the United States being the predominant investor, and advances – even more radical than in the 1870s – taking place in transport and communications, as well as in production and organisational techniques in the pioneering enterprises. After 1945, it has been pointed out, 'capital, technology and management skills came to represent a closely integrated package of resources to the firm'.[6] Since for various reasons markets in these assets proved inadequate mechanisms for the international movement of resources that was now practicable, and because of the synergy to be sought in asset combinations, FDI became the preferred means of such international resource transfer. Hence the evolution of the modern technologically based MNE: different in degree if not in kind from the ones of 1870–1939.

The composition of MNE activity

Since the period under consideration appears to be a reasonably homogeneous one within which to carry out MNE research, what quantitative evidence do we possess? For this purpose, data from Dunning's path-breaking article of 1983 can be usefully combined with earlier US estimates.

Table 5.1. *Estimated stock of (accumulated) foreign direct investment by country of origin*

	1914		1938	
	Total ($bn)	%	Total ($bn)	%
UK	6.5[a]	45½	10.5	40
US	2.65	18½	7.3	28
Rest of world[b]	5.15	36	8.6	32
	14.3	100	26.4	100
of which:	Whole world (%)	US (%)	UK (%)	US (%)
Supply-orientated (primary products)	55	53	n.a.	35
Railways	20	10	n.a.	4
Market-orientated (manufacturing)	15	18	24	28
Trade and distribution	10	6	n.a.	7
Public utilities banking etc.	?	13	n.a.	26
	100	100	100	100

Notes: n.a. = not available.
[a] Probably an underestimate (Houston and Dunning, 1976 pp. 7, 12).
[b] Next largest investing country = France, 12% 1914, 10% 1938.
Sources: Whole world 1914: Dunning (1983), pp. 87, 89. UK 1938 derived from *ibid.*, p. 94. US 1940: Wilkins (1970), p. 110, (1974) pp. 182–3.

Table 5.1 gives figures of the overall world stock of FDI, the main investing countries' shares, and the broad industrial categories, for 1914 and 1938.

As yet there is no breakdown by categories of Britain's FDI stock in those years. However, it seems feasible that the resource-rich US should have had a relatively lower percentage share of supply-orientated direct investment – and much lower in absolute terms – than Britain. More certainly, Britain's heavy involvement in railways and in trade and distribution was reflected in the higher relevant FDI percentages than in the US. As to market-orientated investment, for the manufacture of goods in host countries, it remains to be determined whether the US was comparatively more active in this category than was Britain. Since about 12 per cent of enterprises quoted on the

London stock exchange in 1914, and believed to be operating wholly or very largely overseas, were manufacturing ones,[7] and many unquoted and predominantly domestic British manufacturing firms are known to have established production subsidiaries abroad by then, the 'whole world' figure of 15 per cent for 1914 seems a reasonable estimate of Britain's manufacturing FDI share.

After 1918 protectionist policies and sagging demand for primary products were behind the relative increase in market-orientated, as against supply-orientated, investment worldwide. In the US the share of the former rose from 18 per cent in 1914 to 28 per cent in 1940: for Britain's equivalent last year of peace, 1938, the share was about 24 per cent. The composition of direct investment by the continental European countries, which provided the bulk of the remaining global FDI, remains to be investigated.

To link up orders of magnitude with MNE characteristics, many and various case studies could be adduced, as suggested in the Introduction. The problem here is how to establish whether such cases are representative of the whole. Instead of constructing generalisations from widely differing case studies, the present note studies one sub-group of MNEs: those making simple and fairly divisible consumer goods. Admittedly these represented only a minor proportion of the total. Taking Britain on its own, if we assume that half the 15 per cent (or thereabouts) in 1914 were manufacturers of non-consumption goods – e.g. agricultural machinery made by Clayton & Shuttleworth or Fowler, Callender's insulated cables, or industrial cleaning materials by Sanitas – then only 7–8 per cent, say $500m or £100m, could be attributed to consumer goods, of which the sample forms a part. A half share of the 24 per cent in 1938 would be about $1,250m or £260m.

So as to build up such aggregate figures, it would clearly be impossible to compute the FDI share of each firm in this sub-group. Instead, the appendix lists seven product groups in the period 1870–1939: beverages, biscuits, confectionery, matches, patent medicines, soap and tobacco, and notes such British and overseas MNEs as have been identified. Since relative size is commonly supposed to be associated with FDI, known market leaders are indicated by (M). FDI successfully undertaken (A), unsuccessful FDI (B), and that considered but turned down (C), are also designated. This sample of firms is studied next, notably to establish their export tendencies.

The sample of firms and their propensity to export

In the Introduction, it was suggested that firms will tend to become international first of all by exporting and then perhaps by producing abroad. Most of the examples cited in the appendix are for Britain and the US, which in table 5.1 were shown jointly to account for 64% of the aggregate FDI

Table 5.2. *UK consumer goods firms – export/turnover percentages*

	1870	1901	1913	1930	1935
Biscuits					
Huntley & Palmers	18–20	32	48	22	16
Peek Frean	7[a]	21	21	16	?
Chocolate					
Cadbury	3[b]	19[d]	24	6	4
Fry	2	9	16	10	6
Patent medicines					
Beecham	10–15	10–15	10–15	?	24[f]
Tobacco					
Wills	1[c]	21	[e]	[e]	[e]

Notes: [a] 1863. [b] 1874. [c] 1883. [d] 1909. [e] Exports taken over by British American Tobacco. [f] 1940.

stock in 1914 and for 68% in 1938. Information for other investing countries may be seriously incomplete. Was there any systematic difference between the export orientation of British and of US firms?

In some (but not all) of the product groups in the appendix, British firms tended to be very active exporters. Anecdotal evidence tells of the patent medicine manufacturers Thomas Holloway and James C. Eno who personally canvassed ships' passengers and crews at the docks, and the striking efforts of legendary overseas representatives of, say, Huntley & Palmers. The actual export orientation of certain British firms is given in table 5.2.

On the other hand, the export record of comparable US firms was more variable, and reluctance to export apparently had some association with lags in setting up manufacturing abroad. The giant combine of 1898, the National Biscuit Company, unprofitably exported on a small scale to Latin America before 1914, did not produce biscuits abroad until 1925 – going then to Canada – and in Britain not until the 1960s. US soap manufacturers do not seem to have exported on any scale to Britain before the early 1920s or to have produced here until the 1930s. The export activity of most US patent medicine manufacturers was low. Only a few medicines, such as Carter's Little Liver Pills or Dr Williams' Pink Pills for Pale People, are known to have been at all heavily exported to Britain before 1914. If and when such firms found well established export markets becoming difficult, how far did they resort to FDI as an acceptable alternative?

Motives for and finance of overseas production

Motives

It has not yet been possible to code the firms in our sample according to the reasons for undertaking FDI, or alternatively considering FDI and then deciding against it. Nor does space permit a discussion of the various FDI motives put forward in the theory of the MNE. Instead, two motives in particular will be briefly discussed: tariffs and the operation of the product cycle.

Tariffs were clearly of overwhelming importance in this period. Until the 1870s exporting firms could use a number of devices to mitigate the effects of recipient countries' tariffs and other barriers to trade. Some British firms engaged in smuggling, even with their own government's connivance, for instance of beer to the Baltic in 1806 and of textiles to German states in the 1830s.[8] Others undervalued their exports on bills of lading. In 1869 Thomas Holloway asked the British supplier of his ointment jars to invoice a consignment at half the price less discount and to send him a second invoice for his overseas shipments, adding:

I am acquainted with a great many houses which ship goods to the United States and adopt the same plan. The duties, which must be paid in gold, have now become so excessive as to be almost prohibitive for English manufacturers, and the commerce of this country with the United States would greatly suffer if means were not adopted to lessen the outlay for duties.

After 1870 the more efficient state apparatus in advanced countries virtually ruled out such expedients. Some detailed research is badly needed on the pre-1914 tariff changes in the US, continental and commonwealth countries, the lead time in the announcement of proposed changes, and the related timing of the investing firms' FDI decisions. Trade journals regularly reported tariff developments: to take the US example, the McKinley Act of 1890 has often been quoted as a spur to FDI there, but the Payne and Aldrich tariff of 1911 requires investigation as having disquieted a number of manufacturers in Britain and no doubt other countries also. For instance, both Huntley & Palmers and Pears quite independently began taking steps for production in the US, Pears relying on the extensive local knowledge of Sir Joseph Beecham, a Pears non-executive director who had been manufacturing Beecham's pills in the US since 1888. In fact, the 1911 tariff proposals were subsequently watered down and Pears abandoned its plans; for Huntley & Palmers see below.

As suggested above, the relatively greater number of production subsidiaries set up after 1918 seem to reflect trading nations' increasingly protectionist policies: Britain adopted tariffs generally for the first time after 1931. In some countries, notably Australia, stringent trade restrictions were reinforced by government-sponsored campaigns to buy home products and even encouragements to overseas firms to start up host-country production.

The product-cycle theory, which implicitly considers the sorts of goods in our sample, postulates that manufacturers in the more advanced countries will seek to secure and maintain a technological advantage over producers in less developed markets.[9] When the former have built up markets extensive enough to justify the trouble and cost of local manufacture, round about the time when exports come under threat from rivals, then they will actively consider FDI. In the present sample, this defensive strategy – when it can be distinguished from the tariff motive – does not appear to be strongly represented.

When Schweppes started going abroad after 1877 and Spratts after 1886, the nature of their comparatively low-cost goods made overseas production preferable to exporting. Beecham, supported by the Anglo-American Convention of 1887 to protect trade marks, started making his pills in the US the following year partly to facilitate the tracking down and prosecuting of counterfeiters. On the other hand, there were aggressive strategies of FDI against firms in tariff-free Britain, particularly from the US: Diamond Match, having failed to license its advance match-making technology to Bryant & May, Britain's market leader, began manufacture here in 1898. Within six years it had forced Bryant & May into an agreement, which in turn induced the latter to start producing overseas. American Tobacco strove to penetrate the UK market by acquiring a small British firm, but, after its British rivals had in 1902 set up a defensive combine (Imperial Tobacco), came to an agreement to form an (at first US-controlled) joint subsidiary, British American Tobacco, to take care of the rest of the world's markets. Apart from two insignificant tit-for-tat direct investments in 1927, the combines acquired no new sources of overseas tobacco manufacture before 1939.

Finance

British market leaders in this sample were on the whole making such handsome profits before 1914 that they could easily finance FDI from their own resources. Perhaps only Schweppes, gravely short of cash after incorporation by the crooked company promoter E. T. Hooley, had to forego FDI opportunities on financial grounds in 1905 and 1919. On the other hand, US companies starting up production in Britain often raised money on the London stock exchange, including Diamond Match, British American Tobacco and four patent medicine firms which followed the US practice of floating companies with heavily watered capital, making handsome flotation profits and then moving on to other fields. All these companies in due course became UK-owned.

The role of entrepreneurship

In an enquiry of this kind, some attention needs to be paid to the entrepreneurs responsible for undertaking FDI. On the British side, Lever established soap production subsidiaries in ten countries by 1914, and the Swedish Kreuger had subsidiaries in about 35 countries by 1930. Weston of Canada was a 'gap-filler' who began making really cheap biscuits in Britain from 1934 onwards, within five years was the single largest biscuit producer here, and brazenly offered in 1938 to buy out the country's most prestigious combine of Huntley & Palmers and Peek Frean. Duke of American Tobacco met his match in Sir William and George Wills, the progenitors of Imperial Tobacco. Barber of Diamond Match personally – and successfully – threatened to whip the shareholders of the moribund Bryant & May 'out of their boots'.[10] Lever, Kreuger, Beecham and the Spratts were all cosmopolitan and energetic men who felt the attraction of the US and enjoyed the toil and journeyings involved in setting up subsidiaries.

As against these, Huntley & Palmers (like Bryant & May) experienced poor entrepreneurship. The gap it left in failing to satisfy newer biscuit tastes was largely filled by four Scottish and Irish rivals, all of which between 1897 and 1914 carried out regional direct investment, setting up factories in England nearer to the main domestic markets. Huntley & Palmers retreated into its export markets; about ten times up to 1939 it turned down proposals to produce overseas, claiming that it lacked the managerial resources for this purpose. Although some circular reasoning is inevitable here – since by definition a 'good' entrepreneur is one who makes a success of production abroad – a refining of the analysis of entrepreneurship might yield some insights which could be valuable from the viewpoint of the histories of MNEs.

Conclusion

It has been shown above that some useful data can be collected on cases of production abroad before 1939. Perhaps these may encourage further case-by-case research, so as to contribute more systematic knowledge of a crucial period in the evolution of what we now term MNEs.

NOTES

1 Thanks are due to John Dunning, Mark Casson and John Cantwell for helpful comments on an earlier draft. References are not usually given for individual companies, but the author will gladly provide further particulars.
2 For testing see Dunning (1981), chapters 3–5; Koutsoyiannis (1982), pp. 260–8.

3 An interesting comparative study (based on Dunlop, Courtaulds and Cadbury) is G. G. Jones' 'The performance of British multinational enterprise 1890–1939' (Hertner and Jones 1985).
4 See, for example, Stopford (1974) and Nicholas (1982). A historical survey of FDI and its motivation by the 250 top UK MNEs is being carried out, by Howard Archer, at the University of Reading.
5 Dunning (1983), p. 86.
6 Hood and Young (1982), p. 12.
7 Houston and Dunning (1976), p. 40. Regrettably, little useful information could be gleaned from the list of British Investments Abroad – which omits those in the US and Canada – in US Federal Trade Commission (1916).
8 Mathias (1959), p. 182 (but in 1822 a British ex-MP scaled the high Russian tariff walls for beer by setting up a brewery at St Petersburg); Clapham (1926), p. 480.
9 For a good survey see Caves (1982), pp. 61ff, 207ff.
10 Southard (1931), p. xiv.

REFERENCES

Caves, Richard E. (1982). *Multinational enterprise and economic analysis*, Cambridge.
Clapham, John H. (1926). *An economic history of modern Britain: I. The early railway age 1820–1850*, Cambridge.
Dunning, John H. (1981). *International production and the multinational enterprise*, London.
Dunning, John H. (1983). 'Changes in the level and structure of international production in the last one hundred years', in M. Casson (ed.), *The growth of international business*, London, pp. 84–139.
Hertner, Peter and Jones, Geoffrey G. (1985). *Multinationals: theory and history*, London.
Hood, N., and Young, S. (1982). 'British policy and inward direct investment', *Journal of World Trade Law*.
Houston, T., and Dunning, J. H. (1976). *U.K. Industry abroad*, London.
Koutsoyiannis, A. (1982). *Non-Price Decisions: The firm in a modern context*, London.
Mathias, Peter (1959). *The brewing industry in England 1700–1830*, Cambridge.
Nicholas, Stephen J. (1982). 'British multinational investment before 1939', *Journal of European Economic History*, 11, 605–30.
Southard, Frank A. Jr. (1931). *American industry in Europe*, Boston.
Stopford, John M. (1974). 'The origins of British-based multinational manufacturing enterprises', *Business History Review* 48, 303–35.
US Federal Trade Commission (1916). *Report on co-operation in American export trade*, vol. 2, Washington, DC, pp. 537–74.
Wilkins, Mira (1970). *The emergence of multinational enterprise: American business abroad from the Colonial era to 1914*, Cambridge, Mass.
  (1974). *The maturing of multinational enterprise: American business abroad from 1914 to 1970*, Cambridge, Mass.

Appendix: *Simple consumer goods: international production 1870–1939*
(*Market-orientated activities only*)

	Date when 'international industry' began	1870–1918 UK firms	US/foreign firms
Soft	1900s	34. Australia 1877 (A) US 1884–92 (B), US 1905 (C)	35. (US) Cuba 1906, Canada *c*.1910 (A) 36. (US) UK 1906 (A) UK-owned by 1937
Beverages Alcoholic	—	[Up to 100 brewing cos. US 1888–99, 11 in New York. Syndicate, not direct, investment. Mostly (B)]	
Human		1. (M) France 1904 jv with 15 (C) US 1911,	
	1870s– 1880s	jv with 4 (C) S. Africa 1911 (C)	
Biscuits		46. Germany. Austria jv 1912	
Canine	—	8. Russian 1886 (B), US 1899 (A)	
Chocolate	1880s?	9. (M) Australia 1911 (C) 15. France 1904, jv with 1 (C)	12. (Germany) US pre-1914 (A)
Confectionery			
Sweets	—	11. US 1904–8 (B), Germany 1906, Canada, Australia pre-1914 (A)	
Matches	1890s	17. (M) 1901 agreement with 18 S. Africa 1904, Australia 1908, New Zealand 1910 (all jvs-A) US-owned 1901–14	18. (US) UK 1895 (A) – see 17 Brazil, Peru, S. Africa, Switzerland pre-1914 (A), Germany 1900–3 (B) 19. (Sweden) US 1910, Norway, Finland pre-1914 (A)
Patent medicines	*c*1885	20. (M) US 1888 (A) 47. (M) US 1860 (B)	21. (US) UK 1896 (C) 22. (US) UK 1884, 1897 ⎱ UK stock 23. (US) UK 1889 ⎰ exchange 24. (US) UK 1890 flotations 25. (US) UK 1901 (B). All UK-owned by *c*1905

1918–39

UK firms	US/foreign firms
34. Australia, US 1919 (C) Belgium 1923, S. Africa 1924. New Zealand 1925, France 1928 (A)	35. (US) France *c* 1920 (B) Licensing then replaces FDI
37. US *c* 1930s (A)	
38. Australia 1927, Canada 1927, US 1934 (A)	
1. US 1925, 1928, 1934 (C) France 1926, jv with 3 1931–51 (B) Germany and Hungary 1929 (C) Canada 1935 (C) Canada 1935 (C) Australia and New Zealand, jv with 9 1930 (C)	2. (US-M) Canada 1925 (A) UK – not until 1960s (shreaded wheat 1925, A)
5. India 1924, Australia 1931 (A)	6. (Canada) UK (cheap biscuits) 1934 (A) UK seek to buy 7, 1938
46. India 1930 (C)	
9. Australia 1920, jv with 10 & 14 (B) New Zealand 1930 jv (A) S. Africa 1937 (A)	13. (Switzerland) UK pre-1938 (A)
10. Canada 1919 jv (bought by 9 before 1931, B)	16. (US) UK 1934 (A)
15. S. Africa 1926 jv (A?) Canada late 1920s (A?)	
11. US 1922 jv (A)	44. (US) Mexico 1927, Canada 1929, UK pre-1933 (B)
14. Australia 1920 jv (B)	45. (US) UK *c* 1935 (A), Germany *c* 1935 (B)
17. Colombia *c* 1920 (A) Brazil 1926 jv (A) Argentina 1930s (A) S. Rhodesia 1937 (A)	18. (US) Canada 1926, jv with 19
	19. (Sweden) Australia 1919, India 1923 (A). 33 countries by 1930 (A). 1927 agreement with 17.
20. Australia 1925 (A) Canada 1925 (A)	21. (US) UK 1920s (A)
	26. (US) UK 1930s (A)

Appendix: (*cont.*)

	Date when 'international industry' began	1870–1918	
		UK firms	US/foreign firms
Soap	1890s	27. (M) US 1897, European countries 1898 onwards, Australia 1900, Canada 1900, S. Africa 1910 (A) Japan 1913 (B) 28. US 1911 (C) 29. S. Africa 1911 (C), 1913 jv with 27 (A), China 1913 jv with 27 (C), 1916 (A)	30. (France) UK *c*1888 (expatriate investment? (A) – UK-owned before 1898)
Tobacco	*c*1880s	39. (M) Japan 1898 (C), Canada 1899 (C), Australia, 1901 (A). Forms 42, 1901. Agreement with 41, 1902, leads to formation of 43 40. Australia 1900 (A)	41. (US) Australia, Canada, Germany, Japan 1890s (A), UK 1901 (acquires 40: leads to agreement with 39, 1902. 40 sold to 42, 1902

KEY

1. Huntley-Palmers
2. National Biscuit Co.
3. McVitie & Price
4. General Biscuit Co. of America
5. Peek Frean
6. Weston Biscuit Co.
7. Associated Biscuit Manufacturers (1. + 5.)
8. Spratts Patent Ltd.
9. Cadbury
10. Fry
11. Mackintosh
12. Stollwerke

13. Nestlé
14. Pascall
15. Rowntree
16. Mars (UK) Ltd.
17. Bryant & May
18. Diamond Match Co.
19. Swedish Match
20. Beecham's Pills Ltd
21. Carter Medicine Co.
22. A. J. White Ltd
23. H. H. Warner Ltd
24. Sequah Ltd

1918–39

UK firms	US/foreign firms
27. India 1922 (B), 1934 (A) Congo 1922 (B), Nigeria 1924. Merger with Dutch co. (to form Unilever) 1929 31. US 1928 (A), Canada 1937 (A)	32. (US) Canada 1914, UK 1930 (A) (defensive v 27) 33. (US) European countries, Canada, Latin America, Australia by 1930 (A)
43. (UK-owned since 1920s) US 1927 (A)	41. (US) UK 1927 (A)

25. St Jacobs Oil Ltd
26. Dr Williams Medicine Co.
27. Lever Brothers
28. A. & F. Pears Ltd
29. Joseph Crosfield & Sons Ltd
30. Vinolia Ltd
31. Yardley & Co. Ltd.
32. Procter & Gamble
33. Colgate-Palmolive-Peet
34. Schweppes Ltd
35. Coca-Cola
36. Horlicks Ltd

37. Cantrell & Cochrane
38. Distillers Co. Ltd
39. W. D. & H. O. Wills Ltd
40. Ogden & Co. Ltd
41. American Tobacco Co.
42. Imperial Tobacco Co. Ltd
43. British American Tobacco Co. Ltd
44. American Chicle Co
45. W. R. Wrigley Co.
46. Carrs of Carlisle
47. Thomas Holloway

Notes: (A) Successful FDI. (B) Unsuccessful FDI. (C) FDI proposal considered but rejected. (M) Market leader. jv joint venture. v versus.
Source: T.A.B. Corley: The Nature of Multinationals 1870–1939.

6 International price maintenance: control of commodity trade in the 1920s

JOSEPH BRANDES

Though history may not repeat itself exactly, there were some interesting echoes in the 1970s of the struggle against foreign combinations of raw materials in the 1920s. As Secretary of Commerce, Herbert Hoover fought the cartel-like price-fixing of rubber, potash, sisal, and even coffee. Then, as now, the world's most affluent industrial nation represented the political economy of expansion. Real growth was the key to stability and social progress at home, to power abroad, and growth was seen as depending to some extent on access to, and competitive markets in, key raw materials. But in the 1920s, America was not yet confronted by a rival economic superpower such as Japan of the 1970s and 1980s.

Conditioned by a heritage of limitless resources and productive ingenuity, Americans tended to assume a mastery of their own fate. They seemed unwilling to face the nation's growing dependence on various foreign supplies and on an effective functioning of the international economy. Yet, some policy makers even in the 1920s did perceive dangers that would become an overriding national concern by the 1970s.

It was a crisis long in the making, traceable to America's mass production industries. In the 1920s, the automobile industry, in particular, seemed threatened by foreign restrictions of the rubber supply and sharply rising rubber prices. Then, as now with oil or bauxite or a score of other commodities, a wide range of 'solutions' was offered – including measures to achieve national self-sufficiency and to retaliate in kind. Anti-foreign attitudes rose to the fore, as pressures were brought to bear against the officially sponsored cartels, and this issue became commingled with such other economic foreign policy issues as inter-allied war debts. Naively, perhaps, then as now, Americans sought to ascertain which of their erstwhile allies could still qualify as their friends.

During the Republican ascendancy of the 1920s, the grand marshal of economic policy at home as abroad was Herbert Hoover, a competent and willing leader in the anti-cartel struggle. Among his more moderate weapons was a public relations campaign for conservation, featuring such slogans as

'Economize on Rubber' and 'Help Hoover Against the English Rubber Trust', and accompanied by the patriotic appeal of '1776–1925'.[1] In addition, he was able to bring a wide range of other weapons to bear in the spheres of public and intergovernmental pressure.

Indeed, many of the issues and responses of the 1920s were echoed within the raw materials crises (not oil alone) of the 1970s, as if reflecting a kind of repetitive aspect of industrial America's political economy. In an approach not unlike Hoover's, a senior fellow of the Brookings Institution advised that 'only unity among consumers can effectively counter unity among producers'. Without a revision of international trade rules, he warned, the problem could become just as acute for raw materials dominated by 'several other commodity cartels', including copper, bauxite and coffee.[2] Brazil's 'coffee cartel' (Hoover's old nemesis, the Coffee Institute) also announced steep price increases for 1974, labelling its decision an 'A-Bomb'.[3]

As always, it seems, public policy has had to consider diverse economic interest groups, not to mention the ever-elusive concept of the national interest encompassing the American consumer. Yet the clashing pressures have always been complex. In the coffee trade, for example, the concerns of roasters were not identical with those of the distributors, and among the consumers of rubber from British Malaya were such politically influential US manufacturers as Goodyear, Goodrich, and US Rubber, as well as their ultimate customers for tyres or hot water bags. Behind the Big Three of rubber manufacturing, moreover, were such Wall Street firms as Dillon, Read & Co. and Kuhn, Loeb & Co., involved with foreign investments. Consequently, financial considerations cutting across international boundaries clashed with the notion of safeguarding America from the foreign monopolies' grip. American investment bankers then, as today, did not always agree with the manufacturers.

Assessing the 'morals' of 'multinational' oil corporations in the 1970s, Leonard Silk inquired whether they could ever be expected to pursue other goals than short-term profit maximisation, or display greater obedience to the demands of the United States than to those of Saudi Arabia.[4] Ironically, federal policies encouraging security, culminated in Senator Henry M. Jackson's charges of 'corporate disloyalty' against the Arabian American Oil Company. It had refused to supply even US military forces during the Arab–Israeli War of 1973. In this light, Hoover's early insistence (1922) that 'America should have at least a quarter interest in this [oil] business [as] a matter of national pride...' seems a bit quaint. He was appealing at the time for the broadest possible participation by American firms in the Mesopotamian oil fields and, as he frequently did, was offering advice 'from the point of view of American commercial interests'[5] rather than national strategic concerns.

Perennially, it seems, Americans have disagreed among themselves on issues of private profit and governmental intervention, production quotas and import controls, tax and tariff policies, corporate and social responsibilities, enforcement of anti-trust laws, divestiture, and even nationalisation. A mingling of populist and progressive impulses, with a dose of *petit bourgeoisie*, gave rise periodically to scepticism directed against domestic as well as international big business. Congressional investigations and pressure for more vigilant scrutiny by the Justice Department or regulatory agencies have been the outcome. In this vein were the past complaints of some farm-state congressmen, in the course of 1926 hearings, that profiteering by tyre manufacturers had gone far beyond the actual price increases of crude rubber. New York's fiery Fiorello H. LaGuardia, as well as southern and western congressmen, remained unconvinced that governmental efforts to combat raw materials cartels would benefit anyone except the large corporations. And American industry's defensive efforts – encouraged by Hoover – to create a rubber buying pool were condemned by others as violating the anti-trust laws.[6] A conglomerate of buyers would be as much a violation of the free market as a producers' monopoly!

In a somewhat parallel mood, perhaps, Senator Frank Church of Idaho, Chairman of the Subcommittee on Multinational Corporations early in 1974, found that 'Wall Street lawyers were sent to the Middle East...' and had worked out an 'arrangement...to abruptly reduce the taxes paid by the companies to the United States Treasury while dramatically increasing the tax revenues accruing to the oil producing governments'. Others have noted the interlocking directorates among the oil companies, including a number of investment bankers serving on the boards of two or more oil companies, as cause for punitive actions by the Justice Department, Federal Trade Commission, and the Securities and Exchange Commission.[7] Above all, perhaps, charges of Clayton Act violation have been intended to mobilise public reproach, always a potent weapon in a democratic society. In brief, echoes of the 1920s persisted into the economic foreign policy debates of the later era.

Hoover's attack on foreign combinations: *the 1920s ideology*

The Hoover policies were based on an ideological amalgam of nineteenth-century classical economics with the needs of twentieth-century business in the United States. A 'free' economy was revered by Hoover as the democratic force on which depended the continued progress of all the American people. Not merely the advancement of entrepreneurial interests or material progress, but all the things which made America great stemmed from the competitive business tradition modified by changing circumstances including technological efficiency.

In practice, the application of these principles was shaped by the fact that

Hoover preferred a pragmatic approach to specific issues. On the one hand, for example, he fought bitterly *for free international access* to raw materials, especially those the United States did *not* possess. Relying on nineteenth-century theories of free trade and 'comparative advantage', he assailed the resort to 'monopoly' control of such products as rubber, coffee, potash, and others. International amity was threatened, Hoover asserted, by *foreign* combinations to restrict prices and production. On the other hand, he defended American tariff protectionism as essential to continued national prosperity, minimising the opposition aroused at home and abroad by the Republican trade policies. And American prosperity, he believed, was the cornerstone upon which worldwide recovery and prosperity must rest.

In combating foreign 'monopolies', Hoover appealed to American national feeling and kept himself in the forefront as the champion of American economic rights abroad. Against such foreign interests, he mobilised a counter-offensive which in some respects exerted greater pressure than did the offending 'monopolies'. The Commerce Department, for example, effectively blocked loans to the Brazilian coffee interests and to the Franco-German potash cartel, and British colonial rubber interests were threatened with a well-financed American buying pool.

Efficient service to private American interests became the keynote of the Commerce Department's widespread operations. Yet Hoover had accepted the Cabinet position in Harding's administration partly because of a desire to put into practice his own economic and social principles. His experience as relief administrator in Europe had convinced him more firmly than before that the ways of 'American individualism' were superior to any other system, that unlike some of European capitalism, private enterprise in the United States fostered opportunity for all individuals and was thus an expression of equality and 'social justice'. Belief in these traditional American ideals was the truly 'liberal' approach, Hoover maintained, although he was himself attacked often by self-styled progressive and internationalist groups.

It would be misleading to imply that Hoover's concept of the voluntary partnership between government and business was intended to serve the interests of business alone. The Commerce Department was no passive partner sacrificing its own initiative either to Wall Street or Main Street. Thus, in spite of the opposition of many investment houses, Hoover promoted a program of governmental supervision over foreign lending so that the diplomatic and economic interests of America would be given due consideration. Hoover insisted on adequate loan standards, as a governmental responsibility, to prevent 'unproductive' uses and eventual loss to American investors or consumers.

Surely, as concluded by Peri Arnold, Hoover was 'no simple *laissez-faire* ideologue'.[8] Hoover attempted to co-ordinate governmental actions with private economic interests in the name of the public good. He was well aware of the instabilities and losses resulting from the business cycle, the striving for profit through economies of scale and technological efficiency. Competition was hardly synonymous with productivity. Moreover, he believed, American individualism was uniquely tempered by the necessary co-operativeness of the frontier heritage and its social concerns. By contrast with the still-festering problems of Europe, the actual accomplishments of American society represented 'the one great moral reserve in the world today'.[9]

These virtues could be extended by a judicious partnership of free enterprise 'voluntarism' with the benevolent supervision of the state. 'Regulations to prevent domination and unfair trade practices, yet preserving rightful initiative, are in keeping with our social foundations', Hoover maintained.[10] When the Department of Commerce responded to the needs of American business, whether surveying alternate sources of crude rubber or finding export markets for the finished product, it was going beyond mere service to a limited constituency or clientele. It was, as Hoover saw it, serving the nation by providing aid to its 'most creative and beneficial element',[11] especially when the latter was threatened from abroad.

Thus the effects of artificially high rubber prices were painted by Hoover on a broad canvas. Not only were domestic distributors and manufacturers hurt by fluctuating inventory values, but the British rubber cartel's actions caused an 'arousal of national feeling' and even a determination by the whole 'consuming world to fight militantly for its existence'. We of the wealthy United States 'could take care of ourselves', Hoover proclaimed aggressively, 'we have it within our powers to retaliate'. And a strong national response had become necessary because the normal 'higgling of merchants [was] lifted to the plane of international relations, with all its spawn of criticism and hate'. The international monopolies of raw materials ran counter to the cherished 'belief that economic progress must depend upon the driving force of competition'. Yet the British Stevenson Plan drove up the price of rubber not only from Malaya but even the Dutch East Indies.

Their interference with the 'inalienable right' of buyers to bargain with sellers threatened the basis of international commerce and well-being, 'for no single nation can dissociate its prosperity from the prosperity and good will of all of them'. None could boast the right to monopolise a product which other nations required 'for their standards of living and comfort', especially when prices were raised 'far beyond [a] reasonable profit' because 'no voice at all' was granted to consumers. As such restrictions spread and were backed by governmental patronage or direct legislation, they could 'only lead to mutual disaster'.[12] Government involvement made the rubber cartel even more ominous.

With his first-hand knowledge of world affairs, Hoover knew how distant were the ideals of economic equilibrium and co-operation in the aftermath of the First World War. His wartime commander-in-chief, President Wilson, saw little cause for optimism after peace was achieved. 'It is evident to me that we are on the eve of a commercial war of the worst sort', he warned in 1920, 'and I am afraid that Great Britain will prove capable of as great commercial savagery as Germany has displayed for so many years in her competitive methods'.[13]

Friction had begun during the war when the British, controlling three-quarters of the world's plantation supply in their southeast Asian colonies, had listed crude rubber as contraband. American manufacturers had been 'greatly exercised over [the] embargoes'. And foreshadowing the tensions of the 1920s, Secretary of State William Jennings Bryan had threatened: 'If American manufacturers are not to obtain necessary supplies, prices of American goods which [Britain] may desire will be greatly increased, if, indeed the exportations from this country be not ultimately prevented'.[14] It was a case of nationalism and neutral rights on the part of the Great Commoner, and an issue that had been painstakingly resolved through American reassurances that the finished product would not reach Britain's foes.

With the war over and wartime controls largely scrapped, Hoover saw a 'world rapidly gaining stability'. But he still feared the snowballing effect of new restrictions abroad leading to protectionist pleas at home 'every time some industry fell into trouble'. Fortunately, the United States had not yet followed the example set by foreign combinations. Even the farm relief bills being considered in Congress were characterised by a basic generosity. They offered 'the benevolent aspect of proposing to fix a higher price to our home consumers than to foreigners and to thus bless the foreigner with cheaper food'.[15] But 'we' would have to protect our interests, and the British and other sponsors of price-fixing combinations should realise that their actions were threatening those competitive commitments which were the key to economic progress. Thus we would protect our wheat producers, while opposing governmental protection to British colonial rubber.

As the world's major agricultural exporting nation, America could not be counted upon for unlimited generosity or patience in the face of provocation. Britain was a foremost importer of foodstuffs and raw materials, Hoover liked to note, vulnerable to the threat of an American cotton producers' combination, for example. Although distasteful ideologically, retaliation might nonetheless be required 'from a national point of view'. This was a reality which the British government should be urged to consider in a 'comprehensive' manner, recognising that 'they' might suffer more than the United States from the same 'currents which they have been to some degree responsible for putting in motion'.

In short, Hoover hoped that the British government could be persuaded diplomatically to desist from the harmful effects of price fixing on 'the whole

fabric of international commerce and of wholesome international relations...[even] world welfare....'[16] Such was Hoover's explicit advice to
Secretary of State Kellogg, to be transmitted through the US ambassador in
London, Alanson B. Houghton, toward the end of 1925. But Britain did not
yield on its efforts to raise and maintain rubber prices.

Nor were Hoover's ideas without detractors at home. His opposition to
loan flotation on behalf of the accused cartels inspired a *Wall Street Journal*
plea 'begging him not to overburden himself'. Could not the nation count on
a capable Secretary of the Treasury, Andrew Mellon, and his equally
effective colleague, Frank Kellogg, to conduct economic foreign policy? 'Mr
Hoover's Helpfulness' in aborting a $40,000,000 flotation for the German
Potash Syndicate – 'Something of a monopoly in its way' – was a disappoint-
ment to Lee Higginson & Co. and to other financiers. The journal claimed
that potash was used mainly in cotton and truck farming, but little in the
major wheat and corn belts where substitutes were available.

Moreover, Hoover might 'wisely let the Brazilian coffee industry alone',
and discontinue his persistent tie-in between foreign pricing policies and
access to American financial markets. The combinations were able to obtain
their loans in London, anyway. Worse still was Hoover's use of loan
restrictions as 'a club for the collection of foreign debts'. Generally, the
journal found, Wall Street might need 'Washington's advice but not
Washington's control'. 'Mr Hoover is not really necessary in such councils',
concluded its New Year's editorial of 1926. Obviously the investment
banking community held a friendlier view of the commodity cartels.

Hoover did not shrink from such blunt challenges. In a press release
marked specifically for the *western farm* papers, the Secretary of Commerce
relished the role of America's progressive conscience, speaking out against
Wall Street opportunism. When the time of reckoning came for 'the
American banking community', Hoover predicted, 'the commissions which
might be collected on floating such loans would be no compensation'. There
would be a 'justifiable criticism...from the American potash and coffee
consumers when [they] become aware that American capital was being
placed at the disposal of these agencies through which prices were held
against our own people and which if located upon our own soil would be a
violation of our laws'.[17] But could foreign organisations be held accountable
to US law or US policies?

In an official memorandum, Hoover acknowledged the availability of
European funding for the Brazilian coffee valorisation program. It only
confirmed his view of the occasionally irresponsible Europeans willing to
'enter into a gamble to hold the price of coffee'. Still, 'it was better that it
be done by some outsider than done by American bankers against the
interests of the American public'. If the government was responsible for the
welfare of farmers requiring potash, at least equal care was demanded by the

'numerical importance of the coffee consumer'. It was, he said 'wholly impossible for the American Government to be either directly or indirectly a party to further conspiracies against the American consumer', and hence imperative that loans to Sao Paulo or similar foreign combinations be disapproved.[18] Thus Hoover tried to mobilise US credit resources against the commodity cartels.

While Hoover's acceptance of classical economics included at least a limited recognition of comparative advantage in international trade, it did not extend to the totally free flow of capital across national boundaries. The national interest, defined as the greatest good for the nation's greatest numbers, sometimes required that the 'invisible hand' of the world's market places be superseded. Millions of jobs, after all, were tied to the continued prosperity of the American automobile industry, now threatened by British rubber restrictions. And because of this, the federal government was justified in launching an intensive search for alternative sources. Whether plantations 'under American control' in the Philippines, or encouragement to Firestone's mammoth projects in Liberia, or synthetic production at home, there was a need for engineering developments that the 'invisible hand' had not brought forth.

'It may be that Mr Hoover has an exaggerated idea of government help', was the plaint of some of his opponents.[19] At times, his hard line on loans and the 'sensational speeches' of his antimonopoly allies in Congress (such as House Majority Leader John Q. Tilson) caused diplomatic repercussions in Latin America as well. Even the *Times* of Argentina was cited as predicting a 'come-back' of British economic influence because Hoover 'interfered so very definitely in the matter of lending money to the Brazilians'. Insensitive to 'South American dignity', he had failed to seek the tactful screen of a bland rejection by Wall Street intermediaries, preferring a blunt statement of official policy.[20]

Hoover's disclaimer was a model of statesmanlike rectitude:

No one wishes to maintain the good will of foreign nations more than I do, but I would be serving the American people badly if I did not bespeak their interest as consumers against the monstrous imposition which has been imposed upon them in many directions. Furthermore, unless the growth of foreign monopolies directed against consuming countries can be halted, we shall all be confronted with an era of international friction such as we have never hitherto conceived.[21]

Further, in a typical display of national confidence, Hoover warned that the United States was 'strong enough' to take the lead in combating foreign monopolies. The diplomatic pressures of those 'few' governments fostering such restrictions would be more than outweighed by the gratitude of fifty-odd consuming nations. And in separate advisory letters to Kellogg, he urged continuing counter-pressures against Britain to 'shift their policy', not only on rubber but also on the financing of potash and coffee restrictions.

Through such financing, he concluded, the 'British become parties to further impositions upon our consumers'.[22]

Classic ideals of economic growth mingled with consumer protection and moral indignation. In a little over a year, from the spring of 1924 to summer 1925, coffee prices rose from thirteen to thirty cents a pound through artificial restrictions, a condition condemned by Hoover for 'mulcting the American people at the rate of $200,000,000 annually'. With profits of 65% and higher, the managers of the Brazilian valorisation scheme – 'nothing but a group of speculators' – grew fearful of declining consumption. For American resistance ultimately proved effective, creating unmanageable surpluses. Having realised the 'folly of their program', the Brazilians vainly sought loans to prevent 'general disaster'. They could not have these, Hoover maintained, nor 'any contract entered into for restraint of trade and plunder of the American people'.

Only if direct participation were granted to 'American consumers...a strong hand in the control of the valorization scheme itself', could a loan to Sao Paulo be considered. And it would be much better if there were a complete abandonment of such foreign combination schemes. If allowed to fail, their collapse 'might be one of the best lessons the world has had that the American people cannot be perpetually held up'.[23]

As if to amend Harding's classic statement, Hoover pronounced that 'it is the business of the Administration to give such protection to the American consumer as it can' in the face of foreign conspiracies, even if Wall Street preferred to finance them.[24] To a degree, this was consistent with his definition of American individualism as the motor for profitable efficiency but also as a 'constant militant check upon capital becoming a thing to be feared'.[25] Government-supported cartels stifled consumption as well as competition. Consequently, through 1928, Hoover continued a wary opposition to funding for Brazil's Coffee Institute, refinancing proposals included.[26]

By 1928, Hoover managed to mobilise American industry into a defensive National Coffee Council. The latter could eventually advise 'Candidate Hoover' that having 'become the dread of Brazilian Coffee Interests' he might well relent in his new role as presidential nominee and assure Latin Americans that no hostility was intended except for the monopoly's 'excessive and artificially maintained prices'.[27]

Ultimately, commodity prices dropped precipitously – more a portent of the Great Depression than Hoover's victory over the cartels.

NOTES

The author is entirely indebted to the Herbert Hoover Presidential Library Association (West Branch, Iowa), which made this research possible.

1 *New York Times*, 27 December 1925.
2 C. Fred Bergsten, 'Some vital commodities are subject to "resource"', *New York Times*, Sunday, 27 January 1974; Eric Sevareid's TV editorial, 'The era of product diplomacy', 20 February 1974.
3 'Brazil is raising prices of coffee', *New York Times*, 24 December 1973; for Brazil's governmental Coffee Institute in the 1920 struggle, see Joseph Brandes, *Herbert Hoover and economic diplomacy: Department of Commerce policy, 1921–1928* (Pittsburgh, 1962), pp. 133, 137, *passim* (available in reprint edition, Westport, Conn., 1975: Greenwood Press).
4 Leonard Silk, 'Multinational morals', *New York Times*, 5 March 1974.
5 'Aramco concedes denying oil to US military since October', *New York Times*, 26 January 1974; Hughes to Hoover, 'Confidential', 17 August 1922; Hoover to Hughes, 19 August 1922, Herbert Hoover Papers (Herbert Hoover Presidential Library, West Branch, Iowa), Commerce Section, Hughes.
6 United States Congress, House, Committee on Interstate and Foreign Commerce, *Hearings on Crude Rubber, Coffee, Etc.*, 69 Cong., 1 Sess. (Washington, 1926), 55–6, 273; LaGuardia and others, in *Congressional Record*, 70 Cong., 1 Sess. 5 April 1928), 5971, 5983–4, 5996.
7 Senator Church Hearings, *New York Times*, 31 January 1974; '25 on boards of oil companies scrutinized in antitrust inquiry', *New York Times*, 12 March 1974.
8 Peri Ethan Arnold, 'Herbert Hoover and the Department of Commerce: a study of ideology and policy', Ph.D. diss. (University of Chicago, 1972), p. 22.
9 Herbert Hoover to Woodrow Wilson, in Hoover, *Memoirs*, 3 vols. (New York, 1951–2), vol. 1, p. 457.
10 Herbert Hoover, *American individualism* (Garden City, 1922), p. 55.
11 Arnold, 'Hoover and the Department of commerce', p. 81.
12 Herbert Hoover, 'Foreign combinations now fixing prices of raw materials imported into the United States' (Washington, 1925), pp. 3–4, 6, 8–9, 11.
13 Woodrow Wilson to Undersecretary of State Franklin L. Polk, 4 March 1920 (Polk Mss, Yale University Library), in John A. DeNovo, 'the movement for an aggressive American oil policy abroad, 1918–1920', *American Historical Review*, 61 (July 1956), 858–9; Frank R. Chalk, 'The United States and the international struggle for rubber, 1914–1941', Ph.D. diss. (University of Wisconsin, 1970), p. 33.
14 Bryan to Ambassador Walter Hines Page, 12 November, 2 December, 1914, in *Munitions Industry, Report on Existing Legislation*, 74 Cong., 2 Sess., Senate Report No. 944, Part 5 (1935), 99–100, cited in Chalk, 'Struggle for rubber', pp. 11–12.
15 Hoover, 31 October 1925, in *Munitions Industry, Report*, cited in Chalk, 'Struggle for rubber', p. 97.
16 Hoover to Kellogg, letter and memorandum, 28 November 1925, Hoover Papers, Commerce Section, Secretary of State Kellogg.
17 'Mr Hoover's helpfulness', *Wall Street Journal*, 1 January 1926, and 'Statement by Secretary Hoover regarding foreign monopolies,' 4 January 1926, Hoover Papers, Commerce Section, Foreign Comb., Misc.

18 Hoover Memorandum, 25 August 1925, Hoover Papers, Commerce Section, Foreign Loans.
19 *Wall Street Journal*, 1 January 1926.
20 *The Times of Argentina*, 16 November 1925, article enclosed by H. F. McCreery of Hard & Rand Inc., 22 December 1925, Hoover Papers, Commerce Section, Foreign Loans, Sao Paulo. For additional background on Hoover's anti-monopoly stand, as well as a fresh, comprehensive, scholarly treatment of related themes, see Joan Hoff Wilson's, *American business and foreign policy, 1920–1933* (Lexington, 1971), especially pp. 171–5.
21 Hoover to McCreery, 5 January 1926, Hoover Papers, Commerce Section, Foreign Loans, Sao Paulo.
22 Hoover to Kellogg, 28 November 1925, Hoover Papers, Commerce Section, Secretary of State Kellogg.
23 Hoover memorandum, 25 August 1925, Hoover Papers, Commerce Section, Foreign Loans.
24 *Ibid.*
25 Hoover, *American individualism*, p. 38.
26 Hoover to Charles Evans Hughes, 8 February 1928, Hoover Papers, Commerce Section, Foreign Loans.
27 Berent Friele, National Coffee Council (US), to Julius Klein, 25 June 1928; Klein to Friele, 6 July 1928, Bureau of Foreign and Domestic Commerce Records (National Archives, RG 151), 640 (Brazil).

7 Financial operations of US transnational corporations: development after the Second World War and recent tendencies

MONIKA ŠESTÁKOVÁ

The basis of contemporary transnational corporations (TNC) presents capital export in the form of foreign direct investment (FDI). Capital export from the USA began at the end of the nineteenth century and in 1897 had reached $600m.[1] Until the First World War it was growing at about 9% a year. In the period between the two world wars the capital export growth rate slowed down. Nevertheless after the Second World War it accelerated again (in the 1950s and 1960s to about 10%, in the 1970s to 11% a year), the main form of private foreign investment becoming direct investment. In this period capital export was already closely connected with TNCs' global strategy. TNCs became typical international monopolies of the day, integrating and controlling within the framework of one complex all phases of the reproduction process.

Between 1946 and 1964, 187 US industrial corporations (belonging to the 500 largest corporations of the USA) have founded or acquired about 60% of existing affiliates abroad.[2] These constitute the basis of contemporary international monopoly complexes, taking advantage of international specialisation and co-operation of production. At the same time US foreign investment began to be directed to industrially developed countries, and this trend intensified in the following period. While in 1950 48.6% of US FDI was directed to industrially developed capitalist countries, in 1960 the figure had increased to 59.2%, in 1970 68%, in 1975 73.2% and in 1983 75%.[3] This orientation of FDI is conditioned, *inter alia*, by the contemporary scientific-technological revolution, which was connected with the deepening of international specialisation and co-operation of production (inclusive of the growing intensity of intra-industry international division of labour).

At the same time that the internal integration of monopolistic complexes advanced, the importance of financial operations was growing too – as a basic instrument of TNCs' economic policy and as a means of central control over the whole complex of activity. TNCs implement capital mobilisation from several countries and resources allocation within their monopolistic complex by means of various financial operations. For TNCs, financial operations are not only employed as a safety instrument that protects against several risks connected with operations on an international scale, but they also offer an opportunity to gain advantages. For example, emanating from fluctuations in exchange rates, from differences in inflation trends in various countries and so on, they thus obtain long-run global profits from the whole complex.

TNCs' financial operations are one of the main forms of international profit re-distribution. Especially in this sphere it often happens that TNCs' interests are in contradiction to the economic and political aims of national governments. That is why it was this sphere of TNCs' policy which became a subject of critique in both host and home countries, and still receives a great deal of attention on the platform of the United Nations Organisation (UNO).

Foreign affiliates financing and methods of withdrawing funds from abroad

TNCs' financial policy is a complicated system, including foreign affiliates' financing methods: it is closely connected with methods of profit transfers into a parent company (or into a holding company in tax havens) and with methods of financial resource transfers between affiliates in several countries.

The forming of TNCs' financial operations system, naturally, has been a continual process of improvement running in parallel with the 'maturing' of the TNC itself. At the very beginning of foreign expansion, when the foreign operations capacity was small, the use of a global system of financial resources mobilisation and allocation was not possible. Intra-system financial relations increased in parallel with the growth of the foreign involvement rate.

The parent company provided its foreign affiliates with financial resources partly in the form of equity capital and partly in the form of intra-company credit (the latter is preferable from the point of view of taxation and also for political reasons). Further, by means of roll-over accounts for goods and services, by transfer-pricing and dividend policy, US TNCs aim at financial independence of their foreign affiliates, so that they can finance their activities from their own resources as soon as possible. That is why in the very first years after the founding of an affiliate only a minimal amount of dividends is withdrawn, while the bulk of the income is reinvested in the foreign affiliates.[4] As soon as the position of affiliates on the market is stabilised, the rate of withdrawing money from foreign affiliates begins to exceed the inflow of funds from the parent company.[5]

The capital outflow in the financing of US TNCs' foreign operations is continuously decreasing. In the 1970s the FDI of US corporations was financed mostly by the reinvestment of earnings and by depreciation allowances. In 1980 the US FDI position rose 14%. The share of net capital outflow in financing was $1.5 billion. Meanwhile the share of reinvested earnings was $17 billion.[6] At the same time the difference between levels of earnings reinvestment within industrially developed and developing countries is growing. Between 1950 and 1963 US TNCs have exported capital amounting to $11.7 billion into developed countries and reinvested earnings of $8.6 billion. In the same period they have exported $1.5 billion to developing countries and reinvested $5.5 billion. In the following decade the sum of reinvestments in developed countries ($35.2 billion) has exceeded the net capital outflow ($30.5 billion). Nevertheless, in developing countries an inverse proportion can be observed ($9.1 billion and $12.5 billion). The lower share of reinvestment in developing countries was not a consequence of a lower profit rate from this investment, but much more a consequence of the fear of risk connected with investments in these countries. At the same time it represents an international income redistribution that is disadvantageous for developing countries.

Methods of withdrawing funds from foreign affiliates are subordinated to global TNCs' strategy. The manoeuvring possibilities are greater the higher the equity share of a parent company in a foreign company. That is why, *inter alia*, US TNCs sought for the greatest possible share in the capital of foreign companies. When choosing methods of withdrawing funds TNCs try, on the one hand, to minimise the whole sum of taxation (using the differences in tax systems of different countries) and, on the other hand, to insure against the risk following from exchange rate fluctuations. The manoeuvring possibilities in this sphere are very broad – from more or less legal forms of tax avoidances to directly illegal methods of tax evasion. In principle, TNCs seek to transfer as high a proportion as possible of their earnings to the states with the lowest tax rates (these countries are known as 'tax havens'), then to withdraw the money as soon as possible from the country menaced by currency devaluation. In that respect the tactics of 'leads and lags' and the mechanism of transfer pricing are used. Both these tactics can be widely used in taxation minimisation as well as in overcoming credit, monetary and other restrictions imposed by national governments.

In the financing of foreign affiliates (and in some cases even in the mobilisation of funds for parent companies) an important role is played by credit, acquired on local capital markets and international financial markets (e.g. the Euromoney market and Eurobond market). In the primary stage of foreign expansion the use of local credit was limited by insufficient development of local capital markets. The importance of foreign credit for US TNCs has increased in the 1960s. This increase was connected with a rapid growth of foreign investment, with the US administration's measures to restrain capital export on the one hand and with the instability of international monetary relations on the other. 1967 is seen as a turning-point in US TNCs' financial strategy. In the years 1967–70 foreign indebtedness has increased by $7.5 billion. Since then TNCs' global financial strategy has begun to be enforced.

Endeavouring to avoid national government control and to overcome national credit barriers led to increasing TNCs' interest in the Eurodollar market (short-term credit) and in the Eurobond market (long-term credit). The 1960s are a kind of turning-point in the exploitation of these international financial markets. In the years 1968–9 the Eurodollar market volume almost doubled, and TNCs had a great share in that increase.[7] The Euromoney market offers many advantages for TNCs: it is not subjected to national financial authorities control; it offers the possibility of obtaining large sums of financial means (syndicate credit); there are many manoeuvring possibilities in taking advantage of the differences in rates of interest from credits of different maturity or in taking advantage of 'floating' exchange rates. US TNCs' interest in Euromarkets oscillated in conjunction with US credit policy measures, development of international financial relations and the general business situation. Considerable swings have come about in the 1980s, too. For example, in 1982 US corporations borrowed $12.8 billion on the Euromarket, but in the first six months of 1983 only $3 billion (compared with $8 billion in the first six months of 1982).[8] The rapid growth of the Euromarket has been a source of high profits for large American banks (Morgan Stanley, Morgan Guaranty, Credit Suisse First Boston, Merrill Lynch, Goldman Sachs). On the whole the huge amount of TNCs' operations on the Euromarket was a source of instability for international economic relations; having used 'hot money' transfers, they engendered inflation in many countries and limited the efficiency of national governments' monetary and credit policies.

Intra-firm transactions and transfer pricing mechanism

The tightening of the internal integration of TNCs' international complexes transforms every enterprise, every affiliate, merely into a part of a global system in which activities of several elements are mutually conditioned and are aiming at increasing economic efficiency for the whole complex. This tendency is objectively conditioned by scientific–technological progress and the development of division of labour. But this integration within the framework of TNCs is implemented without respecting interests in the economic development of national economies (especially of host countries) and in regional economic integration.

In intra-system control within TNCs an important role is played by transfer pricing policy. The higher the degree of intra-firm transactions and the higher their share in the total foreign trade volume of individual countries, the stronger is the influence of transfer pricing policy on the fulfilment of the economic and political objectives of national governments. If the transfer prices deviate from arm's length prices considerably (whether caused by tax considerations or in consequence of exchange speculation or other strategic aims of TNCs), the conflicts between TNCs and national governments consequently deepen. Transfer prices manipulations both distort the information function of prices in international trade and can exert a negative influence upon the international division of labour.

The goals of transfer pricing policy deepen the hierarchic dependence of developing countries on parent companies. Transfer prices (including profit transfers and royalty payments) lead to the redistribution of financial resources to the disadvantage of developing countries; they render the possibilities of accumulation and technological progress more difficult in these countries, they weaken the competitive position of local firms, and exert a negative influence upon the balance of payments of host countries.

In the last few years many countries have endeavoured to control export and import prices of TNCs' affiliates. However, they have encountered problems: e.g., it is too difficult to determine objective arm's length prices; the real amount of intra-firm transactions is distorted by TNCs' accounting practices; national governments often lack the necessary 'negotiating capacity' in respect of large TNCs, and so on. It seems also that it is not enough merely to monitor individual export and import prices; it is also important to monitor the whole financial operations system of TNCs (with special regard to the possibility of flexible changes of tactics and methods of fund transfers). Intensifying competition itself between TNCs will not automatically solve this problem. Efforts to control the activities of TNCs, (including their financial operations) is a part of the whole struggle for the New International Economic Order.

Some contemporary tendencies and problems

The US FDI position has experienced important changes in the last few years. Capital inflow into the USA grew in the last decade at such a rate that the USA has become a net importer of capital. In 1985 net FDI outflow from the USA made up $18.75 billion; meanwhile FDI inflow into the USA made up $25.36 billion.[9] Foreign capital plays an important role in investment financing inside the USA. In this respect a problem of capital outflow from various countries into the USA arises and this affects the chances of economic growth in these states. This problem is specially topical in West Europe.

In the last few years some new forms of TNCs' foreign expansion have come to the fore. Besides the participation in foreign companies' capital, there are licensing agreements, sub-contracting, turnkey projects, management and marketing contracts and co-production agreements, to name a few. The practice of joint ventures has also spread. At a glance it could seem that the spread of non-equity arrangements, where the connections with financial flows are not so obvious, would lead to a reduction of the importance of TNCs' financial operations. In fact, these forms of expansion are also closely connected with long-term financial strategy, and in their implementation, too, financial instruments are used. At the same time, these measures give transnational corporations the opportunity to reduce risk and reach 'satisfactory returns on their technological, managerial and marketing assets'.[10]

In connection with the spread of TNCs' foreign operations and their growing influence on national economies, the interest of national governments and non-state organisations (for example, unions) in TNCs' accounting and reporting principles is increasing. These problems are being discussed in international organisations, too, and on the initiative of the Commission on TNCs of the UN Economic and Social Council, 'International Standards of Accounting and Reporting' are being elaborated. The question does not concern merely the unification of accounting principles (these differ between countries and corporations) to make international and interfirm comparisons possible, but also some open problems such as accounting for research and development costs; financial reporting by segments of TNCs; effects of inflation on financial information; and accounting for effects of exchange rates changes.

The solution of these problems is not only of technical, merely accounting interest, but it has a great social and political impact. Until now, financial aspects of TNCs' activities were probably mostly hidden from the public. The improvement of data systems on TNCs' financial policies, of course, cannot solve all the problems connected with effective control of their activities. Nevertheless, it could enable national governments to formulate their economic and political strategy based on a more realistic evaluation of the probable consequences of TNCs' activities. At the same time, it might be an important step on the path to a more equitable order of international economic relations.

NOTES

1 S. M. Robbins and R. B. Stobaugh, *Money in the multinational enterprise. A study of financial policy*, (New York, 1973), p. 7.
2 J. B. Vaupel and J. P. Curhan, *The making of multinational enterprise* (Boston, 1969), p. 4.
3 In *Survey of Current Business* for corresponding years.
4 15% of the foreign affiliates of 187 US TNCs have not paid any dividends at all and 10% of affiliates paid dividends just once in eight years (1960–7) (M. Z. Brooke and H. L. Remmers, *The strategy of multinational enterprise. Organization and finance* (London, 1970), p. 169).

5 For instance, in the period 1960–5 the rate of fund withdrawing from US affiliates in West Europe exceeded the net capital inflow by 25%.

6 J. Sneddon Little, 'Multinational corporations and foreign direct investment: current trends and issues', *Annals of the American Academy of Political and Social Science*, vol. 460 (March 1982), 56.

7 For a more detailed analysis, see Andrew F. Brimmer, 'Multinational banks and the management of monetary policy in the United States', *Journal of Finance*, 28 (May 1973), pp. 439–54.

8 *The Banker*, September 1983, p. 81.

9 *Survey of Current Business* (August 1986) 44, 78.

10 See *Transnational corporations in world development. Third survey* UN–CTC (New York, 1983), Sales No. E 83 II. A 14, p. 4.

8 Multinational enterprise – financing, trade, diplomacy: the Swedish case

KLAUS WOHLERT

Introduction

Efforts to maintain political neutrality and economic independence are some of the basic, historically rooted features of Swedish foreign trade policy. Although situated in a remote corner of Europe and rather small in terms of population, Sweden has developed into a technologically sophisticated industrial country, particularly since the Second World War. Compared to home market sales the volume of Swedish foreign trade, always relatively large and decisively important for economic growth, has increased proportionately as Sweden's economy, like that of other industrial nations, has gone through a prolonged process of concentration. To what extent the degree of concentration is comparable to that of other countries is hard to judge, as a comparative study of the development of Swedish enterprises along the lines drawn up by Professor Alfred D. Chandler, Jr, has yet to be made. Still lacking, too, is a modern history of the banking economy. However, these gaps should be filled before long.[1] The purpose of this paper is to provide some insight into the interrelations between the Swedish export economy and the major powers.

Sweden as a strategic component of the economies of the Great Powers

Obviously, sustaining neutrality and independence involves special problems. Thus the lack of coal on the part of neutral states during the First World War enabled Britain to pursue a stiff price policy. Her coal exports served as an argument for depressing the prices of vital British imports. At the same time, Britain pressured Sweden to counteract German exports in order to keep any re-exported German goods from competing on the British home market. Harm Schröter and others claim that the Great Powers, and notably Britain, were intent upon hampering the ongoing industrialisation of the Scandinavian countries to secure them as sources of raw materials and as markets for finished goods, as well as to counteract future competition from those countries.

Immediately after the First World War, large German enterprises in the fields of iron and steel, coal and coke, chemistry and electrotechnology were already launching a company-level Scandinavian export offensive resulting in a 30 % share of Scandinavian import markets during the 1920s. Britain, on the other hand, suffered a 50 % loss of her share. The major reasons for such German competitiveness were to be found not so much in the Scandinavian 'cultural proximity' to Germany (in terms of language, the decimal system, the adoption of technical standards, etc.) as in structural conditons, such as company-level international industrial agreements, a tight organisational web of associations representing industrial interests, and the intimate collaboration between banks and industrial enterprises.[2] Only brief mention shall be made here of the extent to which big business penetration into foreign realms contained political components. In 1916, for instance, the Swedish government passed legislation prohibiting the acquisition of Swedish ore fields by foreigners.

The fact that foreign companies were able to establish themselves in spite of this legislation was due to Swedish middlemen. Foreign firms frequently established subsidiaries in the neutral Netherlands, whence undercover affiliates would then be set up in Sweden. In this connection, Stockholms Enskilda Bank – a large Swedish bank belonging to the brothers Jacob and Marcus Wallenberg – played the role of invisible middleman between IG Farbenindustrie AG and the Dutch Chemicaliën Handels Maatschappij (Chemamij), a camouflaged subsidiary of IG Farben through which the IG effected a complex realignment of its foreign affiliates. In their account of such ties, Gerard Aalders and Cess Wiebes refer to similar affiliations in the case of Robert Bosch AG. Particularly precarious in this context was the task of disguising the daughter companies in the United States, that is, the American Bosch Corporation (ABC). After the Second World War, the Americans allegedly used the involvement of Jacob Wallenberg in these transactions to justify sabotaging the Swedish–Russian credit agreements of 1946. In addition, according to Aalders and Wiebes, the Americans pressured Jacob Wallenberg into resigning as general manager in 1946, to be succeeded by his brother Marcus. As the authors admit however, the evidence for both of these sensational allegations is inconclusive.[3]

From what precedes, three interesting conclusions may be drawn. In the first place, the growth strategies of multinational enterprises may come into conflict with the legislation of the individual states where the company headquarters have established affiliates. It follows, secondly, that the government of the resident country of the company's headquarters may assist the multinational by exercising political pressure to the extent permitted by the strength of its economic independence and geopolitical position. Thirdly, the government of the country which has become host to an affiliate of a multinational company may or may not be able to resist any political pressure brought to bear upon it, again according to the strength of its economic independence and geopolitical position.

In terms of economic strategy, Scandinavia was interesting to both Germany and Great Britain. However, quite unlike the situation in the Danube monarchy and Czechoslovakia, as analysed by Professor Alice Teichova,[4] Scandinavia was not in the immediate line of fire between the USSR and Germany between 1939 and 1945. Until the outbreak of the First World War, Sweden was a net importer of capital, albeit exclusively in the form of government loans and foreign funding. No direct foreign investments were allowed,[5] and, consequently, there was no control or command of Swedish multinationals by foreign members of their governing boards. The point is important: for this reason, particularly important strategic information could not easily be forwarded to foreign business concerns, diplomats, and governments.

Promotion of the interests of the export industry

Given the central position of foreign trade in the Swedish economy, the smooth conduct of international trade in goods and currencies is vitally important to both import and export industries as well as to the Department of Foreign Trade. The purpose of this chapter is not to expand on Sweden's membership in international bodies but rather to give a few examples of industrial associations based on common interests. In addition to official organisations, amalgamations of unofficial groups and committees have been highly influential.

These associations came about mainly for two external reasons – the under-representation of industry in the Swedish parliament, and dissatisfaction with the leading industrial federations for their inadequate attention to the interests of the export industry.

Hardly any organised interests have stood to lose as much through democratisation, numerically as well as in terms of parliamentary representation, as have industry and commerce. Following the first House Reform of 1919, big business representation dropped from about fifty to thirty seats. As early as 1937, these were further reduced to eighteen with only a handful of MPs left today.[6] To counter this trend, commerce and industry seek to promote their political interests by other means. Politically, they are organised in the Swedish Employers' Association (SAF), and for economic purposes, industrial entrepreneurs belong to the Swedish Export Association, with a supporting membership comprising insurance companies, banks, and trading companies with export interests. Characteristically for Sweden, the situation has been compounded by the politically determined notion of

Table 8.1. *Firms with exports and sales from foreign subsidiaries about 1933 and share capital of five Swedish joint stock companies*

Name of firm	Branch	Foreign subsidiaries	Sales %	Share capital (SEK)
AB Separator/ Alfa-Laval	Dairy machinery, engineering machines	28 (1933)	70	82 million
SKF	Ball and roller bearing applications	42 (1934)	85	84 million
Electrolux	Electrical machinery and engineering	20 (1930)	60	60 million
ASEA	Electrical machinery, engineering, applications	15 (1933)	55	75 million
LM Ericsson	Telephone	25 (1931)	53	101 million

Source: M. Fritz, *Ett världsföretag växer fram.* Alfa-Laval 100 år. Stockholm 1983; B. Steckzén, *SKF Svenska Kullager Fabriken,* Göteborg 1957; *Sveriges offentliga utredningar* SOU 1981: 43, Stockholm 1981; H. Runblom, *Svenska företag i Latinamerika.* Uppsala 1971; A. Attman and U. Olsson, *L. M. Ericsson 100 år,* band II. Örebro 1976.

'neutrality', repeatedly a source of acrimonious dispute, between government and industrial representatives on the one hand, but also internally among the entrepreneurs themselves and, more specifically, between export and home market interests. As economic activities are bound to take place within a legal and political framework ultimately delineated by parliament and the government, the Swedish export industry felt obliged to assert its own interests more determinedly in relation to other groups.

In the 1920s and 1930s, an important issue was the distribution of state subsidies: while these were much sought after, businessmen were at the same time unwilling to renounce their economic independence of the state. Gustaf Söderlund, who became president of the Employers' Association in 1931, decided to make a clean sweep of party politics. In the face of mounting Social Democratic strength, Söderlund maintained that the renunciation of a partisan stance was the best way to ward off any political interference with free enterprise.

In the fateful year of 1933, the presidents of the five leading export industries formed a directorate, commonly known as the TBF ('The Big Five' or 'direktörsklubben'), for the promotion of common economic interests. The names of the firms involved, the types of produce, the number of foreign subsidiaries, the ratio of foreign sales in percentages of total sales, and total concern share capital in Sweden, are shown in table 8.1.

Later on, these five were joined by AGA (industrial gas, lighthouse) with twenty-seven foreign affiliates. It should be noted that no distinction has been made in the above table between actual exports and goods produced abroad. Furthermore, the ongoing depression should be kept in mind. Beginning in mid-1935, the turnover not only of the TBF but of the export industry in general experienced a boom which went on until the beginning of the Second World War. In this connection, the imports of essential raw materials such as coal, oil, rubber, precious metals, chemicals, or consumer goods have not been taken into consideration.[7]

During the inter-war period, all the multinational companies mentioned here were solidly linked up with the major Swedish banks. In 1932, Marcus Wallenberg took a seat on the board of LM Ericsson and Jacob Wallenberg became a member of the board of SKF. While AGA and ASEA belonged in the spheres of interest of Svenska Handelsbanken and Enskilda Banken, respectively, Alfa-Laval at that time still maintained relations to various large banks. Foreign banks were not involved with Swedish multinational enterprises.

With increasing capital growth in the Swedish industry, credit supply to industry from the big banks began to taper off in the second half of the 1930s, an aspect of which further mention will be made later on.

Between 1933 and 1942, the TBF directorate was convened seventy-four times altogether, and membership attendance was high. At the same time, the members belonged to other business associations as well and also sat on the boards of other enterprises. They frequently saw leading members of the banking community, maintained contacts with parliamentarians and government members, submitted proposals to political decision makers, and delivered formal opinions on various matters. Some of them received special expert commissions by the government. In all of this, the Wallenberg family played a major role.

Banking and diplomacy

One of the largest Swedish banks was the Stockholm Enskilda Banken ('Enskilda'), where Jacob Wallenberg held a directorship from 1920 and became managing director between 1927 and 1946. In 1927, it had a capital of SEK 116 million, with hidden assets at SEK 25 million.[8] Four years later, Jacob Wallenberg became chairman of the board. Beside Svenska Handels-banken (1926 capital: SEK 117 million), Enskilda is still the largest banking firm in Scandinavia and has remained from its inception in 1856 to 1985 the private property of the Wallenbergs. During the interwar period, and particularly in the 1930s and 40s, Jacob Wallenberg was frequently commissioned to negotiate on behalf of the Swedish government or the Association of the Swedish Industry. He also dealt indirectly with representatives of the German government and the Allies in important matters of economic policy. Thus in 1934 Jacob Wallenberg went to

Germany accompanied by the managing director of the SKF, Björn Prytz, who was also the head of the Swedish Export Association. Together with a diplomat, Ambassador Gunnar Hägglöf, and a Swedish Under-Secretary of State, Wallenberg negotiated an agreement with the Reichswirtschaftsminister Hjalmar Schacht to safeguard the voluminous exchange of goods and payments between Germany and Sweden. An additional concern was the protection of Swedish assets in German private and government bonds amounting to several hundreds of millions of SEK. At about the same time, the SKF negotiated deliveries of machinery (at the rate of SEK 10 million) and ball bearings (SEK 15 million) to the Soviet Union, for which the SKF granted a twenty-year credit in the form of an 8 % government bond. In that same year (1934), the Swedish parliament turned down a government bill proposing state credits in the amount of SEK 100 million to the Soviets. In 1937, the SKF was forced to close down its subsidiary in Moscow. Nevertheless, both parties went through with the deal.

In 1939, Jacob Wallenberg again negotiated large deals in Germany, this time in close agreement with his Minister of Finance, the social democrat Ernst Wigforss. His mission was, *inter alia*, to barter 10 million tons of iron ore for 300,000 tons of merchant iron, 85,000 tons of potash, and 130,000 tons of Glauber's salt. Wallenberg wanted the prices of the German deliveries to be tied up with Swedish ore quotations.[9]

No less diplomatically alert was Marcus Wallenberg, who made Europe and the US his permanent sphere of activity during the interwar years. An interesting background study and a well researched analysis of the German banking crisis has been presented by Manfred Pohl. For an account of the complications of banking policy and diplomacy in this context, including the roles played by M. Wallenberg, Brüning, and Schäffer, see Eckard Wandel.[10]

Industries, banking, institutions

In the study of multinational corporations, two main aspects come to the fore: firstly, the financing of their establishment abroad and, secondly, the size of their earnings and the way the latter have been invested.

Before the First World War, the AB Separator/Alfa-Laval financed only a minor part of the expansion of foreign affiliates with the capital of the parent company. As a rule, mortgage loans were taken in the respective countries on security given by concern headquarters. In some cases, a combination of real capital investment and escalating increment funding (chain-establishment or Stufengründung) was used (New York, Vienna, Paris, Hamburg). The parent company always kept a controlling interest in its foreign affiliates. The company's headquarters in Stockholm always aimed at maximum combine profits, not maximum profits for individual subsidiaries. During their first years in business, all new subsidiaries reported losses for several straight years. In some instances, Vienna being a case in point, it took as much as ten years to bring in satisfactory profits. Financial subsidies from headquarters were exceptions, losses were charged to Stockholm and goods consignments credited in advance. This strategy made it possible to fight the competition successfully on the home market as well as in the countries where the subsidiaries were operating. The personal separation between managerial functions on the one hand and property or capital ownership on the other had been completed as early as 1910, both at the combine level and in all subsidiaries. As all leading directors were thus actually employees, it became possible for the centre of the combine to implement efficient management throughout the organisation. During the build-up stage, all employees were Swedish citizens with the exception of the Czechoslovak, Hungarian, and Romanian affiliates. In Paris, a Scotsman was managing director. More than half of the senior staff had had officers' training before they entered the service of the company, while the rest had a background as civil servants in positions of responsibility. All factories at home and abroad were patterned on the American subsidiary in that they were equipped with the latest machine tools and adopted American methods for structuring work processes and production lines.

Up to the 1907 take-over of its largest European competitor, the Bergedorfer Eisenwerk in Hamburg-Bergedorf, more than SEK 100 million (118 million Reichsmarks) had flowed into the coffers of the Stockholm headquarters. The last major competitor before the First World War, the separator department of Burmeister & Wain in Copenhagen, was acquired in 1910, a deal financed entirely by the American subsidiary. In this case, furthermore, the purchase-sum of SEK 1.8 million was never even entered in the books at headquarters, which was otherwise a normal procedure in internal transfer operations. In connection with the Bergedorfer purchase, the Dresdner Bank apparently participated by temporarily financing part of the transaction at the rate of RM 260,000. To what extent the Stockholm banks were involved in this deal remains uncertain.[11]

For obvious reasons, it is hard to gain an insight into the internal financing devices of the foreign subsidiaries. Hence their short-term importance can hardly be assessed. However, it would seem that credit financing outside normal channels may still play a certain role in international modes of payment despite the extended services of financial institutions. The arrival of multinational corporations and, above all, the establishment of subsidiaries abroad largely took place before the Second World War. These companies have had excellent relations with the respective foreign governments. It is significant that most Swedish multinationals have been able to report relatively high net financial gains during the following periods: Up to and through the First World War; the mid-1930s to 1944; and the 1980s.

A common feature of these periods is the decreasing utilisation of bank credits. The companies with which we are concerned show a relatively high degree of self-financing. In 1983, for instance, Alfa-Laval had liquid funds of more than SEK, 2,000,000,000, tied up in Sweden without any possibility of being invested abroad. The Swedish market shares of Alfa-Laval, SKF, ASEA, Ericsson and AGA are so large that further expansion for their traditional products is hardly possible. Since the beginning of 1980, even Enskilda and Svenska Handelsbanken, the two largest Swedish banks, have begun launching subsidiaries abroad. At the same time, foreign banks have been licensed to open up offices in Sweden. The cause given for the formerly forbidden establishment of Swedish bank affiliates abroad is that they ought to be able to serve Swedish foreign ventures even in the future.

Another innovation is the organisational alignment of savings banks and association: Under the umbrella of the 'Sparbankernas Bank Gruppen', an amalgamation of 162 savings banks claiming total assets of SEK 71 billion now emerges as the fifth largest Swedish bank and has already included foreign trade in its sphere of activities.[12]

NOTES

1 Alfred D. Chandler, Jr and H. Daems, *Managerial Hierarchies* (Cambridge, Mass. 1980). H. Pohl, 'Zur Geschichte von Organisation und Leitung deutscher Grossunternehmen seit dem 19. Jahrhundert', in *Zeitschrift für Unternehmensgeschichte* 3 (1981). Research in progress by C. Wohlert, The emergence of the Swedish corporate economy, published hitherto: C. Wohlert, Concentration tendencies in Swedish industry before WW I in H. Pohl (ed.), *The concentration process in the entrepreneurial economy since the late 19th century* (Stuttgart, 1988). About Swedish research in banking history, see K. Wohlert 'Kurzreferate über den Stand der bankhistorischen Forschung' in *Bankhistorisches Archiv – Zeitschrift zur Bankengeschichte* 2 (1982) pp. 46, 65–7, 83–4.

2 H. G. Schröter, *Aussenpolitik und Wirtschaftsinteresse*, (Frankfurt a. Main, 1983) O. Åhlander, *Staat, Wirtschaft und Handelspolitik*, Lund Studies in International History, 20 (1983).

3 G. Aalders and C. Wiebes, 'Stockholms Enskilda Bank, German Bosch and IG Farben', in *Scandinavian Economic History Review*, 23:1 (1985).

4 A. Teichova, 'The Mannesmann concern in East Central Europe in the interwar period', in A. Teichova and P. L. Cottrell (eds.), *International Business and Central Europe*, 1918–1939 (Leicester, New York, 1983), pp. 103–37.

5 L. Jörberg, 'Konjunktur, struktur och internationellt beroende' in *Meddelande från Ekonomisk-historiska institutionen* (Lunds universitet, 1982); L. Jörberg 'Den svenska ekonomiska utvecklingen 1861–1983' in *Meddelande från Ekonomisk-historiska institutionen* (Lunds universitet, 1984).

6 S. A. Söderpalm, *Wallenberg och Branting* (Lund, 1970); and *Direktörsklubben* (Stockholm, 1976).

7 E. Ambjörn, *Svenskt importberoende 1926–1956* (Uppsala, 1959).

8 *Finansman Företagare Förhandlare*. 'Till Jacob Wallenberg på 80-årsdagen den 27 September 1972' (Stockholm, 1972).

9 G. Hägglöf, 'Jacob Wallenberg och Tyskland under andra världskriget', in *Finansman Företagare Förhandlare*. B. Steckzén, *SKF Svenska Kullagerfabriken* (Göteborg, 1957).

10 M. Pohl, *Konzentration im deutschen Bankwesen (1848–1980)* (Frankfurt a. Main, 1982). E. Wandel, *Hans Schäffer: Steuermann in wirtschaftlichen und politischen Krisen 1886–1967* (Stuttgart, 1974). K.-G. Hildebrand, *I omvandlingens tjänst Svenska Handelsbanken 1830–1955* (Stockholm, 1971).

11 K. Wohlert, 'Ein multinationaler Konzern entsteht' (with a summary in English) in *Zeitschrift für Unternehmensgeschichte* 3 (1983) pp. 188–213; K. Wohlert, *Framväxten av svenska multinationella företag* (with a summary in English) (Stockholm, 1981).

12 S.-I. Sundqvist, *Sveriges största börsföretag 1984* (Borås, 1984). *Dagens Nyheter*, 1982-06-13.

9 Foreign penetration of German enterprises after the First World War: the problem of Überfremdung

GERALD D. FELDMAN

On 23 May 1919, the German Minister of Economics Rudolf Wissell presided over a very confidential meeting with sixty or seventy of Germany's leading industrialists to discuss ways and means of dissuading the Allied powers at Versailles from carrying out their intentions in the Saar and Upper Silesia. The chief proposal under consideration was that Germany offer the Allies economic inducements in the form of participation in German enterprises. Wissell pointed out that, 'however painful it might be for the individual branches of industry to have strangers in their own house, where they had previously ruled alone, the distress of the Fatherland requires a renunciation of individual interest.[1] Reich Treasury Minister Gothein presented the issues more hopefully, reminding his listeners that foreign capital had played an important role in Germany's industrialisation until favourable conditions had enabled Germany gradually to free herself from it. Germany was once again in need of capital, but her military defeat made it impossible to borrow without offering direct foreign participation in the ownership of German industrial enterprises in return. American business circles had sent out feelers along these lines. The German government, therefore, entertained the hope that a means had been found both to deflect Germany's former enemies from some of their territorial ambitions and to procure the capital needed for reconstruction.

As we know, the Allies at Versailles had no intention of trading the territorial and economic advantages they were writing into the Treaty for the schemes inspired by unnamed American businessmen, and the wishful thinking of Germany's government leaders need not detain us. The issue of foreign participation in German enterprises, however, continued to have importance throughout the Weimar Republic's history, and it became linked – whether rightly or wrongly is another matter – with the question of Germany's capacity to retain her economic sovereignty despite the economic and political misery and heavy dependence on foreign capital which characterised the Weimar Republic. It is an instructive case study in the efforts of a Great Power to deal with the tensions between concerns for its

87

national interest and sovereignty, on the one hand, and its dependence upon international capital and participation in the world economy, on the other.

Germany's rise to Great Power status before 1914 had, as Gothein's remarks suggested, been accompanied by the liberation of her industrial development from dependence on foreign capital and, indeed, by her assumption of the role of an important capital exporter. Not only could Germany, like the United States, boast important multinational enterprises (for example, Siemens and Mannesmann), but her capitalists also invested in foreign enterprises. In the case of French ore mines in Normandy, for example, such investment reached levels that permitted actual control of certain of the enterprises in question. While prewar Germans sometimes fretted about the 'American danger' and the 'trust threat' from the USA, neither the German government nor the German business community were particularly fearful of foreign investors and certainly were aware of their own stake in freedom of movement on the capital market. Prior to 1914, only three German industries had been 'foreignised', in the sense that non-German interests dominated German manufacture and the German market through enterprises they had either set up on their own or over which they had gained control: the British–American Tobacco Company controlled about 25% of the German market through its purchase of the Dresden-based G. A. Jasmatzi & Co.; 60–70% of the German margarine industry was controlled by the Dutch firm of Anton Jürgens and the Anglo–Dutch firm of Van den Bergh Ltd; six of the eight German firms in the plate glass cartel were controlled by the Franco–Belgian 'Société Anonyme des Glaceries et des Produits Chimiques de St Gobain, Chauny et Cerey'. Obviously, the 'American danger' was more projection than reality. The incursions of other nations were not particularly sensational either. When war came, Germans were distressed to find that English interests owned some of their leading urban gas works as well as such a natural resource as the Apollinaris mineral water enterprise. Thus, while patriotic Englishmen were telling their compatriots to drink Perrier rather than German water, their German counterparts were railing against Apollinaris for being an English drink.[2]

So much for the prewar menace of 'foreignisation'. Furthermore, the war was used by all countries to 'nationalise' their capital to a greater extent than ever before. Not only were the holdings of enemy persons and corporations seized and placed in the hands of trustees or liquidated, but in the German case, the decision to finance the war by means of internal loans created a remarkably high reliance on domestic sources of capital. The loss of the war combined with the tremendous waste to capital resources which the war had entailed dealt a harsh blow to this 'nationalisation' process. They threatened to make Germany even more dependent on foreign capital than she had been during the course of her industrialisation. The implications for her international status were also significant. Germany, after all, was not Austria or one of the successor states – or was that to be her fate? It is noteworthy, for example, that the Austrian Republic, after an initial effort to prevent 'foreignisation' in order to push forward Social Democratic socialisation plans, reversed policy in the first half of 1920. On the one hand, Austrian corporations actually competed with one another to permit foreigners to provide capital and gain a voice in the management of their enterprises. On the other hand, the government sold off stock it had purchased during the brief period when it had toyed with socialisation ideas and even gave foreign holders of stock in Austrian enterprises tax benefits.[3]

These things were not to happen in Germany, but the Austrian case is not only interesting for the great power–small power contrast. It is also significant because it reminds us that the problem under discussion had relevance for domestic economic and social policy and that it involved decision making on both the private and the public levels. It is conceivable that private capitalist interests could encourage 'foreignisation' for reasons of necessity, profit or convenience and that they could even see it as a means of escaping from unwelcome policies on the part of their own government. At the same time, governments could either encourage the sacrifice of the private autonomy of their own capitalists in order to attain perceived national benefits, as was the case when Wissell argued that a measure of foreign economic penetration might help Germany's efforts to retain the Saar and Upper Silesia, or they could fight against foreign economic penetration in order to promote socialisation schemes or retain their ability to pursue various policy goals. Finally, the readiness of foreigners to penetrate the German economy – or any economy – was very much a function of their perception of the investment climate in general and of their evaluation of the domestic balance of forces.

This was well illustrated by the 23 May 1919 meeting, where the major industrialists present took a very sober and realistic view of the entire matter, but by no means presented a very coherent or united position.[4] The chemical industrialist Carl Duisberg, among others, pointed out that the German mark had depreciated so badly that it would be very easy for foreign capital to penetrate the economy. As one solution to this problem, he turned to German corporation law, which made possible the issuance of preferential stock (*Vorzugsaktien*) with multiple voting rights. Such stock could be reserved for the original founders of the company or a small group of German stockholders. If one used this device, then in Duisberg's view it would also be possible to control the situation further by offering the enemy powers stock in German enterprises, especially in those enterprises producing coal, nitrates and potash, since the enemy was demanding indemnities in the form of these raw materials anyway. The costs, of course, were to be born by the government, and Duisberg proposed that the Reich pay the costs of issuing the new stocks and bonds required or purchase certain mines and plants outright. He also suggested that the negotiations on this question not only be conducted from government to government but also between the German and non-German interest groups involved. What was essential – and here Duisberg's posture was typical of both the industrialists and the government leaders – was that the terms be set by the Germans in such a manner as to prevent foreign domination of the German economy.

The machine builder Ernst von Borsig shared Duisberg's positive approach, pointing out that the government's proposal was the 'only way out of the mire'. He thought his own industry particularly suitable for American investment because of its technical superiority, and even suggested that individual plants might be purchased by the government and given over to foreign control. The latter suggestion may not have been entirely disinterested, since he noted that the competition in his own field of locomotive building had been greatly increased by the entry of Krupp and the AEG into the field, and one wonders exactly whose plants he had in mind for this purpose. In any case, he urged the strongest possible organisation of his industry. Surprisingly, he emphasised that this should be done under state leadership so that there was an agency with the authority needed to defend common against special interests. This enthusiasm for the state organisation of industry in connection with the effort to secure foreign participation in German enterprises was strongly seconded by Hans Krämer of the cellulose and paper industry and by the banker, Fritz Andrae, who urged that 'one has to think of a huge concern which includes everything, that is, all of industry and which negotiates with America. The organisation must take place under the leadership of the state!!'

These enthusiasms were not shared by all the industrialists, some of whom urged caution about making proposals and were less sanguine about the chances of preventing foreign control. They wondered if it was wise to anticipate enemy intentions by offering that which had not yet been requested, and they doubted that foreign business interests would content themselves with an ownership that brought no control. Carl Friedrich von Siemens feared that the Americans were out to destroy Germany's competition in the electrotechnical field and that even a high degree of German organisation to prevent this would not succeed in averting American control if the Americans set themselves to the task. He emphasised that the offer of shares was a pure business arrangement and could not be confused with demands for the compensation of war damages. In contrast to the Americans, the French did have an interest in the prosperity of his industry so that the Germans would have the money to pay reparations. The French, however, did not have the money to buy German shares. Siemens, therefore, warned against taking any initiative as well as against entering into any participation arrangements unless the Allies retreated from their 'ruinous' economic demands.

Siemens' reservations were echoed by Dr Kind of the Steel Works Association (*Stahlwerksverband*), who served as a spokesman for the powerful heavy industrialists. Kind also stressed that the enemy powers had different interests, the French wanting German coal, the English viewing the German iron and steel industry as a dangerous competitor, the Americans simply wanting to enrich themselves. To each of them, therefore, 'participation' in German industry meant different and often irreconcilable things. In Kind's view, the government should first find out if the enemy had any interest in trading territorial demands for participation in German enterprises and, if so, in what enterprises. As another businessman hinted, there was a considerable amount of presumption in the assumption that foreign economic interests were anxious to invest in Germany since 'circumstances in Germany at the present time are very unclear [and] one undoubtedly can count on heavy taxation and perhaps with a levy on industrial wealth...That certainly would not be any incentive for foreign capital!' The representative of the potash industry even questioned the idea, generally accepted at the meeting, that a high degree of organisation was desirable. He warned against creating a potash monopoly, since this would enable the enemy to demand payment in potash itself, and he urged the government to give the industry a free hand in issuing shares and bonds on its own.

This certainly presents a confusing picture, and it reflects the great uncertainties of the last month before the signature of the peace treaty. The problems were compounded by the fact that some of the industrialists, at this time, were trying to come to terms with the corporatist, planned economy schemes contained in the *Gemeinwirtschaft* program of the Economics Minister, Rudolf Wissell and his leading adviser, Wichard von Moellendorff, and which had been popularised and advocated by Walther Rathenau of the AEG. These plans had strong supporters among some of the industrialists and bankers – Krämer and Andrae, for example – but were viewed with suspicion by others as a continuation of wartime bureaucratic management of the economy.[5] Nevertheless, a high degree of organisation was very characteristic of German capitalism, and it was not surprising that both the industrialists and the government leaders wished to promote an organised approach to the question of foreign participation in German enterprises. This was all the more the case at this time, when Germany was undergoing a veritable organisational mania in the plausible but somewhat naive belief that this was the ideal way to be prepared for all eventualities, both foreign and domestic. The basic questions were whether the state was going to dominate this organisational process or whether it was going to be carried out under private auspices and in what manner.

The 'foreignisation' debate thus existed from the outset of the Republic's history, and it was closely linked to basic problems of domestic and foreign policy. It attained prominence during the two major phases of Weimar's economic history, the period of inflation from 1919 to 1923, and the period of stabilisation from 1924 to 1929. It received particular public attention, however, early in the former years and at the end of the latter, and this discussion will focus its main attention on the years 1919–20 and 1929–30.

On the surface at least, the post-war inflation of 1919–23 provided a marvellous opportunity to 'buy out' and to 'buy up' Germany. This was especially the case during the periods of rapid mark depreciation from the fall of 1919 to the spring of 1920 and after the fall of 1921. At these times, there was a considerable amount of 'buying out' (*Ausverkauf*) of Germany by foreigners who used their strong currencies to procure German goods 'for a song'. German ability to resist such incursions was limited. If the Allies were co-operative, the German authorities could attempt to plug up the 'hole in the West', that is, the border between the occupied and unoccupied zones, through customs control. At the same time, the various branches of German industry could be compelled to form export syndicates that would agree on minimum export prices to be enforced at the borders. The Germans could also charge foreigners an 'exchange surcharge' (*Valutazuschlag*) for their sojourns in German hotels and resorts.[6]

It was one thing to place such irritating and much resented barriers in the way of cheap Alpine vacations, it was another to inhibit the flow of foreign capital seeking to make the most of Germany's currency depreciation. There was no problem in accepting what became the chief source of such capital between 1919 and 1922, namely, foreign speculation in marks and mark denominated assets. Germany was able to escape hyperinflation for as long as she did in large measure because of the willingness of foreigners to speculate on the mark when it was low in the expectation of 'making a killing' when it someday would allegedly increase in value.[7] Not all German businessmen were prepared to advise their foreign friends to embark upon such adventures. Richard Merton of the Metallgesellschaft, warned a Dutch colleague against purchasing fixed interest mark denominated assets because of the risk of depreciation and urged the purchase of 'first class industrial paper', however low its immediate rate of return. He pointed out that 'an industrial share is something which, completely independent of the fact that it is denominated in marks, is the part ownership of an enterprise which more or less retains its intrinsic worth irrespective of the situation of the mark.[8]

Such friendly advice was not meant to encourage unfriendly takeovers, of course, but the danger that control of Germany's industrial assets could be bought up was very real. One need only compare the mark and dollar cost

Table 9.1.

	31 December 1913 $1 = 4.20 M$	26 February 1920 $1 = 100 M$	31 December 1920 $1 = 72 M$
Harpen Mining	1720 M. $410	4500 M. $45	5530 M. $71
Phoenix	2340 M. $557	5850 M. $58.50	6550 M. $91
German Potash	1260 M. $300	5250 M. $52.50	4550 M. $66
BASF	5580 M. $1330	6390 M. $63.90	5700 M. $90

of a 1,000 mark share of four of Germany's leading concerns at the end of 1913, February 1920, and December 1920 to realise the possibilities (see Table 9.1).

The figures for late February 1920 are particularly significant because share purchases for foreign accounts during that month were the highest for the postwar period while the mark was at its lowest level since 1914. While the mark improved in the course of the relative stabilisation which followed, share prices remained remarkably cheap for foreigners. The potentialities are even more impressive when one notes that the first three enterprises had not increased their capital stock to any great extent in 1919, and only the BASF had doubled its capital in December 1919.[9]

Why was German industry not 'bought up'? Retrospectively, the reason is fairly clear. As Oskar Schlitter of the Deutsche Bank pointed out almost a decade later: 'there were not enough people abroad who could evaluate German conditions sufficiently, and also not enough people who had the necessary confidence. You have to imagine as if someone today [i.e., 1928 – GDF] would go and buy shares in Russia. Foreigners found German conditions just as alien as we today find many things in Russia alien from a commercial point of view.'[10] As the opportunities provided by the decline of the mark diminished with the relative stabilisation, the worsening business conditions in the United States and Great Britain imposed caution on businessmen there. When the mark began a new series of plunges after the fall of 1921, Germany's domestic and foreign policy problems were such that foreigners no longer even had much of a taste for their mark speculations.[11]

In retrospect, therefore, the danger of a systematic and sustained effort to 'foreignise' German enterprises from without during the inflation was fairly limited. That was not, however, how Germans themselves viewed the situation in the fall and winter of 1919–20, when the danger appeared greatest, or subsequently with somewhat less alarm prior to the stabilisation.

Foreign penetration of German heavy industry was a source of particular worry. The territorial arrangements imposed by the Versailles Treaty had disrupted the connections between the plants of various concerns, while raw materials requirements, operating and long-term capital requirements, and the problems of reconstructing foreign trading networks also increased the danger that the leaders of these industries might yield to the temptations offered by foreigners. The Gelsenkirchener Bergwerke and the Stumm concern, for example, had sold control of their plants on the left bank to French interests, and in early 1920, Mannesmann followed suit by giving 60% control of its Saar holdings to a French group. The 30 million francs paid Mannesmann translated into 103.38 million marks and thus exceeded the value of its capital stock. As a consequence, Mannesmann did not have to undertake to raise capital by issuing new shares and bonds, as was the case with most concerns at this time, and was even in a position to pay its impatient stockholders a decent dividend.[12]

Far more sensational was the combined 'internal' and 'external foreignisation' of the Phoenix Concern at the turn of 1919–20, when a substantial albeit not absolutely controlling share of its stock was bought up by the Cologne iron merchant, Otto Wolff, on the one hand, and Dutch interests with whom Wolff had close connections, on the other. The manoeuvre was much resented by both the management, which 'deeply regretted' that a substantial portion of Phoenix stock had come into Dutch hands, and the Chairman of the Supervisory Board, S. Alfred von Oppenheim, who remarked with reference to Wolff that 'one sees everywhere the bad consequences of the war and revolution profiteers, who are insatiable and who ruthlessly seek to expand their interests further'.[13] Apparently, some of the large stockholders did not know who was behind the sensational stock purchases until the process was completed. It was rumoured that American interests were buying up the stock, and there was much relief to learn that the Dutch were involved instead. Where America competed with Germany on the world market for these products, Dutch and German interests were complementary. Nevertheless, many found the case troubling because it *could* have been the Americans, and 'the domination of leading German enterprises by foreign capital from countries where the preconditons for economic collaboration are not present, but rather whose domination threatens to lead to an enslavement of the German economy, is a danger which the harmless events surrounding Phoenix have brought clearly into the open'.[14]

Not every such danger was brought out into the open or was equally harmless. No less a personage than the chief executive officer of the Krupp firm, Otto Wiedfeldt, seemed to feel that the best way out of the firm's reconversion difficulties and financial problems was a surrender of some independence. Given a choice between dictation from the seemingly insatiable Hugo Stinnes, who had built up his gigantic vertical trust, the Siemens–Rheinelbe–Schuckert Union, at this time and an arrangement with US Steel, Wiedfeldt preferred the latter. Thus, in July 1921, Wiedfeldt proposed that Krupp use its Mendelssohn bank connection to approach Rockefeller and US Steel and offer 100 million marks in Krupp shares in return for an American seat on the Krupp Board of Supervisors. He argued that the criticism of Krupp that this would entail would be sufficiently compensated for by its greater independence of the other Ruhr works, especially of Stinnes, foreign trade advantages, and desperately needed capital. Nevertheless, Gustav Krupp von Bohlen und Halbach rejected the Wiedfeldt proposal, which he found incompatible with the special character and reputation of the firm, and decided to find other means of autonomous survival.[15]

This option was not open to Rheinmetall, a former major producer of weapons in which Krupp was a major shareholder. Rheinmetall's efforts to switch from war production to locomotives and typewriters had reduced dividends from a wartime high of 26–8 % to nothing. Its location on the left bank of the Rhine and impressive facilities, however, could be of great value to the French. The latter's acquisitions from Gelsenkirchen, Stumm and Mannesmann, and reports that the French were buying into the South German finishing industry, alarmed Carl Friedrich von Siemens, who feared that 'the policy of France perhaps is to cut off the Rhenish economic area from that of the rest of Germany and gradually to make a second Saar territory out of it'.[16] France would then control a region rich in raw materials and manufacturing plants and be in a position to dump raw materials and iron on the rest of Germany while being relieved of the need to import machinery and other manufactured products. Siemens, therefore, suggested to his business allies in the Siemens–Rheinelbe–Schuckert Union, that they create a consortium with some banks and secure Krupp's cooperation in gaining control of Rheinmetall. Stinnes showed some interest, but the rescue operation finally was conducted by the AEG and the Otto Wolff interests.

There were other occasions, however, when Stinnes could play, or claim to play, what in today's parlance is called a 'white knight'. When the speculative banker, Hugo Herzfeld, secured majority control of the Bochumer Verein stock in the fall of 1920 and seemed prepared to sell to Dutch interests, Stinnes prevented foreignisation by purchasing the stock and integrating the firm into the Rhine–Elbe-Union.[17] If German bankers welcomed Stinnes' move on this occasion, they had more mixed feelings when 40,000 shares of the Karl Fürstenberg's bank the Berliner Handelsgesell-schaft first found their way into the hands of the Hungarian–Romanian speculator, Emil Cyprut, who then sold them to Stinnes in March 1922. Czech capital also appeared to be behind Cyprut's operation. Until this time, the German banking community had been rather complacent about the dangers which 'foreignisation', either domestic or foreign, posed to them because of the huge amount of capital this would require and their feeling that their shares were well and safely placed. The Cyprut–Stinnes affair, however, demonstrated that under conditions of galloping inflation even they were not safe, and they began to follow the lead of their industrial brethren in seeking ways and means of achieving a measure of solidarity and employing 'self-help' in warding off such incursions.[18]

However 'organised' German capitalism and patriotic its leaders, there were real limits to solidarity. German industry did need foreign capital, and the notion of organising both individual branches of industry and all of industry for the purpose of procuring and distributing it, which had been discussed prior to the signing of the treaty, continued to be a subject of lively interest in 1919–20. Apparently, the machine building industry or a group of firms in the industry tried to approach American investors collectively in the spring of 1920 only to discover that the Americans involved wished 'to choose the individual flowers for the bouquet themselves'.[19] Of greater significance were the proposals emanating from some leading industrialists in the Reichsverband der deutschen Industrie, the economic writer Georg Bernhard, and various officials of the Economics Ministry, most notably the State Secretary Julius Hirsch, for a pooling of industrial credit through the establishment of an Economic Bank that would direct both domestic and foreign capital investments. These schemes failed as well. The banks vigorously opposed such potential competition and claimed that they were 'swimming in capital'. They brushed aside the point that most of it was speculative capital that could be withdrawn with disastrous consequences. As for industry, it became increasingly wary of the *dirigiste* implications of such schemes, and the Finance Ministry vigorously opposed anything that might further increase the government deficit.[20]

In the last analysis, both government and industry felt compelled to fall back upon the device of the preferred share with multiple voting rights as the chief weapon against 'foreignisation'. Although there was considerable pressure on the government to do something positive in 1919–20, the economic clauses of the Versailles Treaty prohibited the Germans from imposing economic restrictions on her former enemies which were not imposed upon Germans as well.[21] While the government could seek to prevent Dutch middlemen known to be in the business of buying up German shares and property for foreigners from crossing the border,[22] discrimination against former neutrals hardly was in Germany's interest either. The government, therefore, encouraged industry to use the legal means already available under German corporation law.

If German corporation law had made provision for the issuance of special shares with multiple voting rights, the prewar use of such shares had primarily been in cases where new ownership had been called in to rehabilitate (*Sanierung*) a company in financial difficulties by giving the new owners the voting rights they needed to reform the company successfully.[23] The purpose had not been to disenfranchise the stockholders. It was not inappropriate, therefore, that one of the first persons to advocate the use of such shares to prevent foreignisation publicly, Ernst Sontag, entitled his 1918 discussion of the subject, 'The Corporation in Conflict between Power and Law'.[24]

Tampering with the principle of majority role was an uncomfortable business, but the dangers of letting this time-honoured principle hold sway were dramatically illustrated at the end of 1919 in the case of the vegetable oil industry. When the management of the Bremen–Besigheimer Oelfabriken and the Oelfabrik Gross–Gerau sought to prevent foreignisation at the hands of the Dutch margarine interests by securing approval for the creation of preferential stock with multiple voting rights, the stockholders objected on the grounds that so much of the stock was already in foreign hands that the necessary majority could not be secured and further that the foreign participation was necessary to secure the needed raw materials. In the former case, it was a large German stockholder who carried the day for the foreign interests. In a much publicised letter to its German membership, the Association of German Vegetable Oil Firms vehemently criticised the defeat of the pro-German forces in this incident and warned that the foreignisation of the industry would mean that the foreigners would walk off with the profits, press the technically well equipped and efficient German plants into the service of foreign economic interests, and could even simply remove plants and machinery from the country if they so desired. The association alleged that only shares with multiple voting rights would provide protection against the exploitation of Germany's monetary misery for the purpose of placing German enterprises at the mercy of foreigners. It appealed to the patriotism of the industry's shareholders as well as their egotistical interests in order to prevent 'German labour' from falling into 'tributary service' to foreigners. All this was to no avail, and the Association soon came to terms with van den Bergh and Jürgens, who dominated the industry throughout the Republic's history and did so without the dire consequences predicted.[25]

In 1919, however, nothing was quite so predictable, and the policy was to prevent the worst. Thus, on 4 December 1919, the German Chamber of Industry and Commerce wrote to its members endorsing the issuance of shares with multiple voting rights in order to fight 'foreignisation'. While the organisation pointed out that foreign investment was to be encouraged as a means of interesting Germany's former enemies in the success of German industry, in moderating their demands, and in assuring that Germany had enough raw materials, it was important to prevent them gaining control for the purpose of undermining German economic development and competitiveness. The possibilities of preventing foreignisation by passing legislation setting up certain prerequisites for stock ownership were limited because foreigners could always use straw men for their purposes, and the 'nationalisation' of the supervisory boards and the boards of directors provided no guarantee either. The crucial thing was to neutralise the ability of foreigners to take advantage of their presence at the stockholders meetings, and the issuance of stock with multiple voting rights was a means of ensuring special voting powers on questions of membership on the boards of supervisors or directors and on matters pertaining to basic policy. Chamber of Commerce members were called upon to pay particular heed to instances of 'open or veiled purchase of stocks by foreigners' and to take appropriate steps where the danger of foreignisation existed.[26]

To illustrate the possibilities, the Chamber of Industry and Commerce provided the example of the Hamburg–Amerika line (Hapag), which had made an exchange of preferred stock of limited financial value but with multiple voting rights with the Hamburg–South America Steamship Company. By this means, either company could come to the rescue of the other in the event that foreigners tried to use their share holdings to control one of these companies. This advice, however, only revealed more or less official approval of what the major concerns were doing anyway. The leading firms of the chemical industry, the so-called 'Anilin Group', which was to become IG Farben, had already done precisely what their leading executive, Carl Duisberg, had advised and issued preferred shares with multiple voting rights. Their original contribution to this effort, however, was to arrange that the member firms of the trust would hold one another's multiple voting right stock. This practice continued throughout the Weimar Republic and seemed particularly necessary because of the great foreign interest in holding shares in this industry. In fact, most of the great corporations and many of the smaller ones issued shares with multiple voting rights in the course of 1919–20, and this practice continued in later years so that, by the late 1920s, about 50% of the leading corporations had protected themselves in this manner.[27]

The creation of blocks of shares with multiple voting rights which were reserved, as in the case of Siemens, for family members, or for friendly shareholders, reliable banks, and German nationals was extremely problematic and easily led to abuses. There was a considerable number of instances in which the threat of foreignisation was used as a justification for issuing such shares, while the real purpose of the issue was for a minority of stockholders, sometimes in collusion with the management, to disenfranchise the majority of stockholders or even take control from the original stockholders. While the Prussian Ministry of Commerce, which had the power to approve new stock issues, encouraged the issuance of shares with multiple voting rights to prevent foreignisation, it very rapidly had reason to warn against the misuse of such shares for other purposes and called upon the Chambers of Commerce to report such cases.[28]

Among the great concerns, Siemens' big competitor, the AEG, distinguished itself during the inflation by finding a means of securing foreign participation without resorting to the crudities of issuing shares with multiple voting rights. It was in part able to do so because it was the most highly capitalised of the great concerns at that time. In order to secure needed raw materials, especially copper, it sold 25 million marks worth of its shares to the American Smelting and Refining Company through the banking house of Kuhn, Loeb & Co., whose owner, Otto Kahn, was related to the AEG's general director, Felix Deutsch. The shares were sold at a price which gave the AEG the equivalent of 50 million marks in dollars, while the danger of foreignisation was prevented by treating the shares as a block and placing both their disposition and their votes under the control of a committee composed of two Germans and one American. As a consequence, the management actually strengthened the power of the AEG's management against any opposition. Walther Rathenau praised his concern's stock sale to the Americans as 'a pioneering arrangement',[29] but it was not one easily emulated. The lignite industrialist, Paul Silverberg, felt more secure issuing multiple voting shares for the Rheinische Braunkohlengesellschaft, and when asked by August Thyssen why he had done so, Silverberg bluntly replied that 'without them we would have lost control either to Petschek [a Czech industrialist – GDF] or to Stinnes or to you'.[30] How much proteciton such shares provided in the long run remained a real question, however, and critics often pointed out that foreignisation could be eased if those in control of the shares with multiple voting rights decided it was in their interest to sell out to foreigners.[31]

In the last analysis, therefore, if one asks why much more of German industry was not 'foreignised' during the inflation, the answer is not to be found in the issuance of multiple voting shares. This undoubtedly had a chilling effect, but had economic and political conditions encouraged a concerted effort by foreigners to buy up German industry, it is doubtful that this mechanism would have sufficed. Most of Germany's great industrial leaders were committed to prevent 'foreignisation', and it was this that gave potency to the devices they employed. At the same time, 'external foreignisation' was also fought by 'internal foreignisation', that process of vertical concentration for which the period was famous. This answered the need for capital and raw materials felt by the smaller firms which surrendered their independence to the larger ones and was considered preferable to foreign domination.[32] At the same time, Stinnes' taking over of the Bochumer Verein, and the AEG's interests in the Rheinmetall and the cable producer, Felten & Guilleaume, was explicitly motivated by the desire to prevent foreign control of those enterprises.[33] In this respect, Germany proved that she was not like Austria or one of the weaker successor states. If anything, the Treaty of Versailles had strengthened German resolve to prevent foreignisation during the inflation, and where the prospect of foreign participation in German enterprises had been considered as a possible trade-off for territorial and political concessions before the Treaty was signed, German heavy industry persistently refused to consider schemes for French participation in German heavy industry between 1920 and 1923 unless Germany would also be allowed to participate in French heavy industry and unless the French gave up occupation of the Saar and the Rhineland.[34] For Germany, the 'foreignisation' issue was intimately linked to German nationalism and to the problems arising from the role foreign capital would play in the reconstruction not only of her economy, but also of her tarnished Great Power status.

A major consequence of the stabilisation of the mark, the ending of the Ruhr occupation, and the Dawes Plan was the reintegration of Germany into the world economy and a much less anxious posture toward 'foreignisation'. As is well known, Germany became very dependent upon short-term foreign capital, especially from America, while her stabilisation process and the rationalisation programmes conducted by industry created a welcome environment for foreign capital. Most of the real 'foreignisation' of German industry, such as it was, took place between 1924 and 1929, but it was only toward the end of this period that it began to attract significant attention once again. Whether it was an issue or not was more a function of politics than economics. The basic conflict was between a moderate internationalist, economically liberal position and a nationalist and, in the broadest sense, protectionist position. The debate was one touchstone of whether or not the Weimar Republic would be able to retain a distinctive foreign policy of international understanding, as well as find ways and means of using her economic potential to recover her international position within a liberal and internationalist context.[35]

For those who wished to see the Weimar Republic recover her position within such an environment, the problems of 'foreignisation' had to be taken in stride. The more liberal organs of the business community, like the *Frankfurter Zeitung* and the *Magazin der Wirtschaft* voiced this attitude. Along with those who took the opposite position, they fretted over Germany's dependence on short-term capital after 1924, but they refused to engage in a revival of the alarmism over 'foreignisation'. The noted economic writer, Georg Bernhard, warned particularly against proposals that the Reich or the states buy up firms in danger of 'foreignisation', pointing out that such suggestions hardly were in conformity with demands for economic freedom and reduced government expenditure and taxes. It was contradictory, he argued, to declare approvingly that Germany was once again integrated into the world economy and then forget that this involved the integration of capital markets as well. It was better for foreigners to pay the bill for poorly run or uncompetitive German firms than it was for Germans to do so, and Bernhard was particularly critical of the notoriously troubled German motor car industry for its ceaseless propaganda to 'buy German automobiles' and to raise customs barriers. If Germans wished to export, they had to be willing to import. He went on to ask if 'it is not better that an American, a Belgian, a French or an Italian automobile firm participates in a German work and has its models produced here, than that it set up a competing factory of its own, in which, for example, it puts togethr parts made in America or directly imports foreign cars?'[36]

If Bernhard thought it was high time that Germans ceased to perceive 'the so-called foreignisation as a misfortune instead of a natural fructification of Germany's capital weak economy', he noted that the growing alarm over 'foreignisation' had increased in intensity 'since Reichsbank President Schacht has brought the German people to fear foreign capital'.[37] It was no accident that the issue heated up in 1929 in the context of the development of the Young Plan, which Schacht was to oppose with all the drama and destructiveness of which that megalomaniac was capable,[38] and the bitter debate within Germany over its acceptance. While the plan certainly offered Germany clear advantages over the Dawes Plan, it underscored the fact that Germany would remain dependent on foreign capital for a long time to come and did so at a time when economic conditions were taking a turn for the worse. Interest rates on short-term capital continued to be high, and the danger that such money could be withdrawn and that its sources would dry up was ever present. The bond market was proving unsatisfactory. Under these circumstances, foreign participation in German enterprises was increasing in importance as a source of industrial capital formation. While continuing to condemn foreign investment that might have the purpose of shutting down German competition, reducing production, and thereby creating unemployment in Germany, the *Frankfurter Zeitung* welcomed what it called a 'purely capitalistic foreignization, which one today begins to view not as a danger, but rather as a chance for a quicker development of the German economy...'.[39] The paper argued that the use of preferential shares with multiple voting rights had not worked to keep foreigners out, but went on to urge that German corporation law and economic practice be readjusted not to discourage but rather to encourage foreign engagement in German economic life. In so far as foreign penetration might be found harmful to general German economic interests through the unjustified shutting down of plants or other untoward measures, the creation of a government Securities Office (*Aktienamt*) that would have the power to sanction countermeasures was viewed as a solution. The newspaper sharply attacked protectionism, panic, and xenophobic responses as harmful and unjustified.

When the *Frankfurter Zeitung* took a close look at some 100 cases of alleged 'foreignisation' of German corporations, it came to the sobering conclusion that in the overwhelming number of such cases a minority not a majority of shares was involved, the management was retained in German hands, and the corporations affected had a long history of foreign participation. Furthermore, foreign participation in these corporations had not been accomplished against the will of their owners or management, but rather with their approval or even as a consequence of their initiative:

Not infrequently our businessmen themselves offered the foreigners the opportunity; weak or tired portfolios of securities were seeking out a new owner: the Prussian Mortgage Bank to Krüger via Barmat; Stinnes' Koholyt to Inveresk in London; Stinnes-Mülheim to Stinnes-New York; Michael's Iduna firms to Globe Underwriters in New York...; Sauch's Vox Records to Duophone in New York; Köslin Paper Works and Konschewski's Alfred-Gronau works to Combined Pulp and Paper – indeed everywhere the desire came from the German side.[40]

Furthermore, the Germans themselves were involved in the organised purchase of foreign shares, as in the case of the Svenska-Gruppe, Montecatini, Norsk Hydro, and the Polish Cement Firm of Firley, and they even managed investment trusts and enterprises in Switzerland and Holland. Germany, after all, was a participant in an international process of trustification, interchange and competition in which financial advantages, patents, licenses, raw materials needs, and other economic considerations played the major role. Mannesmann, Wrigley Chewing Gum and Citroën all operated multinationally for such reasons. The principle of 'reciprocity', therefore, was in order, and while the *Frankfurter* recognised that Germany's capital shortage made it likely that she would be more the object than the perpetrator of international capital penetration during the coming years, its writers suggested that Germany's conservative tariff and patent regulations as well as her financial and labour methods did their share to increase German vulnerability.

This revealing article pointed up the limitations and dilemmas of a quantitative approach to the problem or a mere listing of firms and percentages of foreign participation.[41] When the Reich Statistical Office tried to investigate the question, it found that foreigners held shares of 724 German corporations at the end of 1929. These holdings were worth 2.5 billion marks. It then rounded its estimate off to 4 billion marks to take into account holdings which were not public and affiliates of foreign companies in Germany. Between 1926 and 1929, foreign holdings in German enterprises had doubled in value, while the value of German holdings abroad had remained constant. Clearly, German firms had become much more dependent upon foreign capital participation, but only the most minute analysis could determine how much and with what significance. For example, if a German corporation decided for tax or other financial reasons to found a holding company abroad, and its German shareholders then transferred their shares to the holding company, the Reich Statistical Office considered the corporation to be 'foreignised'. Thus, the German linoleum and synthetic textiles industries appeared 'foreignised'. In reality, the Zürich-based Continental Linoleum Concern, was nothing more than a holding company for the stock of the German producers and the transfer of the stock of the Vereinigte Glanzstoff–Fabriken to the Dutch concern Aku in no way changed the German character of the ownership or the German control of its non-German holdings.[42]

For those anxious to discount such evidence or with an interest in sounding an alarm, General Motors' takeover of Germany's leading automobile manufacturer, Adam Opel AG, between March and July 1929, and the International General Electric's securing of 25–30 % of the AEG in August of 1929, provided just the sort of sensationally unwelcome news they needed. Opel had led the chorus of German automobile producers in their collective dirge over foreign penetration of the market and industry and had done its utmost to play upon nationalist sentiments. Its outgoing letters had born a stamp declaring that 'until the German balance of trade is active, we request that you only visit us and deliver to us in German vehicles'.[43] The Opel family's decision to transform its firm into a corporation and then sell out to the Americans, therefore, was an event that could not go unnoticed, and certainly not one that had anything to do with Germany having an active trade balance. Economic commentators recognised that it was the unavoidable consequence of the German industry's failure to concentrate and to adopt American methods, and they pointed out that the Germans might also have warded off the Americans by joining together with European producers. At the same time, they remarked favourably on the possibility of Germany becoming a centre of the American effort to penetrate other European markets. Even the liberal press, however, noted with discomfort that the new ownership had shown no interest whatever in Opel's bicycle producing subsidiary, the Elite–Diamant Werke.[44]

Furthermore, if the Opel family had become understandably reticent, others were quite prepared to make political and nationalist use of the company's plight. General Director Vögler of the Vereinigte Stahlwerke and Schacht made direct reference to the affair in reporting to the Cabinet on the Young Plan negotiations. They argued that conditions

naturally are totally catastrophic for Germany over the long run. The events at Opel during the last week are very typical. With its economy continuing on its present course, Germany runs the great danger of becoming an American labour province. President Schacht described this as his view of Germany's future for the next 40–50 years. Under present circumstances, Germany would become a land of workers and employees, without having much share of its own substance, since the economy would have to indebt itself abroad more and more labouring under its present burdens. General Director Vögler agreed completely.... We are now wasting our substance. Since it is not bringing any return, the prices of easily alienated values naturally diminish first, that is, shares and real estate and they both go first to foreigners....[45]

Shortly after this report, Schacht made reference to the 'foreignisation' issue again, pointing out that the Americans had a very unrealistic view of Germany's economic capabilities, and that, in the process of pursuing their interests, Germany would be bought up:

One must once and for all understand the differences between the American and German economies. So great and generally respected a German enterprise as Opel was recently bought up with a fraction of a year's income by General Motors. The total yearly income of this American firm is much higher than all the German dividends put together. As a consequence the Americans operate from completely different perspectives than we. Our ideals are a matter of complete indifference over there. The Americans only want to do business. Europe for them is only a very large conglomeration, and for the Americans it hardly matters to examine whether they are dealing with Romania, Poland, Germany or some other land. Only where they find concrete individual cases for making a profit on the European market do the Americans move in. He assumes, for example, with complete certainty, that IG Farben, the AEG and other first class German works are already today in large measure in American possession....[46]

There was, of course, a contradiction between Schacht's description of America's economy and motives and the tendency of himself and his colleagues to attribute America's penetration of the economy to the reparations burden. In reality, all of Europe suffered from a capital shortage, and Germany was not alone in complaining and worrying about the 'foreignisation' of her enterprises.[47] It would be a mistake, however, to dismiss the fact that this problem, like most of the significant economic, social and political issues in the Weimar Republic was linked to the reparations question. It was the latter that seemed to legitimise the alarmism and bitterness with which 'foreignisation' was treated, and its recrudescence in 1929–30 was symptomatic of the manner in which the oncoming depression would be combined with the struggle against reparations as well as with the retreat from the liberal institutions of the Weimar Republic itself.

The business community was by no means united in their posture, and some of the differences came out much more clearly in the case of the International General Electric's increased participation in the AEG. The AEG's leaders in 1929 certainly could not repeat Walther Rathenau's boast of 1920 that his concern had concluded a 'pioneering arrangement' with General Electric in which the latter gave money while eschewing the right to control the AEG. In 1929, the AEG stock, in contrast to its competitor

Siemens, was very widely scattered. There was no extremely large German shareholder, so that a minority share of 25–30 % had great significance. Also, the AEG agreed to have five Americans, one of whom was the Reparations Agent, Owen D. Young, sit on its thirty-two member Supervisory Board. Finally, it gave General Electric the right to acquire up to 49 % of its stock.[48]

This arrangement marred the harmony of the September 1929 meeting of the Reich Association of German Industry to celebrate its tenth anniversary. Dr Werner Kehl of the Deutsche Bank, reflecting the policies being pursued by the great banks at this time, argued that it was necessary and important for Germany to get an increasing amount of foreign capital in the form of 'long term and responsible participation' through the sale of shares. In so far as Kehl recommended this for government and municipal owned enterprises, his remarks were universally approved by an assemblage long anxious to fight 'cold socialisation' with privatisation, but the enthusiasm for his argument with respect to private enterprises was decidedly mixed. Director Sempell of the Vereinigte Stahlwerke sharply criticised those who would permit strong minorities representing powerful foreign corporations from gaining decisive influence over major German industrial enterprises. This scarcely veiled reference to AEG provoked an immediate response from Director Meinhardt of the Osram firm, who stressed the value of 'minority participation at a good price which does not endanger the management of the enterprise and which promotes exports'.[49] Hermann Bücher, the General Director of the AEG, rose even more strongly and aggressively to the defence, arguing that it was a mistake to call the willingness of foreign capitalists to risk their money on a German enterprise 'foreignisation' and insisting that the leadership of a firm was really a question of 'personality'. From his point of view, it was more dangerous to cover debts and operating costs through the issuance of high interest bonds, and it was the path taken by the AEG that was truly 'patriotic'.

This probably was a veiled attack on the AEG's competitor, Siemens, which in February 1930 was to issue 35,000 participating debentures, through Dillon Read & Co. The American General Electric Company was to hold some $11 million of these debentures, which were scheduled to mature in 2930, to which no voting rights were attached, and whose interest rate was dependent on profits.[50] In any case, Carl Friedrich von Siemens used the occasion of the celebration of his firm's founding on 12 October 1929 to deliver an address which clearly took the side of Sempell against the AEG by declaring that 'many leaders of the once so proud German electrotechnical industry have prematurely given up the steering wheel and taken on foreign pilots...'. In so doing, they had not 'eased the work of those who hope to hold their German ship in a position of leadership in the competition with foreign nations through their own strength and only with their own crew'. He warned that these 'foreign pilots' would 'use their German captains as instruments to serve the will of foreigners'.[51]

Bücher and his colleagues at the AEG did not appreciate all this passion and pathos from their competitor. Rather unconvincingly Bücher claimed that the thousands of German citizens who owned AEG stock demonstrated that the firm had not been 'foreignised', as if the widely distributed AEG stock was some protection against General Electric or compared with the power exercised by the majority holding enjoyed by the Siemens family. With greater cogency, the AEG reminded Siemens that the latter was a participant with the AEG in the sale of Osram stock to General Electric. What could not be said publicly, of course, was that Siemens was financially stronger and technologically ahead of the AEG and that Siemens had largely been responsible for rejecting overtures from the AEG for the formation of a community of interests (*Interessengemeinschaft*). The press did indeed think it inappropriate for the AEG's chief competitor to make such criticisms, and Siemens himself did something to correct the situation by giving a more sober statement to the press in which he admitted the legitimacy of selling stock to foreign interests and that he was not in a position to judge individual cases. Nevertheless, he did feel that there was an entire group of instances in which firms had become too dependent on foreigners.[52]

It would be a mistake to make too much of these episodes, and if Siemens and the AEG were illustrative of anything, it was of the close relationships and strong support which truly competitive and powerful German firms could have from the United States in this period. If the Opel affair caused some bad blood, it was because of the messy state of the German industry, and both the German government and German industry made a point of cultivating General Motors, a policy which extended even to the first period of Hitler's rule.[53]

The significance of the 'foreignisation' issue is twofold. From the perspective of Weimar history, the issue is interesting because of its instrumentalisation for foreign policy and domestic political purposes, and it enjoyed brief importance in 1919–20 and 1929–30 precisely for these reasons. What Georg Bernhard objected to in Siemens' attack on the AEG was that it reflected the 'carrying over of narrow concepts of power from politics to economics' and a surrender to a set of 'clichés and slogans' which had become part of 'the arsenal of a politics that is bad and lacking in ideas'.[54] From Bernhard's point of view, American participation in the German economy was a means of strengthening Germany's economic role in Europe and Europe's economic role in the world. For the extreme nationalists, however, it was evidence in their battle against Versailles and an argument for their protectionist and autarchic postures. Even for more moderate elements, however, the 'foreignisations' were useful as arguments against the social policies of Weimar, which were blamed in large measure for the inadequate capital investment in German industry. Not only Vögler and Schacht, but also Gustav Stolper's *Der Deutsche Volkswirt* could argue that the most extreme and undesirable forms of 'foreignisation' could only be avoided if there was a satisfactory financial and economic reform that would permit Germany to have a 'halfway normal capital market'.[55]

On a broader level, the 'foreignisation' controversy is an early demonstration of the conflict between the 'nationalisation' of capital promoted by the First World War and the interventionist state, on the one hand, and the interdependence of modern industrial societies and the internationalisation of capital markets, on the other hand. The controversy was brought to an end in Germany by renewed internal chaos and international depression and then by the extreme 'nationalisation' of capital under the Nazi régime. In the post-war era, it has remained muted because of the prosperity and commitment to a liberal international economic order, at least among the western nations. It is hardly a dead issue.

NOTES

1. Report of Director von Holtzendorff, 24 May 1919, HAPAG Archiv.
2. Hans Jürgen von Kleist, *Die ausländische Kapitalbeteiligung in Deutschland* (Berlin, 1921), pp. 30ff.; Charlotte Leubuscher, 'Die Nationalisierung des Kapitals', *Archiv für Sozialwissenschaft* 42 (1916–17), 505–34; Thomas R. Kabisch, *Deutsches Kapital in den USA. Von der Reichsgründung bis zur Sequestrierung (1917) und Freigabe* (Stuttgart, 1982); Fritz Blaich, *Amerikanische Firmen in Deutschland 1890–1918*, Zeitschrift für Unternehmensgeschichte Beiheft 30 (Wiesbaden, 1984).
3. Simon Kurz, *Die Überfremdungsgefahr der deutschen Aktiengesellschaften und ihre Abwehr*, Betriebs- und Finanzwirtschaftliche Forschungen, Heft 13 (Leipzig, 1921), pp. 58ff.
4. This discussion is based on the protocol cited in note 1.
5. See Hans Gotthard Ehlert, *Die wirtschaftliche Zentralbehörde des Deutschen Reiches 1914 bis 1919. Das Problem der 'Gemeinwirtschaft' in Krieg und Frieden*, Beiträge zur Wirtschafts- und Sozialgeschichte, Bd 19 (Wiesbaden, 1982), pp. 225ff.; Gerald D. Feldman, *Iron and steel in the German inflation, 1916–1923* (Princeton, 1977), pp. 100ff, and 'Der deutsche Organisierte Kapitalismus während der Kriegs- und Inflationsjahre 1914–1923', in Gerald D. Feldman (ed.), *Vom Weltkrieg zur Weltwirtschaftskrise. Studien zur deutschen Wirtschafts- und Sozialgeschichte 1914–1932*, Kritische Studien zur Geschichtswissenschaft, Bd 60 (Göttingen, 1984), pp. 36–54; also in Heinrich August Winkler (ed.), *Organisierter Kapitalismus*, Kritische Studien zur Geschichtswissenschaft, Bd 9 (Göttingen, 1974), pp. 150–71.
6. See Feldman, *Iron and steel*, pp. 130, 192f. These matters will be discussed in greater detail in my forthcoming *The great disorder: A social and political history of the German inflation, 1914–1924* (Oxford, 1988).
7. In so far as such investors did not see the light earlier, they lost their money in the

hyperinflation of 1922–3. See Carl-Ludwig Holtfrerich, 'Amerikanischer Kapital-export und Wiederaufbau der deutschen Wirtschaft 1919–1923' *Vierteljahrsschrift für Sozial- und Wirtschaftsgeschichte* 64 (1977), 497–529 and 'U.S. capital exports to Germany 1919–1923 compared to 1924–1929', *Explorations in Economic History* 23 (1986), 1–32.

8 Richard Merton to R. van Hemert, 19 January 1920, Privatbriefe Richard Merton, Historisches Archiv der Metallgesellschaft, Frankfurt-am-Main.

9 Kurz, *Überfremdungsgefahr*, pp. 8–10.

10 Auschuss zur Untersuchung der Erzeugungs- und Absatzbedingungen der deutschen Wirtschaft, *Verhandlungen und Berichte des Unterausschusses für allgemeine Wirtschaftsstruktur (1. Unterausschuss). 3. Arbeitsgruppe. Wandlungen in den wirtschaftlichen Organisationsformen. Erster Teil. Wandlungen in den Rechtsformen der Einzelunternehmungen und Konzerne* (Berlin, 1928), p. 4. (Hereafter cited as Enquete 1/3/1.)

11 Carl-Ludwig Holtfrerich, *Die deutsche Inflation 1914–1923. Ursachen und Folgen in internationaler Perspektive* (Berlin and New York, 1980), pp. 279ff, and Feldman, *Iron and steel*, p. 226.

12 *Plutus. Kritische Zeitschrift für Volkswirtschaft und Finanzwesen*, 5 May 1920, 152ff.

13 Schaewen to Heinrichsbauer, 18 December 1920, Mannesmann-Archiv, P/1/25/33 and S. Alfred von Oppenheim to Schaewen, 8 April 1920, Mannesmann-Archiv, P/1/25/38.

14 *Plutus*, 24 March 1920, 105f.

15 Feldman, *Iron and steel*, pp. 263f.

16 Siemens to Vögler, 24 March 1921 and related correspondence to Nachlass Hugo Stinnes, Bestand I 220, Nr. 253/2 in the Archiv für Christlich-Demokratische Politik der Konrad-Adenauer-Stiftung.

17 Feldman, *Iron and steel*, p. 235, and 'Kapitalistische Expropriateure', *Plutus*, 1 March 1922, 81.

18 *Plutus*, 25 October 1922, 424ff, 428, and *Frankfurter Zeitung*, No. 759, 24 October 1922, 2ff; No. 772, 28 October 1922, 1.

19 Feldman, *Iron and steel*, p. 226.

20 On these schemes, see Gerald, D. Feldman, 'The political economy of Germany's relative stabilization during the 1920/21 world depression', in Gerald D. Feldman et al., *The German inflation reconsidered. A preliminary balance* (Berlin and New York, 1982), pp. 180–206, especially pp. 196ff. See also 'Reichswirtschaftsbank', *Plutus*, 27 October 1920, 331–7.

21 Kleist, *Ausländische Kapitalbeteiligung*, p. 102.

22 An example is to be found in the files of the Handelskammer Koblenz reporting on the refusal of a passport to one Dirk Hendrick van Schuppen, who had the intention of 'buying up larger German enterprises', Rheinisch-Westfälisches Wirtschaftsarchiv zu Köln (Hereafter WWA Köln), Nr 3/5/63.

23 Enquete 1/3/1, p. 191.

24 Ernst Sontag, *Die Aktiengesellschaft im Kampf zwischen Macht und Recht* (Berlin, 1918).

25 *Plutus*, 15 January 1920, 26f.; 'Ein Appell an die deutschen Oelmühlen-Aktionäre und Oelmühlen-Besitzer', December 1919, Zentrales Staatsarchiv Potsdam, Zentralarbeitsgemeinschaft, Nr. 112, Bl. 21f.; Enquete-Ausschuss, *Die Deutsche Ölmühlenindustrie. Verhandlungen und Berichte des Unterausschusses für allgemeine Wirtschaftsstruktur (1. Unterausschuss), 5. Arbeitsgruppe (Aussenhandel), 7. Band* (Berlin, 1930), pp. 37ff.

26 Deutscher Industrie- und Handelstag an die Mitglieder, 4 December 1919, WWA Köln, 20/507/2.

27 Kleist, *Ausländische Kapitalbeteiligung,* pp. 74f.; Frank Allen Southard, *American industry in Europe,* Ph.D. Diss., University of California at Berkeley (Berkeley, 1930), p. 274. For a detailed listing of the measures taken by various leading corporations and the different mechanisms employed, see Kurz, *Überfremdungsgefahr,* pp. 63ff.

28 See *Frankfurter Zeitung,* No. 87, 2 February 1920, 2; No. 544, 26 July 1920, 2; No. 545, 26 July 1920, 2; Kurz, *Überfremdungsgefahr,* pp. 54ff. The question of legal reform of German corporation law in connection with such abuses received considerable discussion later in the decade. See Enquete 1/3/1, pp. 52ff., 179ff.

29 *Plutus,* 19 May 1920, 165f.

30 Enquete 1/3/1, p. 188.

31 'Antwort an das Reichjustizministerium, II', *Frankfurter Zeitung,* No. 678, 11 September 1929, 4.

32 See Manfred Nussbaum, *Wirtschaft und Staat in Deutschland während der Weimarer Republik* (Berlin, 1978), pp. 37ff., and Feldman, *Iron and steel,* chapter 4.

33 *Plutus,* 19 May 1920, p. 165.

34 Peter Wulf, *Hugo Stinnes. Wirtschaft und Politik 1918–1924* (Stuttgart, 1979), pp. 329ff.

35 On the problems and possibilities of Weimar in the field of foreign affairs, see the imaginative study of Peter Krüger, *Die Außenpolitik von Weimar* (Darmstadt, 1985). For an important recent investigation on the problem of the American loans, see William C. McNeil, *American money and the Weimar Republic. Economics and politics on the eve of the Great Depression* (New York, 1986). An imaginative and important analysis of the structural problems of the German economy is provided by Harold James, *The German slump. Politics and economics 1924–1936* (Oxford, 1986).

36 Georg Bernhard, 'Das Gespenst der Überfremdung', *Magazin der Wirtschaft,* 22 November 1928, 1799–1801. On the automobile industry propaganda, see Southard, *American industry,* p. 120; Werner Link, *Die amerikanische Stabilisierungspolitik in Deutschland 1921–1932* (Düsseldorf, 1970), pp. 377ff.

37 *Magazin der Wirtschaft,* 22 November 1928, p. 1800. See also McNeil, *American money,* pp. 173ff., 231ff.

38 Link, *Die amerikanische Stabilisierungspolitik,* pp. 431ff., 453ff.; Heinz Habedank, *Die Reichsbank in der Weimarer Republik. Zur Rolle der Zentralbank in der Politik des deutschen Imperialismus 1919–1933* (Berlin, 1981), pp. 165ff.

39 For the quote, see the first of the following three illuminating discussions of the problem by the *Frankfurter Zeitung,* 'Eine neue Ära des Kapitalimports', No. 450, 22 June 1929, 4; 'Überfremdung? – Ausverkauf,' No. 532, 23 July 1929, 2 and No. 544, 24 July 1929, 4.

40 *Frankfurter Zeitung,* No. 544, 24 July 1929, 4.

41 The Economic Policy Section of Siemens drew up such a list of 105 'foreignised' concerns, probably in 1930. Werner von Siemens Institut für Geschichte des Hauses Siemens, München, SAA LS/209.

42 Georg Katona, 'Die Auslandsverschuldung Deutschlands', *Der Deutsche Volkswirt,* Nr 10, 5 December 1930, pp. 309–11. In the list drawn up by Siemens (See note 41) the Linoleum-Werke AG is listed as 100 per cent 'foreignised' and the Vereinigte Glanzstoff-Fabriken is listed as over 50 per cent 'foreignised'. One wonders how such misinformation influenced Carl Friedrich von Siemens to take the negative position on foreign penetration to be discussed shortly.

43 'Statt Autotrust Überfremdung', *Magazin der Wirtschaft*, 21 March 1929, 441–4. For a sober analysis of the problems of Opel and the German automobile industry, see Fritz Blaich, 'Die "Fehlrationalisierung" in der deutschen Automobilindustrie 1924 bis 1929', *Tradition* 18 (1973), 18–33.

44 Southard, *American industry*, p. 121.

45 'Bericht der beiden Hauptdelegierten über die Pariser Sachverständigenkonferenz', 22 March 1929, Martin Vogt (ed.), *Das Kabinett Müller II. 28. Juni 1928 bis 27. März 1930. Akten der Reichskanzlei. Weimarer Republik* (Boppard-am-Rhein, 1970), p. 509. Apparently, there was a large amount of foreign capital in IG Farben, but there is no evidence that it exerted any significant influence on company policy. See Enquete 1/3/1, p. 195.

46 'Besprechung über die Reparationslage,' 1 May 1929, Vogt (ed.), *Kabinett Müller II*, p. 618.

47 See Southard's well documented criticism of the German tendency to blame on reparations what was happening everywhere, *American industry*, pp. 270ff.

48 Southard, *American industry*, p. 45 and *Der Deutsche Volkswirt*, 18 October 1929, 69.

49 *Magazin der Wirtschaft,* 26 September 1929, 1493f., 24 October 1929, 1632.

50 Southard, *American industry*, pp. 49f.

51 *Ibid.*, p. 280, and *Der Deutsche Volkswirt*, 18 October 1929, 70.

52 *Der Deutsche Volkswirt*, 18 October 1929, 70 and Georg Bernhard, 'Elektropolemik', *Magazin der Wirtschaft*, 24 October 1929, 1631–3. On the question of an IG between the two concerns, see Heidrun Homburg, 'Die Neuordnung des Marktes nach der Inflation. Probleme und Widerstände am Beispiel der Zusammenschlussprojekte von AEG und Siemens 1924–1933 oder: "wer hat den längeren Atem?"', Gerald D. Feldman and Elisabeth Müller-Luckner (eds.), *Die Nachwirkungen der Inflation auf die deutsche Geschichte 1924–1933*, Schriften des Historischen Kollegs, Bd 6 (Munich, 1985), pp. 117–56.

53 Link, *Die amerikanische Stabilisierungspolitik*, pp. 377–81.

54 *Magazin der Wirtschaft*, 24 October 1929, 1632f.

55 *Der Deutsche Volkswirt*, 18 October 1929, 70.

10 International industrial cartels, the state and politics: Great Britain between the wars

CLEMENS A. WURM

For an understanding of multinational enterprise it is necessary to include an analysis of international cartels. Between the wars they formed an important structural characteristic of the world economy. According to contemporary reckoning in the 1930s between 30% and 50% of world trade was controlled or influenced by international agreements or 'loose associations'. Up until the early years after the Second World War they held the attention of scholars, journalists and politicians in the same manner as the multinational concerns have since the 1960s. And like the latter they have been judged in highly differing, or contradictory manners.

International cartels performed a number of functions, which are fulfilled today by multinational enterprises. In individual cases an international cartel could even become a multinational concern[1]; occasionally it is described as a 'forerunner' of multinational enterprise. International cartels are generally less stable and their resources more limited than those of multinational concerns or national cartels, although they can, as Alice Teichova has pointed out, react to changes swiftly and with flexibility, and represent a more effective instrument of economic penetration than direct investment.[2] Mainly – although not always – large enterprises were the driving force in the formation of international cartels. They preferred, according to region and product, to secure the market by direct investment or an agreement with competitors.

International cartels do not abolish competition. They shift the arena and change the rules according to which it takes place. They are economic creations; in general, they owe their formation to private initiative. During the inter-war period, however, the state was also involved in their creation; the government of the day was more often the driving force than was industry. Their promotion became a 'tool of politics',[3] a means by which to strengthen the position of national groups on the world market or to suppress the activity of rivals. In a period which was characterised by extreme economic nationalism and increasing concentration of political and economic power, the massive intervention of practically all governments in

111

foreign trade and the protection of the flank by the state formed – next to classical factors like competitiveness and technical know-how – a decisive element in the negotiating strength and capacity of firms to maintain their hold on world markets.

The following sections examine the co-operation, or lack of co-operation, of British industry and government in the formation of cartels in the country's 'old' industries. They refer principally to the iron and steel industry, the cotton industry and coal mining. They proceed methodically from the premise that international cartels can only be suitably analysed if the widely diverging questions of economic and political historiography are brought closer together. In contrast, for example, to the chemical industry, which, from 1926, was dominated by a single firm, the branches considered here are composed of an abundance of firms, highly differentiated in size, structure, technology and market position. They are sectors in which national production methods were decisive. In the steel industry alone and for some of the products of its rolling mills, multinational enterprises played a big role (Stewarts & Lloyds; Dorman Long & Co.; Guest, Keen and Nettlefolds etc.). Historically determined structural conditions and the lack of modernisation made them dependent on political action to an extraordinary degree.

I

To improve our understanding it is necessary to introduce briefly the essential facts about the international cartelisation of the industries under consideration. In iron and steel, the European Steel Cartel (Internationale Rohstahlgemeinschaft (IRG)) was created in 1926 by the most important continental producer countries (Germany, France, Belgium, Luxemburg as well as the Saar). The British industry remained apart from this institution. However in 1935–6 they did join the successor organisation, the International Steel Cartel (Internationale Rohstahlexportgemeinschaft (IREG)) and its marketing association, which were formed in 1933. There was a whole series of cartels for special products like rails, pipes and tinplate, in which British industry was involved to a large extent. In coal mining, the Anglo-Polish Agreement, signed in December 1934, limited Polish seaborne coal exports to 21% of the British. In 1937, after the creation of several smaller cartels between national groups from Germany, Britain, the Netherlands, Belgium and Poland, a comprehensive agreement was signed to cover the price, market share and sales conditions for coke. The coal agreement signed in January 1939 between the Mining Asociation of Great Britain and the Rheinisch-Westfaelisches Kohlensyndikat, according to which Britain got 46.27% and Germany 32.08% of total European exports, did not come into effect before the outbreak of the war. The British attempt, in 1933–4, to divide up the world cotton textile market with the Japanese failed because of Japanese resistance.

II

Even before the First World War British industry had made various international agreements. According to the estimates of P. T. Fischer and H. Wagenfuehr, in 1929 it was involved in 'at least 40 international cartels'.[4] Examples are the chemical, artificial silk and copper production industries, as well as aluminium and linoleum manufacturing. However the degree of participation in the 1920s should not be over-estimated. In important branches like steel, the British stayed out of agreements (although admittedly British companies did play an important role in the refounding of the rail cartel). In coal mining, their disapproving attitude was viewed – whether rightly or wrongly – as the main obstacle to the international cartelisation of a complete industrial branch. 'England', judged G. von Haberler at the beginning of the 1930s, 'is not a member of most international cartels.'[5]

The reasons for the British restraint are very complex. Contemporary observers have, by way of explanation, referred to the peculiarities of English law, the individualism of the entrepreneurs and the continued effect of 'Manchester-liberal' opinions. Research has shown the decisive reason to be organisational deficiencies and a lack of inner unity amongst British industry. Also the government, the Civil Service, influential bankers like R. McKenna (Midland Bank) or R. H. Brand (Baring Bros), representatives of leading concerns in the 'new' branches like Sir Alfred Mond (ICI) or Sir Hugo Hirst (General Electric Co.) and important press organs like *The Times* or *The Economist*, all viewed collaboration in national associations as an indispensable precondition for successful international negotiation and co-operation: only united national industries were able to hold their own with highly-organised foreign concerns. As Sir Hugo Hirst told steel industrialists in 1925, 'You cannot make international agreements unless you are united at home.'[6]

Without doubt fragmentation and the low degree of concentration were a serious handicap to successful cartel formation. However it remains to be seen whether other factors were not more important in individual cases. The continued faith of the government in free trade – not organisational deficits – was the decisive reason that the British steel industry remained apart from the European Steel Cartel (Rohstahlgemeinschaft) in the 1920s.[7] For a long time the British pit owners rejected the majority of international agreements absolutely. They wanted to reconstruct the competitiveness of their industry with wage cuts and win back lost market shares *before* any negotiations, in order to be better armed for the battle over quotas. Only from about

1928 – and then only gradually – was a stronger degree of support given to the view, 'that, in the future, international arrangements would be necessary'.[8]

Very little is known of the position of the cotton industrialists during the 1920s. It appears that in this period, international cartel agreements did not play a big role in their deliberations. An attempt at the end of 1929 by the Lancashire Cotton Corporation, made with the consent of the Governor of the Bank of England, to open talks with Japanese industry, met with little accommodation amongst manufacturers of the Far Eastern Empire and came to nothing.

The world economic crisis formed an important date in the inter-war cartel movement. The changes which it brought about in the politics, economy and society of Britain, created new conditions for British cartel policy. With the protective tariff, industry found the instrument that made it possible to speak as equals to foreign competitors. The devaluation of the Pound Sterling improved its competitiveness; in individual cartels this led quickly to higher quotas for British companies. Traditional obstacles to international cartels, such as the fear of exploiting the consumer or the gradual erosion of liberal economic principles, which still played a role in the 1920s, no longer determined the limits to action. Changes of view on economic policy and the widely held opinion that unregulated competition had worsened the depression by causing price falls allowed an economic order to develop, which, compared with the prewar years, was new and whose features were fixed prices, production and competition control, and a tendency to suspend the market as a regulative force.

In the strategy of individual branches or large concerns, international cartels took up a more important place than before. Market arrangements supplemented or took the place of direct investment. A study carried out for the British government during the Second World War on British participation in private international industrial agreements showed what a high proportion of the country's exports and total manufacturing at the end of the 1930s had been gained by internationally cartelised products. The study came to the conclusion that for 1938, the proportion of the export trade directly affected by international arrangements of various sorts can be put roughly at three-tenths of the total value of the exports of goods wholly or mainly manufactured. For the total gross output [in value] of the United Kingdom factory trades in 1935, the figure was around 16%. An estimate based on employment shares came to the same result.[9]

There is much to be said for the view of Geoffrey Jones, that the reduction in direct British investment abroad in the 1930s, in comparison with the 1920s has a lot to do with the fact that firms attempted to defend or win markets through agreement. 'The mirror image of the decline of multinational activity was the increased participation by British companies in international cartels.'[10] International cartels were also of importance for the geographical direction of British exports: the increased movement of British goods to the Commonwealth is, besides the Ottawa Agreements and the advantages of the Sterling Area, attributable to the preference of many – although not all – international cartels to allocate Empire markets to British firms. Finally, in many cases the existence or lack of cartel agreements was a decisive factor for company profits in individual markets. 'British companies prospered where market sharing or other arrangements were in existence and experienced difficulties where they were not.'[11]

If in the 1920s the government limited its activity in connection with international cartels to classical state functions, then in the 1930s it encouraged the participation of industry in international agreements through direct measures. Not the least of its objectives in fostering the internal cartelisation of individual branches such as coal and steel was to make possible its successful collaboration in agreements. The Import Duties Advisory Committee (IDAC), which was created in 1932 – convinced 'that the regulation of trade by international agreements is of advantage to industry in this country'[12] – recommended several times the raising of tariffs, in order to improve the negotiating position of the British group, and to secure the continued existence or make possible the re-establishment of an agreement. The best-known example is the iron and steel industry and its 'General Agreement' with the International Steel Cartel (Internationale Rohstahlexportgemeinschaft (IREG)) in 1935: the raising of the tariff to the prohibitive level of 50% forced continental firms which were dependent on the British market (according to a Treasury official) to capitulate and secured for British industry a long-term agreement to their conditions. In the case of the coal industry, the British government used its strong position in trade negotiations with Poland – which needed the British market for its agricultural produce – in order to bring about an agreement between the Mining Association of Great Britain and the Polish industry in December 1934. This established not only prices, but a fixed relationship between the total quantity of British coal exports, and Polish sea-borne exports and local border deliveries to Germany. The Scandinavian market especially was relieved of Polish price pressure through this agreement.[13] Finally, in the case of the cotton industry, the Board of Trade took the initiative, without either the knowledge or prior agreement of most of the industry, in the unsuccessful talks which the English manufacturers had with Japanese textile magnates over division of the world market. 'Lancashire', according to the deputy chairman of the LCC, John Grey, 'had been pushed into the Japanese conversations.'[14]

During the international negotiations, Whitehall and the representatives of industry kept in close contact with each other. The widespread notion that

British industrialists, in contrast to French or German, carried out their negotiations autonomously or independent from the government, is – at least in so far as it concerns the branches dealt with here – a myth. The steel industry and the IDAC were in regular contact during the talks with continental firms. The Board of Trade was informed promptly – occasionally by telephone – by British industry, over the course of important meetings with continental groups. The import quota, which the British Iron and Steel Federation (BISF) offered the international steel cartel for the provisional agreement, corresponded to the ideas of the IDAC, not the BISF. The trade conference between delegates from Lancashire and Japan from 14 February 1934 to 14 March 1934, in which the English delegation sought to win from the Japanese cotton industry a strict limitation and regulation of their exports (against the prospect of higher prices), took place in the rooms of the Board of Trade. The British manufacturers wanted this on 'psychological grounds', but it appeared that, in view of the superior competitiveness of their rivals, the power of the state was the only instrument capable of making the Japanese give way. Although the British side, in contrast to the Japanese, did not send an official observer to the talks, Sir Horace Wilson, the government's chief industrial adviser, was kept constantly informed of their progress. In the last phase of the discussion the course of proceedings was worked out in close consultation between the Board of Trade and the Lancashire delegates.

Whitehall exercised influence not only in the run-up to new agreements on quotas and in negotiations, but in individual cases Ministries pressed for higher shares in existing agreements or the reservation of particular markets for British companies. For example, officials of the Department of Overseas Trade (DOT) and the Foreign Office pointed out to the Secretary of the British group at the International Railmakers Association (IRMA), R. Lyttleton of GKN, that Britain claimed a 'considerably higher share' of the total quota (the share amounted to 23.8%), because devaluation, protective duties and bilateral trade negotiations had strengthened her position in the meantime. The exercise of direct political influence on international cartels, often complained of by contemporaries, was therefore by no means, as generally assumed, restricted to the dictators of National Socialist Germany, although the influence exercised there was more direct, more comprehensive and more decisive.

III

The motives of the government for its active role varied from case to case and do not permit generalisations. Considerations of an economic and general political nature stand in the foreground, such as the need to improve the country's balance-of-payments through the encouragement of exports (hence the pressure for higher export quotas) and to reduce unemployment, or generally the desire to stabilise market and sales conditions, and increase returns to the companies. The agreement of the BISF with the IREG, for example, formed an important element, in the view of the government, of the IDAC-determined policy which it had been following since 1932, the object of which was to revitalise the iron and steel industry.

The goals of government and industry were by no means always identical. W. Runciman of the Board of Trade wanted to raise exports by joining the International Steel Cartel; it sought the highest possible British export share against concessions on imports. In contrast, the primary matter of concern to the manufacturers was 'to put their own house in order' and that of the world steel market, as well as to achieve better prices. They gave precedence to the security of the domestic market. For them the agreement with the IREG represented the keystone in a building which effectively – indeed more effectively than customs duties – safeguarded the monopoly position of manufacturers in the domestic market. The government satisfied itself with the pricing policy undertakings of the BISF, which was not even responsible for pricing policy according to the association statutes, but represented instead a moral self-restraint on the part of the companies, which could not have stopped the later, much-criticised price rises (above all, the increase of May 1937).

Various estimates and priorities existed, especially where the government exercised pressure on industry to join an international agreement (for example, mining) or where it seized the initiative itself in the negotiations. The British government, in contrast to the pit owners, was convinced that an agreement was more necessary for them than for the Polish competitors, who since the middle of the 1920s had increasingly pushed British coal out of its markets with low prices, particularly in northern Europe. At the same time it was convinced that British mining, because of structural deficiencies (for example, lack of control of the export trade) was not in a position to realise an effective international cartelisation and – more important – was not even ready to take a serious initiative in that direction, since a portion of the coal owners had not given up the hope of beating the competition out of its own resources, because Poland, according to their estimates, was 'financially near breaking point' and Polish industry could not withstand the price war much longer. Also some pit owners believed they detected some easing of German competition. 'It must be anticipated therefore', Whitehall felt, 'that no serious move will be made by the British coal owners towards an international agreement with the other producing countries unless very strong pressure is exerted upon them by the government.'[15] By pushing towards market agreements, the government believed it knew the 'real' interests of the coal mining industry better than the industrialists themselves.

The example of the cotton industry shows that it was by no means just economic considerations that played a role with the political leadership. Lancashire called loudly for drastic state intervention to stop the progress of Japanese competition on the world market: 'whatever the trade might do internally, it would be absolutely impossible to bridge the gap between the English and the Japanese prices'.[16] However, in a situation of political crisis (the conflict in Manchuria), the government did not want to worsen further its relations with the Far Eastern country through action on trade, but on the contrary wanted to signal accommodation to the offer of talks. The cartel venture of the government was launched not the least out of foreign policy considerations. This example illustrates also that it would be false to deduce too quickly from the government's cartel initiatives a high degree of readiness to state intervention. Often the opposite was the case: direct negotiations between the parties concerned relieved the government of the necessity to be active itself on behalf of industry.

IV

The Coal Agreement between the Polish and British pit owners reduced competition in northern Europe and led to higher prices in a series of markets. However altogether it was an agreement of limited range. The hopes, harboured on both sides, that the agreement would lead the way to a comprehensive international cartel with the participation of all exporting nations, did not fulfill themselves.[17] Whether the agreement with Polish industry had helped British coal exports or merely caused a diversion in trade direction – the coal forced out of the Baltic and Scandinavian markets now made more competition for British goods in West Europe and the Mediterranean – is hard to judge and disputed in historiography.[18] On the other hand, it is certain that the agreement created an advantage for the English pit owners of the North Sea coast at the cost of those in South Wales. It is possible that the most significant result of the agreement was in its inter-regional consequences.

The treaty of the BISF with the IREG produced fixed export shares for the British steel industry and prevented loss-making competition. By raising export prices – a declared objective of the IREG – the steel cartel contributed to the improvement of export proceeds and the sales position of the companies. Export figures at the end of 1936 represented a doubling of the low point reached in 1932, while lying admittedly considerably under the level of 1929. From around December 1936 prices rose steeply and for a short time in 1937 exceeded the domestic prices of the steel exporting countries. Certainly in the literature the improvement in export figures is attributed less to market-regulating measures of the international selling associations than to world iron sales and other factors, chiefly of a political nature. However, without doubt, the International Steel Cartel contributed to the raising of export prices and the stabilisation of export profits, above all in the crisis of 1938.

The agreement ensured greater freedom of movement in price fixing in the domestic market for British industry through the regulation and control of imports from the Continent – they were distributed to consumers under the direction of the BISF. Whether and to what extent the agreement was responsible for the later increase in British steel prices cannot be determined with certainty. Clearly the agreement and involvement in the cartel made the price rises considerably easier. Through the connection of Continental steel sales in the British market to British domestic prices and on the basis of the importance of British quotations for the price structure in Empire markets, the cartel exercised pressure on the prices for steel products in the British domestic market.[19] On the other hand, one would have difficulty arguing that British iron and steel products would have done better on the eve of the Second World War if the industry had not been a member of an international steel cartel. The cartel of the 1930s was different from its predecessors in so far as it did not consider the domestic markets of the participants when fixing quotas and left their regulation up to the parties involved. Older existing associations for individual steel products such as the International Wire Rod Association, in which the domestic sales were taken into consideration in fixing quotas, were converted to pure export cartels in the course of the 1930s, according to the pattern of the other associations. The boom in British iron production and not the operation of the International Steel Cartel was responsible for the output level.

The BISF has been accused of directing its main attention during negotiations with the Continental groups to the security and control of the home market and neglecting exports. Without doubt, that accurately describes the priorities of the British negotiators: the main interest was command of the domestic market, and certainly a different relationship of import and export shares would have been more favourable. Soon after the signing of the treaty, supply bottle-necks appeared in the British market and showed that imports, especially of semi-finished products, had been reduced all too drastically. Whether the British steel exports would have been higher with better quotas is uncertain and would have to be investigated from case to case. The 'apathy' that the government repeatedly complained of in the export industries was particularly marked in iron and steel. Indeed, it was emphasised by industrialists that higher exports were worthwhile; they responded to the exhortations of government representatives not to neglect export connections as an insurance against the future, despite strong internal demand and the rearmament programme that was viewed by them as a temporary phenomenon. In view of the turbulent domestic demand for steel, however, there remained temporarily little surplus for export. In the financial year 1936–7 British industry was not in a position to use its quota fully in the marketing associations of the International Steel Cartel. During the period from July 1937 to 30 June 1938, however, it exceeded its quota. The International Tinplate Cartel (in which the British possessed by far the highest quota) directly limited British exports in 1935-6.

The agreement with the IREG shifted power within the industry to the steelmaking branch, at the cost of the consumer. It was an expression of the strong position possessed by the steel industry in the country's political-industrial system since the foreign trade upheavals of 1931-2, built up further in the succeeding period and internationally safeguarded by entry into the steel cartel. The steel industry's 'reverse of fortune' in comparison with the 1920s, already observed by contemporaries, occurred thanks to the state – not, or only to a small degree, to entrepreneurial initiative.

The example of the cotton industry and the unsuccessful British–Japanese textile conference makes it clear that negotiations over markets and prices had to march in step with the economic conditions of the moment and the interests of all involved (Lancashire's proposals were unrealistic; Japanese industrialists did not want to bind themselves). Political deals can only work under certain circumstances (as they did especially in the steel industry) and only within the limits of conditions for successful private economic negotiations and agreements.

Nevertheless, this case shows that it was inadmissable to leave the state – even the British – out of the analysis of international cartels. Its functions may have varied from branch to branch and its intervention may have been less noticeable with the 'new' industries, where it was less necessary since conditions were different. Still, even Sir Alfred Mond of ICI got backing from his country's political leadership for his position in the negotiations with IG Farbenindustrie AG. And also in the chemical industry the international cartel structure of the 1920s stood in close connection with the political constellation and power structures, as they arose out of the consequences of the First World War.[20]

NOTES

This article was translated from the German by Peter J. Lyth.

1 H. Nussbaum, 'International cartels and multinational enterprises', in A. Teichova, M. Lévy-Leboyer, and H. Nussbaum (eds.) *Multinational enterprise in historical perspective* (Cambridge, 1986), p. 131–44.

2 Alice Teichova, *An economic background to Munich. International business and Czechoslovakia 1918–1938* (Cambridge, 1974).

3 R. Liefmann, *Kartelle, Konzerne und Trusts*, 8th, extended edition, (Stuttgart, 1930), p. 187.

4 P. T. Fischer and H. Wagenfuehr, *Kartelle in Europa (ohne Deutschland)* (Nürnberg, 1929), p. 152.

5 G. von Haberler, *The theory of international trade, with its applications to commercial policy* (London, 1936), p. 329 (German edition, 1933).
6 Committee of Civil Research, Meeting of 17.7.1925; CAB 58/1.
7 C. A. Wurm, *Industrielle Interessenpolitik und Staat. Internationale Kartelle in der britischen Aussen- und Wirtschaftspolitik während der Zwischenkriegszeit* (Berlin and New York, 1987) (Evidence for the following is found here, where not otherwise stated). An English version is in preparation for publication by Cambridge University Press.
8 J. Craig to Lord Kylsant, 27 July 1928; British Steel Corporation Glasgow, File: 'Lord Kylsant 1928–1929' (David Colville & Sons Papers).
9 Board of Trade (eds.), *Survey of international and internal cartels*, vol. 2, (London 1944, 1946), p. 23 (author, J. D. Gribbin).
10 G. Jones, 'The expansion of British multinational manufacturing 1890–1939, in A. Okochi and T. Inoue [eds.], *Overseas business activities. Proceedings of the Fuji Conference* (Tokyo, 1984), p. 148.
11 *Ibid.*, pp. 146f.
12 Cmd 5436; cited in H. Hutchinson, *Tariff making and industrial reconstruction. An account of the work of the Import Duties Advisory Committee 1932–1939* (London, 1965), p. 69.
13 P. Salmon, 'Polish-British competition in the coal markets of Northern Europe 1927–1934,' in *Studia Historiae Oeconomicae*, 16 (1981), pp. 217–43; H. G. Schroeter, *Aussenpolitik und Wirtschaftsinteresse. Skandinavien im aussenwirtschaftlichen Kalkül Deutschlands und Grossbritanniens 1918–1939* (Frankfurt-am–Main 1983), p. 239.
14 Special Committee on Japanese Competition [Manchester Chamber of Commerce], meeting of 3.8.1933; M8/5/18.
15 Memorandum of the Mines Department of the Board of Trade 12 December 1932: 'The movement towards international agreement in the coal industry'; FO 371/16422 – W 11623/9819/50.
16 Special Committee on Japanese Competition (Manchester Chamber of Commerce), meeting of 25 january 1933; M8/5/18.
17 For the efforts towards international agreement in the coal industry, see J. R. Gillingham, *Industry and politics in the Third Reich, Ruhr coal, Hitler and Europe* (Stuttgart, 1985) pp. 95 ff. At the time of the negotiations of the British steel industry with the IREG (Spring, 1935), Sir F. Leith-Ross pressed for the conclusion of a 'coal convention between Germany and Britain for the whole world'; Record of A. Dufour-Feronce of his discussion with Leith-Ross, 11 March 1935; PA AA, Special Department 'W', Raw Materials and Goods, Coal, vol. 10; on the question of Leith-Ross's role, see also his letter to E. Poensgen 3 November 1936; HA/GHH 400101320/88. Also the Governor of the Bank of England, M. Norman, was active as a mediator between German and British pit owners. In the case of the steel industry he pressed the BISF to conclude an agreement with the IREG.
18 Compare the different estimates of Salmon, *Competition*; W. R. Garside, 'The north-eastern coalfield and the export trade 1919–1939' in *Durham University Journal*, 62 (1969), 9; T. J. T. Rooth, 'Limits of leverage: the Anglo-Danish trade agreement of 1933', in *Economic History Review*, 37 (1984) 225f. The literature concerns itself mainly with the general British trade policy on northern Europe and Poland, not especially with the coal treaty of the pit owners. Coal is thereby used as an example for the positive, negative or insignificant effects of British trade policy in general.

19 See Wurm, *Industrielle Interessenpolitik* (note 7).

20 A. Teichova, 'Changing political constellations and the Anglo-American-German cartel relations in the chemical industry in the first decade of the inter-war period', in G. Schmidt (ed.), *Konstellationen internationaler Politik 1924–1932. Politische und wirtschaftliche Faktoren in den Beziehungen zwischen Westeuropa und den Vereinigten Staaten* (Bochum, 1983), pp. 221–36.

11 Vickers and Schneider: a comparison of new British and French multinational strategies 1916–26

R. P. T. DAVENPORT-HINES

In a recent study Claud Beaud has shown how the French armaments company, Schneider, acting with the Banque de l'Union Parisienne in the Union Européenne Industrielle et Financière (UEIF) which they formed jointly in 1920, made large industrial investments in the ruins of the Habsburg empire, their acquisitions including the Škoda Works and Berg- und Hütten werksgesellschaft in Czechoslovakia, Veitscher Magnesit Werke of Austria, the Huta Bankowa group in Poland, and the Hungarian General Credit Bank. Beaud characterised Eugene Schneider's new strategy in Central Europe as an extension of his previous Russian initiatives, rather than as comparable to his other major multinational enterprises after 1898 in Switzerland, Italy, Spain, Morocco and South America. As Schneider 'had staked technology rather than capital' in the Putilov arsenal project before 1914, he was not chastened by its failure, and believing 'the Bolshevik régime to be on the verge of collapse', envisaged Škoda as 'the arsenal of the Little Entente, replacing or even complementing Putilov'. Beaud suggests that development of his company's East European markets was a 'secondary' strategic motive for Eugene Schneider (1868–1942), who 'desired to play a part, in some way, in increasing France's greatness ... [during] the time of the "Bloc national" when the superior interests of the nation overrode the short term economic goals of a firm'.[1] Schneider himself declared, while leading a French business delegation to the USA in the early 1920s, 'The war did not end with the treaty of peace'; his 'main ambition' after the Armistice was 'the great task of building up French power and influence in Central Europe, even to the detriment of his own firm's short-term financial interests'.[2] The purpose of this chapter is to show that Schneider's great English armaments rival, Vickers, pursued an equivalent policy at the same period, with less success.

Vickers' multinational expansion before 1914 was aggressive, ambitious but intuitive: the company responded quickly and decisively to specific market opportunities, in an 'optimistic, daring and speculative' spirit which permitted little strategic introspection.[3] Indeed, the diplomatic and techno-

123

logical context of their business could alter so rapidly that several contracts whereby Vickers participated in overseas arsenals had only ten years' duration. Although Vickers' decisions to make direct foreign investments after 1905 in Italy, Japan or elsewhere were taken in the light of the company's political analysis, the British Foreign Office was scarcely consulted, and the directors often preferred to regard their commerical or multinational strategy as independent of considerations of international *haute politique*. Few of these multinational factories were fully operative in 1914, and their orderly development was entirely disrupted by the outbreak of world war.

Vickers' leading directors were men of strong political convictions. Albert Vickers, chairman from 1909 to 1919, endorsed Joseph Chamberlain's brand of imperialism and tariff protection.[4] His nephew and successor as chairman, Douglas Vickers, twice contested a Sheffield parliamentary constituency as a Conservative before sitting in Parliament during 1918–22. As president of the nationalistic British Engineers Association he worked for British hegemony in overseas engineering markets,[5] and in politics he was an imperial protectionist.[6] Of the other powerful Vickers directors, Sir Trevor Dawson and Sir Francis Barker in 1916 founded a pressure group called the London Imperialists intended to secure the election of protectionist members of parliament[7], while Sir Vincent Caillard epitomised business imperialism with his passionate belief in tariff reform, British racial superiority and the civilising mission of empire.[8] After 1915 all of these men fell under the influence of an industrial financier, Dudley Docker, 'a very wide minded man',[9] who held even fiercer political beliefs which embraced tariff reform, 'social imperialism', Germanophobia and the need for corporatist revolution in the British parliamentary system.

In 1916 Docker founded the Federation of British Industries (FBI), which in its early phase was strongly identified with Vickers. The FBI founders, like other businessmen and officials, anticipated that 'at war's end Germany would be strong enough economically to undertake a major export push to recover its markets lost during the war...and...that the Germans would be able to undermine the recovery efforts of Entente producers by underselling them'.[10] They were particularly aware of the threat posed by the intimate collaboration which they attributed to the German government, the German great banks and electrical manufacturers like Allgemeine Elektrizitätsgesellschaft (AEG) and Siemens. For these reasons Vickers' directors substituted for their traditional *ad hoc* multinational expansion a new policy designed to meet what they considered as a crisis in national industrial and imperial strategy.[11] Economic considerations, and traditional business criteria, were not excluded from this policy, but they were approached with an attitude which was fundamentally political. Vickers did not court losses, or abandon rational analysis of profit potential in its new enterprises; but its assessment of strategic propositions became even more coloured by directors' political views than before 1914. They claimed to be acting in the national interest because they thought it would help their dealings with shareholders and government; but at a deeper, more complex level, they believed their own claim. Vickers had after all just played a central part in the wartime munitions effort: the prosperity of private arms manufacturers was essential to doctrines of industrial preparedness to maintain national security. For Vickers' directors, the principle that what was good for the company was good for the country did not seem crude.[12]

In association with Docker (who joined their board), Vickers bought for £1.2 million the British Westinghouse Electrical Company, which was renamed Metropolitan-Vickers (Metrovic). As Docker declared in 1918, electrical engineering was 'a key industry' which previously had 'been almost entirely controlled by other nations...because there were too many competing interests' in Britain, 'each suffering from insufficient equipment'. Vickers' diversification into electrical products would, so Docker told investors, 'not only be to the ultimate good of the shareholders but a matter of considerable importance to the country itself. In pursuing this enter- prise...we are helping the whole of our national commerce, and...[are] asking you to be generous in your support, to take the broad view, and to study the national as well as your individual interest...upon electrical enterprise rests the fate of nearly every industry in the country.'[13] This public declaration of motives was not cant, but is reflected in the Vickers directors' private correspondence.[14]

In 1918 Vickers supplanted Siemens from a Sardinian hydro-electric contract, prompting Caillard to tell the Foreign Office, 'Hitherto the Electrical Industry in Italy has been almost entirely in the hands of the Germans, and this is the first order for large Electric Generating Plant that has ever been placed by the Italians with a British firm.' Vickers, so Caillard avowed, 'are making strenuous efforts to promote British Engineering interests in Italy'.[15] As part of this attempt to oust the Germans from the Italian market Vickers also took (during and after 1917) minority share participations in various Italian companies (see table 11.1). Later in 1918 Docker tried to persuade the Foreign Office to ensure that the Armistice terms withheld copper supplies from AEG so as to paralyse their production and give Metrovic a market advantage.[16]

At the same time Vickers turned to the Swiss electrical industry, as the only one on the European mainland which had evaded German dominance. In July 1919 they took a holding worth about £380,000 in the Baden company, Brown Boveri. A financial and technical agreement was signed[17], and two Englishmen joined the Swiss board of directors: Barker, representing Vickers' old guard, and Sir Ernest Hiley, on behalf of the new Docker interests.[18] But the Swiss electrical venture failed, chiefly because in 1919

Table 11.1. *Depreciation in value of Vickers' Continental electrical investments, 1917–39*

Company	Date of investment	Cost or value of investment[1]	Percentage of shareholding	Date of sale of investment	Sale price of investment
Società per le Imprese Idrauliche ed Elettriche del Tirso	1917	1,666,500 lire (£45,040)	20.83%		Sold to Società Elettrica Sarda in exchange for Sarda shares
	1925	2,000,000 lire (£19,048)	25%	1925	
Società per la Forze Idrauliche della Sila	1917	1,100,000 lire (£29,730)	11.53%		Sold to Società Elettrica Meridionale in exchange for shares and cash
	1925	1,500,000 lire (£14,286)	6%	1925	
Società Elettrica Sarda	1918	1,666,000 lire (£45,027)	16.6%	1926–9	£58,222
	1923	4,249,000 lire (£42,919)	16.6%		
	1929	4,136,000 lire (£45,955)	4.3%		
Società Meridionale di Electricita	1925	£28,695		1934	£23,733
Sécheron of Geneva	1919	1.5m francs	15%	1923	Written down to nil
Picard– Pictet, Geneva	1919			1923–5?	
Brown Boveri, Baden	1919	7m Swiss francs (£380,000)		1925–7	
Tecnomasio Italiano	1919	£108,525		1937–9	Sold at nominal value of approximately £1 per share
Brown Boveri	1922	10,000 lire (£109)	33.3%		
	1930	9,240 lire (£103)	15.3%		
Cie Lorraine pour l'Eclairage Automatique	?	£29,445		1928	£4,000

Notes: (1) Because of fragmentary evidence and fluctuating foreign exchange rates, some values (especially sterling equivalents) in this column are approximate.
Source: Luciano Segreto, 'More Trouble than Profit: Vickers' Investments in Italy 1905–39', *Business History*, 27 (1985), 316–37.

Vickers bought the largest British rolling-stock company in a highly over-capitalised deal which in effect cost almost £14 million. To pay for the deal, Vickers issued share capital was increased by almost £2 million ordinary shares, £1.5 million 7% seven year notes and over £6.75 million 6% cumulative preference shares. Interest payable on the latter was a burden which, coupled with the collapse of industrial orders after 1920, the effect of the Ruhr occupation on raw material prices, and the need for further investment to sustain Vickers' peacetime diversification programme, precipitated a liquidity crisis which raged until 1926. In 1920 alone the cost of paying debenture interest, preference dividends and Corporation Tax (without the 7% notes) exceeded £2.5 million, when profit after tax was only £541,260. Ordinary dividends were unpaid in 1920 and 1923–6, and the group became steadily more uncompetitive as lack of investment led to higher manufacturing costs.[19] Investment for development was impossible. The mesalliance with Docker's Metropolitan Carriage Wagon and Finance Company (MCWF) deprived Vickers of the financial means to support Brown Boveri; but additionally its directors and managers were soon so distracted with improvising responses to the immediate cash crisis and industrial recession in Britain, that they had no time to pursue their continental electrical strategy. Brown Boveri itself was the victim of a liquidity crisis aggravated by the high interest rates and accelerating production costs which marred the Swiss economy between 1919 and 1923, and had responded to Vickers' overtures precisely because they wanted to be rescued by foreign capital investment. In the event, with their high costs, Brown Boveri could only secure foreign orders by taking contracts at losses. Worse still, the technical agreement between Vickers and Brown Boveri negotiated by Barker had several questionable features for the British company, notably clauses which excluded them from direct Italian electrical business, where they had hitherto concentrated their continental electrical efforts. By December 1925 many of the financial ties and technical obligations between Vickers and Brown Boveri were reduced or eliminated by mutual agreement.

As the failure of their larger electro-engineering strategy became clear during the 1920s Vickers sold their continental electrical holdings, frequently at depreciated values, as shown in Table 11.1. Their only investment which substantially appreciated was in the Brussels-based Société Financière de Transport et d'Entreprises Industrielles (Sofina), which had been German-controlled until after the First World War. Nine thousand, three hundred and seventy-eight shares (acquired through Docker and MCWF) valued in 1928 at £429,395 were sold in 1936–7 for £868,671.[20]

Docker helped to form the British Trade Corporation (BTC), which received a Royal Charter in 1917 to serve as an 'Imperial Bank of Industry' to imitate and supplant the great German banks' international role. Caillard testified to the government committee which recommended BTC's formation, and he, together with the Vickers company and four of its directors, Barker, Dawson, Docker and Vincent Vickers, were among the earliest subscribers to its capital.[21] BTC's strategy to attack German trade and finance, and to support White Russians against the Bolsheviks, proved a complete failure by 1923 both because it was based on non-commercial considerations and because the British government did not provide the diplomatic support which was implicit in granting BTC's Royal Charter.[22]

Vickers, using similar (and sometimes identical) information, analysis and personnel, pursued a related policy, sending its more intrepid young men into the Soviet interior and investing in arsenal projects in Poland (1920), Estonia and Romania (1921), and Yugoslavia (1922). These states all in varying degrees felt menaced by Soviet Russia, and wished to amass their own armaments manufacturing capacity. They were, however, poorer clients, representing a smaller potential market, than the powers with whom Vickers had done their greatest business before 1914. Financial packaging, rather than technological quality, was the criticial factor in the inter-war arms business. Whereas Schneider's formal co-operation with the Banque de l'Union Parisienne in UEIF strengthened their East European strategy, the looser links between Vickers and BTC were of less benefit to the British armaments company, primarily because both parties were in severe straits for cash. The lament of Douglas Vickers, that 'when political considerations are involved in any degree, the French always seem ready to find money at a price', is the key to much of the divergence between Vickers and Schneider in the inter-war period, as officials recognised as well as armourers.[23] When UEIF became 'endangered by the liquidity and debt problems of its subsidiaries' after 1921, it turned for rescue to the London capital market, where Škoda's British & Allied Investment Corporation raised loans in 1923–30 totalling £5 million. It would have been unthinkable, however, for the Paris market to have provided funds to rescue a comparable British strategic industry, especially given the closer control exercised by the French government over foreign lending.[24] Fuller details of the ventures in Poland, Estonia, Romania and Yugoslavia are given elsewhere[25], and here only a summary is given of the salient features.

None of these new arsenal projects was a success for Vickers. After the collapse of ambitious hopes of Anglo-Polish industrial development, comparable to the great schemes of Vickers and Lord Cowdray's Pearson group for Russia's Sakhalin oilfields in 1914–16[26], Vickers were forced to reach terms with Schneider; together they agreed with the Poles in 1920 jointly to develop the Starachowice Mining and Metallurgy Company as a national arsenal, in return for a government guarantee of ten years to place all arms orders with Starachowice. Neither foreign company invested cash in

Starachowice, which was probably a device for them to utilise their excess munitions capacity in England and France by exporting surplus machinery for installation in the Polish factory. This was certainly among the main motives for Vickers' decision of 1924–5 to participate, together with its Romanian ally Uzinele de Fier şi Domeniile din Reşiţa S.A., in the ill-starred national arsenal Uzinele Metalurgice din Copşa-Mica şi Cugir S.A. In Poland, at least, despite the influence and enthusiasm of their Polish-born legal director, Count Leon Ostrorog, they had no impact comparable with Schneider, who bought out most of their interest in Starachowice in 1926, at the time when the English company was reorganised with its capital reduced by over £8.2 million (largely to remedy the results of the rolling-stock merger of 1919).

In Estonia Vickers in 1921 signed a ten-year technical agreement with the Anglo-Baltic Shipbuilding Co. concerning the naval works and yards at Reval. Anglo-Baltic was an English limited liability company serving as a front for the Russian speculator who had jockeyed control of the yards in the confusion after the 1917 Revolution. Although he had a good legal title to the property, it was ingeniously contested by Schneider, whose associates had financed much of its pre-war development. The French, 'under the cloak of a pre-war debt', mounted 'most strenuous opposition' to Vickers' work and reconstruction programme at Reval, prompting a British claim 'that Schneider is waging a world-wide contest with Vickers over the armament question'.[27] In addition to pressure mounted by Schneider and the Quai d'Orsay, Vickers were woven into a skein of financial and political perplexities by some of their Estonian associates, and, as elsewhere, lacked the financial power to make a success of Reval. Thus Vickers pared a recommendation of 1922 to support Reval with £250,000 over five years down to £50,000, although the Estonians found other means to extract cash advances. In 1923–4 Vickers extricated themselves from an active role at Reval, although the legal tangle persisted for some years.

As to Société Serbe Minière et Industrielle (Sartid), the Yugoslav subsidiary, in which Vickers held 10,900 shares costing £31,164 by 1923, it secured no government orders during Vickers' direct association with it (1923–34) and was sustained by modest civilian work. Vickers' ways in inter-war Romania with the Reşiţa and Copşa-Mica şi Cugir companies were labyrinthine, with greater influence on the London company's policies than the sums and market might suggest. (Vickers held 30% of Reşiţa's shares, worth £94,941 by 1922, but instead of a direct cash investment in Copşa-Mica şi Cugir, supplied it with machinery worth £263,000 in 1925–9; Romanian arms orders placed with Vickers in 1925–34 were worth £424,863). Vickers were again thwarted by Schneider, mainly through their Czech subsidiary, Škoda: the Franco-Czech combination was more adept both in handling Bucarest's ruling camarilla and as financiers, although even they had difficulty in obtaining payment from the Romanians.[28] The English company liquidated its Romanian holdings in 1934–9.

The story of these Vickers investments stands in sharp contrast to Schneider's experience with Škoda. As the main national arsenal of the Habsburg empire, the Pilsen works had a much higher technological ability than Vickers' counterpart factories in Eastern Europe. Baron Karl Škoda (1877–1929), the dissolute owner of the factory, frightened by workers' demands for a forced sale of one third of the company's shares with a guaranteed dividend of 9%, sold his holding to Schneider for 7 million francs[29], and by September 1919 the French company held 325,000 out of 450,000 shares. 'The incorporation of the largest armaments works in Central Europe with the Schneider combine corresponded with the intention of French power politics and...constituted a decisive step towards...a foothold in Central Europe for further expansion into Eastern and South-Eastern Europe', according to Teichova: it marked 'the first serious attack on German economic interests in the area'. All important decisions, including finance and production, were taken in Paris rather than Pilsen, and Schneider's iron grip on Škoda contrasts with the limp grasp by which Vickers clutched at their foreign arsenals. Škoda expanded 'along the lines of a horizontal monopoly, which gradually dominated the whole Czecho-slovak engineering industry, encroached upon the electrical industry and played a significant part in...foreign trade...through its commercial organisation, Omnipol'.[30] Škoda dividends rose steadily from 5% in 1920 to 28.5% in 1930, and by 1937, after several increases of Škoda's capital, Schneider owned 46.5% of the joint stock capital of 220 million crowns.[31] Three months after the Munich Agreement, in December 1938, when Škoda shares were quoted in Paris at 565 francs, Schneider sold its holding 'on fairly favourable terms to a consortium of Czech banks'.[32] Throughout Schneider treated Škoda ruthlessly, whether in their division of world markets agreed in 1922, the arrangements over patents, or the imposition on Škoda of product diversification 'which prevented thorough reconstruction and rationalisation'. Altogether, as the Czech Director of Ordnance at Pilsen complained, 'The Schneider engineer representatives are very unpopular, being socially most offensive and arrogant.'[33]

The subsidiary theme of this study is liquidity. Schneider controlled its subsidiaries with the minimum outlay or immobilisation of capital: they created 'an elegant, almost classical example of domination by the cheapest way possible': preferred shares with plural voting rights enjoyed by founding shareholders, or the syndicating of such shares' blocks.[34] Vickers, though perpetually cash-starved after the rolling-stock merger, developed no such devices. Barker and Caillard instead took minority shareholdings which were too small for Vickers to exert control but contributed to the illiquidity which was crushing all the flexibility and enterprise of the group during 1920–6. They were even less successful when, as in Poland and Estonia, they tried to participate without direct foreign investment. In the electrical investments, too, Vickers' policy of technical alliances with continental companies, with the English company making direct investments in return for electrical engineering orders, crucially differed from the pre-war German methods on which it was loosely modelled. AEG and Siemens had created Swiss or Belgian financial holding companies which carefully fostered developing markets, whereas Vickers' Electric Holdings was not used as an operating intermediary, but merely held a portfolio of (depreciating) investments. The greater intimacy between Schneider and French diplomacy than between Vickers and the Foreign Office, to which all four attested, was equally significant: it was this admixture of financial and diplomatic advantages, rather than quality distinctions in personnel, that made Schneiders' men-on-the-spot so often seem more effective than those of Vickers. This partly accounts for the decline of Vickers' share in international arms markets during the 1920s: by February 1928 they had only two foreign orders for *land* armaments (from Bolivia and Lithuania), and the responsible director lamented, 'Schneider and Škoda seem between them to share the rest of the world.'[35]

All business decisions are influenced by politics, and armaments are an abnormally politicised export: but the political basis for Vickers' new multinational strategy of 1916–25 was transcendent. Its directors were convinced that the world war was in origin substantially a trade war, and that its special conditions of industrial mobilisation were a unique chance to reassert British export hegemony. But British governmental priorities were to re-establish the City of London's primacy in international finance, and to defend the formal British Empire: Vickers' chosen arenas of Eastern Europe and electro-engineering were peripheral in comparison. Eugene Schneider's strategy broadly reflected French high policy: but for readily comprehensible reasons, the British government lacked Douglas Vickers' continental commitment, and its interests in Eastern Europe were officially described as 'confined to maintaining...peace...by advice and moderating counsel through the League of Nations'.[36] As a result, Vickers painfully learnt the risk of subordinating commercial policy to considerations of higher national aims.

NOTES

I am indebted to Mr H. E. Scrope for permission to use the archives of Vickers plc (since deposited at Cambridge University Library), and to Dr Geoffrey Jones, Dott. Luciano Segreto and Jenny Davenport for criticising earlier versions of this paper.

132   R. P. T. Davenport-Hines

1 Claude Beaud, 'The interests of the Union Européenne in Central Europe', in Alice Teichova and Philip Cottrell (eds.), *International business in Central Europe 1918–39* (Leicester and New York, 1983), pp. 377–8; see György Rónki, *Economy and foreign policy: the struggle of the Great Powers for hegemony in the Danube Valley 1919–1939* (New York, 1983), pp. 13–18; Alice Teichova and Penelope Ratcliffe, 'British interests in Danube navigation after 1918', *Business History*, 27 (1985), 283–300.

2 Schneider, quoted in Philip Noel-Baker, *The private manufacturer of armaments* (London, 1936), p. 285; François Crouzet, 'Commentary', in Teichova and Cottrell (eds), p. 411.

3 T. P. O'Connor, *Daily Telegraph*, 16 July 1919. See generally R. P. T. Davenport-Hines, *Dudley Docker* (Cambridge, 1984), pp. 160–1, 170–1; R. P. T. Davenport-Hines, 'The multinational strategy of Vickers before 1945', in Geoffrey Jones (ed.), *British multinationals: Origins, management and performance* (Aldershot, 1986) pp. 43–74; Clive Trebilcock, *The Vickers Brothers* (London, 1977).

4 J. D. Scott, *Vickers* (London, 1962), pp. 41, 76.

5 Douglas Vickers, quoted in *Eastern Engineering*, January 1913, 209–10; June 1913, 371–2; July 1913, 13; Douglas Vickers, speech at Birmingham of 29 May 1913, quoted *Far Eastern Review*, January 1915, 289; R. P. T. Davenport-Hines, 'The British Engineers Association', in Davenport-Hines (ed.), *Markets and bagmen: studies in the history of marketing and British industrial performance 1830–1939* (Aldershot, 1986) pp. 102–30.

6 For his view that AEG deliberately undermined the British Westinghouse Electrical Co. by dumping, see *Sheffield Daily Telegraph*, 7 January 1910; also see 1, 4, 5, 8, 13 January 1910; 23, 26, 30 November 1910.

7 John Turner, 'The British Commonwealth Union and the General Election of 1918', *English Historical Review*, 93 (1978), 528–59; John Turner, 'The politics of organised business in the First World War' in J. A. Turner (ed.), *Businessmen and politics* (London, 1984), pp. 33–49. Vickers and its associated rolling-stock company provided an annual subsidy of £20,000 to this body for three years from 1918.

8. Caillard, *Imperial fiscal reform* (London, 1903); Caillard, 'Trade relations within the empire', *Empire Review*, 5 (1903), 19–28; Caillard, 'An empire in the making', *Monthly Review*, 18 (1905), 30–55, 37–64 (2 parts); Caillard, 'Imperial preference and the cost of food', *Compatriots' Club Lectures* (London, 1905), pp. 144–74.

9 Sir Arthur Steel-Maitland to A. L. Smith, Master of Balliol, Oxford, 5 November 1918, Steel-Maitland papers 181/626, Scottish Record Office, Edinburgh.

10 Peter Cline, 'Winding down the war economy: British plans for peacetime recovery 1916–19', in Kathleen Burk (ed.), *War and the state* (London, 1982), p. 160.

11 Papers of Federation of British Industries (Warwick University Modern Records Centre); Docker, 'The industrial problem', *National Review*, 72 (1918), 301–10; Docker, untitled chapter in Sydney Chapman (ed.), *Labour and capital after the war* (London, 1918), pp. 129–40; Caillard, 'Industry and production', *National Review*, 75 (1920), 58–66.

12 For the role of socio-institutional factors in businessmen's decisions, see Jonathan Boswell, 'The informal social control of business in Britain, 1880–1959', *Business History Review*, 57 (1983), 237–57.

13 Docker, quoted in *The Economist*, 1 June 1918, 954; see *Vickers News*, October 1919, 8.

14 For example, in the papers of Sir Patrick Hannon at the House of Lords Record

Office and of Sir Roland Nugent at the University of Warwick Modern Records Centre (FBI Collection).

15 Sir Vincent Caillard to Foreign Office, 28 February 1918, PRO FO 382/1842.

16 Docker to Lord Robert Cecil, 16 December 1918, PRO FO 382/1837, quoted in Davenport-Hines, *Docker*, p. 159.

17 Luciano Segreto, 'More trouble than profit: the investments of Vickers in Italy 1906–39', *Business History*, 27 (1985), 316–37; Davenport-Hines, *Docker*, pp. 169–70.

18 On Hiley, see Neville Chamberlain to Walter Long, 14 November 1916, Long Papers 947/771, Wiltshire Record Office.

19 Douglas Vickers, quoted *Vickers News*, May 1925. See also Scott, *Vickers*, pp. 140–6, 156–8; Davenport-Hines, *Docker*, pp. 163–9, 172–5.

20 On Sofina, see Davenport-Hines, *Docker*, pp. 199–211; for fragmentary details of these investments, see Vickers file 434; Memorandum on Electrical Holdings, 22 February 1927, Vickers microfilm R.322; Note on Brown Boveri Italiano, 1934, microfilm R.319; Sir Mark Webster Jenkinson to Sir Herbert Lawrence, 20 September 1929, microfilm R.329.

21 PRO BT 13/83.

22 Davenport-Hines, *Docker*, pp. 137–49; my entry on Sir Alexander Henderson in *Dictionary of Business Biography*, vol. 3 (1985), pp. 153–8; A. S. J. Baster, *The international banks* (London, 1935), pp. 194–203; 'The proposals for a British Trade Bank', *Banker's Magazine*, 52 (1916), 538–46; Sir Charles Addis, 'A British Trade Bank', *Fortnightly Review*, 106 (1916), 841–51; Sir R. H. Inglis Palgrave, 'The British Trade Corporation', *Quarterly Review*, 229 (1918), 143–53; B. C. Newton to Sir Arthur Steel-Maitland, 17 July 1919, GD 193/327/31.

23 Douglas Vickers to Prince Barbu Stirbey, 19 June 1930, Douglas Vickers papers; Department of Overseas Trade memorandum on foreign credit and arms exports, 4 October 1930, PRO BT 60/26/7.

24 Beaud 'Interest of the Union Européenne', pp. 396–7; Sir Orme Sargent, memorandum on flotation on the London market of development loans by foreign governments, 8 June 1928, printed in *Documents of British Foreign Policy* (hereafter *DBFP*),series 1A, vol 5 (London, 1973), pp. 105–9.

25 R. P. T. Davenport-Hines, 'Vickers' Balkan conscience: aspects of Anglo-Romanian armaments 1918–39', *Business History*, 25 (1983), 287–319; Davenport-Hines, 'Strategy before 1945', pp. 61–7.

26 Geoffrey Jones and Clive Trebilcock, 'Russian industry and British business 1910–1930: oil and armaments', *Journal of European Economic History*, 11 (1982) 81–5; *DBFP*, 1st ser., vol. 6 (London, 1956), pp. 474, 479. On the difficulties of British business in Poland in the 1920s, see *DBFP*, ser. 1A, vol. 4 (London, 1971), pp. 197–201; ser. 1A, vol. 5 (London, 1973), pp. 492–3.

27 J. D. Gregory to E. C. C. Wilton, 19 September 1921, PRO FO 371/6732; Emile Cohn to Sir Vincent Caillard, 15 September 1922, Vickers microfilm R346.

28 Beaud, 'Interests of the Union Européenne', p. 394.

29 Report of Lt Col. Sir Thomas Montgomery-Cuninghame, British military attaché at Prague, on visit to Škoda at Pilsen, dated 6 December 1922, PRO FO 371/7388.

30 Alice Teichova, *An economic background to Munich* (Cambridge, 1974), pp. 196–7, 202. For 'nauseating' French propaganda on Schneider and Škoda in Yugoslavia in 1929, see *DBFP*, ser. 1A, vol. 7 (London, 1975), pp. 9–10.

31 C.P. (289) 33. Report of Cabinet Committee on Private Arms Industry, 8 December 1933, PRO Cab 27/551.

32 Teichova, *Munich*, p. 216; PRO FO 371/22901.
33 Teichova, *Munich*, p. 213; Montgomery-Cuninghame, (see note 29).
34 Beaud, 'Interests of the Union Européenne', p. 381; Crouzet, 'Commentary', p. 411.
35 Sir Noel Birch, memorandum of 24 February 1928, Vickers microfilm R286. Naval armaments were a different matter. For a fuller discussion, see Davenport-Hines, 'The British marketing of armaments 1885–1935', in Davenport-Hines, *Markets and bagmen*, pp. 146–91.
36 *DBFP*, ser. 1A, vol. 1 (London, 1966), p. 859.

12   J. & P. Coats Ltd in Poland

EMMA HARRIS[1]

In 1918, J. & P. Coats Ltd of Paisley, the Scottish multinational thread manufacturers, were faced with the loss of one of the major components of their European empire: the Russian operation controlled through the Nevsky Thread Manufacturing Company of St Petersburg, which on the eve of the First World War had accounted for some 90 % of Russian thread production, and which had from the 1890s yielded large profits to the parent company. Of the 150 million strong Russian market, only the populations of Poland and the Baltic states (c. 10 million) were still accessible; and of Coats' six main manufacturing units in Russia, only two tattered remnants had – so far – escaped the Bolsheviks: the Strasdenhof mill at Riga, and the Łódzka Fabryka Nici T.A. at Łódź, now in the shakily-reborn independent Polish state. Radical readjustments were therefore required. We should note that in 1918 all decisions on the future of the Łódź mill rested with Paisley alone: J. & P. Coats Ltd, while maintaining the polite fiction of being 'only shareholders' in subsidiary companies, was a highly-centralised operation. Correspondence with the Łódź company may indeed have been conducted throughout in courtly language of suggestion and advice, but this was merely a gloss on a management structure in which all decisions on investment, production patterns, employment policy, supplies and sales (the last through Coats' marketing arm, the Central Agency) were taken from headquarters departments at Paisley. Łódź could not purchase so much as a coffee boiler for the canteen without headquarters' approval.[2]

The Łódź mill – employing 64,000 spindles and 850 workers in 1914 – had after its take-over by the Nevsky company in 1900 been closely integrated into the Paisley-directed Nevsky manufacturing and sales network. It produced spooled thread and Nevsky tickets for Poland and Russian markets, and grey thread for other Nevsky mills. During the war, it had been closed under compulsory German administration, but although subjected to requisitions which included machine parts, damage was not particularly extensive, and the capital outlay required to reinstitute production was in the region of £100,000. Loss of established markets and production linkages

135

were far more serious problems for the company in 1918. Although this was the only large-scale thread mill in the Polish territories, the thirty million strong Polish market was exhausted, and the Southern and Western territories which had previously formed part of the Austro-Hungarian and German empires enjoyed established supply connections with other Coats mills and brands. Indeed, during the 1920s, the Polish market for finished thread was to prove capable of absorbing only about 20 % of the Łódź mill's spinning capacity.[3] Moreover, Poland in the first phase of its inter-war history – through border disputes, the Polish–Soviet war, internal political instability and labour unrest, inflation and the German tariff war, down to Piłsudski's coup in May 1926 – represented a superficially unattractive proposition to all but the most speculative of foreign capital.

In this situation, Coats' policy in Poland in the first years after the war can most readily be interpreted in terms of continued expectations in the Russian market. The company was by no means resigned to the loss of its Russian interests, and like other British firms with long-standing ties in Russia, saw Poland at least to 1921 as a potential stepping-stone towards renewing these contacts at an appropriate future date. Until the conclusion of the Polish–Soviet war in the late autumn of 1920, Coats' strategy amounted to a cautious reservation of options on renewed use of its manufacturing base in Poland should occasion in Russia arise; from October 1920, the company's activities rapidly accelerated in response to the Polish victory; and only from late 1921 can signs be detected of longer-term adjustment to an exclusively Polish context.

The timing of the initiation of an investment programme at Łódź strongly suggests that the decision was taken against a background of Russian expectations. Coats' first purposeful approach to the Łódź company in May 1919 coincided with the opening stages of the Polish–Soviet war, and was apparently made in direct response to an appeal by the MacAlpine commission, which in March 1919 forwarded to Paisley a report on the mill, 'strongly urging the advisability of sending a representative with plenary powers and money as soon as possible, with a view to the resumption of operations'. While MacAlpine's concern was based on a desire to prevent Bolshevism developing behind the lines while the Polish army was away fighting it at the front[4] – a sentiment that Coats might have applauded but were hardly likely to back financially – the possible opportunities afforded by a satisfactory outcome to the war were not ignored in Paisley. Thereafter, the pattern of the company's activity at Łódź to the autumn of 1920 was designed not to reinstitute production, but cautiously to set in place a structure which could be swiftly activated when required. Thus after an exploratory mission to the mill in May 1919, a young man named Samuel Harvey was sent out as mill manager, specifications for replacement machine parts were taken, and orders placed with British suppliers. But the pace of deliveries to October 1920 betrayed no impatience to begin manufacture. The spinning mill machinery, which required relatively few replacement parts, some of which could be supplied locally, was not operational until June 1920. Re-fitting of the twisting mill, which called for a higher level of investment, was carried out even more dilatorily: parts for the frames were ordered in November 1919, but between June and September 1920, materials for only 14 of the 48 frames were dispatched, while in contrast the remaining 34 sets were to be delivered between October 1920 and January 1921. Parts for the polishing machinery were not ordered until December 1920.[5]

The minimal production instituted from June 1920 when the spinning machinery became operational further indicates that this was only a holding operation. Employment in the spinning mill stood at 15 in June, and by October had reached only 41; it was not until early in 1921 that a viable work force was recruited. Recruitment for the twisting mill did not begin at all until November 1920.[6] While Coats were prepared to provide some thread imports to retain their hold on the Polish market, the limited spinning that did take place at Łódź was intended to offer the appearance rather than the substance of activity, to placate the somewhat uncertain quantity of the new Polish government. The raw cotton dispatched to Łódź at this stage was sent in answer to a telegram from the mill in January 1920, reporting an urgent request from the Polish Industry Ministry that they start production as soon as possible; the telegram concluded: 'Send some cotton to show the authorities our earnest endeavour.' In September 1920, following further official approaches, Paisley showed renewed concern, writing: 'It is unfortunate that the Department of Industry has had occasion to ask an explanation ... We think it extremely important that you should endeavour to give the authorities the satisfaction they desire.'[7] Coats' lack of enthusiasm for immediate market prospects can also be observed in their attitude in July 1920 to an enquiry about loan spinning from a neighbouring Łódź mill: Paisley regretted that 'we are not inclined to entertain your proposal'.[8]

Coats' wariness of irrevocable commitment in this turbulent period is highlighted by the pattern of their behaviour during the concluding stages of the Polish–Soviet war, when Poland faced defeat. Contingency plans had been drawn up: in what was obviously a prearranged code, Łódź wired in early August, 'Harvey health worse. Send instructions in case of death', to which Paisley replied in a series of telegrams ordering sales of cotton and yarn 'against sterling if possible'. Even after the Polish victory at Warsaw in August Coats cut off supplies to Łódź while Polish military requisition was still in the offing. It was not until October 1920 that the situation was noted to be 'considerably more settled', and sales of yarn stocks were discontinued.[9]

For roughly a year after this, however, Coats' revanchist hopes took more concrete form. An interesting message sent to Łódź after the Polish victory suggests specific plans: 'Herbert Cooper ... should hold himself in readiness to leave for Russia at fairly short notice'.[10] Certainly from October 1920 Coats abandoned their policy of caution and began full institution of production at the Łódź mill. A special meeting 'to discuss matters relating to the Łódź Thread Manufacturing Company' was held at Glasgow on 19th October; here a decision was taken to send raw cotton to Łódź, and the first post-war investment in new machinery for the mill was approved.[11] Increased urgency in supplying parts of the twisting frames meant that by January 1921 all were operational, and the mill commenced spooling sixcord thread; all polishing machine parts had been supplied by May 1921, when some glace thread manufacture was begun.[12] By mid-1921 this had resulted in a build-up of relatively large stocks of spooled thread at the mill: nearly 20 000 gross, with a current monthly sales average of less than 2000 gross. In view of Coats' tight control of the production: sales ratio, this must at least in part be explained in terms of preparations for the Russian market, a conclusion moreover borne out by the fact that this was largely 'second-grade thread' which was not suitable for marketing under Coats' own-brand labels in Poland.[13] Paisley soon however showed signs of unease, in June advising the curtailment of sixcord production with reference to the Polish market; by October there was a note of agitation from headquarters, who telegraphed: 'Reduce production in all departments in accordance with sales. Keep in touch with Warsaw agents.'[14]

From now on, while not entirely abandoning plans for the Russian market, Coats began to develop a role for the Łódzka Fabryka Nici T.A. outside this framework. At first this was to be expressed through greater interest in the Polish market, although gradually, as the Polish inflation developed from 1922, and domestic sales (given imported raw materials) became ever more unattractive, emphasis was increasingly placed on export of semi-products.

Growing acceptance of the exclusively Polish context can be traced in attempts – mainly unsuccessful – from 1921 to find local suppliers of auxiliary materials;[15] in the accession of the company to the Łódź Association of Textile Manufacturers;[16] and perhaps most evidently in the new share issue of April 1922, annulling shares previously held by the Nevsky company.[17] Łódź finished thread production was now planned on the basis of demand in the Polish market, with extension in some lines into the Baltic states. Although there was as yet no serious competition for Coats brands in this market, Paisley was sensitive to indications of Polish demand, proposing for example from October 1922 the introduction of 'a cheaper quality of knittings... for the Polish market'. A policy was also developed of substitute production at Łódź of other Coats brands established in certain regions of Poland – notably Harland's Eiserngarn in Galicia.[18] A long-term approach was moreover now adopted to domestic brand reputation and future competition, reflected in quality control and a strategic pricing and ticketing policy. In 1921, Paisley recalled that Łódź brands had not enjoyed a high reputation in Poland before the war: 'It may be necessary to sell...at prices, say, 10% lower than for goods of British manufacture, and it must also be borne in mind that the Łódź brands must be in a position to meet eventual foreign competition.' For the marketing of Łódź's large stock of second quality goods in 1921, Paisley advocated the use of a ticket that did not show the name of the manufacturer; and for Lithuania in 1923, they favoured a ticket which did not show the country of origin ('We understand that Polish designations are not very popular in Lithuania').[19]

The evolution of company policy over the period can be traced in their approach to the Polish military market. Whereas in mid-1920 – anxious to preserve their hold on the civilian market, and clearly not placing much faith in the new Polish authorities – Coats had actually complained that the Polish government had bought most of the company's imports to Poland 'for their own purposes'[20], by November 1920 their attitude had shifted perceptibly and they bridled at indications of long-term competition. While Coats had been making haste slowly in 1920, the Scheibler/Grohmann partnership had re-activated the tiny Łowicz Thread Mill. On 5 November Coats wrote to Łódź:

We note that the military authorities are negotiating with the Łowicz Thread Mill for delivery of Thread....As there may be a danger of this Polish mill later being subventioned, we should like to be kept fully informed so that we may claim entirely similar treatment. It may be that this is only a case of the officials concerned having been bribed, and steps should be taken to find out who they are and what can be done to support our interests.[21]

Whatever was done, from 1921 the Warsaw Commissariat began to renew its approaches to the Central Agency, and from 1922 to the end of our period, the bulk of Commissariat supplies came from the Łódź mill, accounting for c. 10–15% of its finished thread production (minimum military sales: 1922 – 3000 gross; 1923 – 5118 gross; 1924 – 12600 gross). In the first years, Coats gave priority to these orders and stressed the importance of retaining this market.[22]

Gradually, however, as inflation developed, a more cavalier attitude evolved. In the years to 1926, Coats exploited their position of virtual monopoly on supply of thread suitable for the military: Department VII of the Commissariat noted in 1923 that 'the Łodzka Fabryka Nici is the only firm in Poland capable of producing high-quality thread up to military requirements', and the Polish inflation made this an unattractive market to foreign producers without a manufacturing base in the country.[23] Coats therefore did not hesitate to bring pressure to bear upon the Commissariat in 1922–4 on the question of the types of thread ordered and method of payment. In June 1922, Paisley had instructed: 'You should persuade them to take as much as possible in (Black) Troika...in order to reduce your large stocks in this brand.' Apparently, this directive was successfully implemented, for the contract signed in March 1923 was questioned by the Chief of Military Administration, who demanded to know 'why Department VII...had purchased black thread now, when all parts of the uniform stipulated for the army are khaki'. Since his objections delayed the signing of the second part of the contract, Węgliński, the director of the Warsaw Central Agency, visited the Chief in person and threatened 'that if the contract were not confirmed on that very day, the firm would break off negotiations'. The Chief therefore signed.[24] Later in 1923, by again threatening to withdraw supplies, Coats ensured in the worst period of inflation that the War Ministry would pay their accounts in Sterling, or sterling equivalent on the day of delivery, in contravention of the original contract, which laid down fixed prices.[25]

Even as general demand somewhat recovered, the Polish and Baltic finished thread market could absorb only 80,000 to 100,000 gross spools, or c. 20% of the Łódź mill's spinning capacity.[26] Having turned their back on the Nevsky past, Coats therefore expanded semi-product manufacture at the mill. In periods of reduced home demand, they agreed to, or even actively encouraged, the use of spare capacity for local loan spinning orders, or the production of weaving yarn for the local market, although maintaining a vigilant eye to the possibility of future competition – refusing orders which might eventually have been used by competing manufacturers of sewing thread.[27] The main stress was however placed on the integration of Łódź semi-products into Coats' European manufacturing network, an arrangement made additionally attractive by low labour costs. From November 1921, 'half the mill' was to be employed regularly in spinning grey thread for the Home Mills at Ferguslie, in quantities varying from 6,000 to 9,000 lb weekly. From February 1922, grey thread was further directed to other Coats Central European mills as required: in addition to the Paisley order, quantities (initially 7500 lb weekly) were sent periodically to the Harland mill at Wilhelmsburg in Austria, and from October 1923, the Paisley thread was occasionally diverted to the Coats mill at Bratislava. From July 1924, although consignments to these two mills continued intermittently, Łódź mainly supplied the Strasdenhof mill at Riga, an old partner from the Nevsky stable.[28]

By 1923–4 these arrangements were being given some priority over the Łódź mill's own finished thread orders[29] – a fact which must be examined in the context of the Polish inflation, compounded, especially following Władysław Grabski's reform measures of 1923–4, by Polish exchange control regulations. Throughout its post-war operation, the Łódzka Fabryka Nici T.A. was theoretically working simply as a loan spinning mill for Coats, who supplied raw materials and paid a spinning allowance – a purely formal arrangement which provided some leeway in evading the impact of controls.

In 1923, when the Warsaw Treasury Department had questioned this structure, Coats wrote to Łódź:

As according to your letter the new Devisen regulations permit you to utilise for the payment of foreign debts the sterling placed at your disposal, we presume you will have no difficulty in arranging that your invoices covering the manufacturing allowances should be purely formal documents. If the authorities require that the sterling should be utilised at all, it should be utilised ... for the manufacture of thread sold in Poland and whose proceeds should be remitted to this country.[30]

Later, Paisley suggested that in view of 'the present difficulty in having the Polish collections remitted home', payments due from Łódź to the parent company should be used to purchase coal in Poland for the Harland mills in Austria.[31] Thus, although in local currency the formal indebtedness of the Łódź company to Coats inevitably soared during the inflationary post-war years (the lending being partly capitalised in the new share issues of 1922 and 1924), the mill was probably able to reduce its debt somewhat in sterling.[32] None the less, the kind of profits to which Paisley had been accustomed from the Nevsky operation were evidently a thing of the past.

NOTES

1 Abbreviations used throughout: WAPŁ – Wojewódzkie Archiwum Państwowe w Łodzi; ŁFN – Łódzka Fabryka Nici T.A., archive in WAPŁ; CAW – Centralne Archiwum wojskowe; FO – Public Record Office, Foreign Office.
2 See E. E. Kruze, 'Tabaczni i nitocznii tresti' – iz istorii imperializma v Rosii', in *Iz Istorii Imperializma v Rosii,* Akademia Nauk SSSR, Trudy Leningradskogo Otdelenija Instituta Istorii, Vypusk 1 (Moskva–Leningrad, 1959), pp. 68 ff.; ŁFN 27, 28, 29, 30, 33, *passim.*
3 ŁFN 30; FO 371–3936, 202703, 8.VI.1920, letter from W. H. Coats to Lord Curzon.
4 FO 371–3894,no. 17710, 21.1.1919; MUN 4/6360, 62341, App. I, p. 15; FO 371–3936, 202703, 8.VI.1920, letter from W. H. Coats to Lord Curzon.
5 ŁFN 27, M14, 8.XI.1919; ŁFN 27, 21, 24.XI.1919; ŁFN 27, 11, 21.1.1921; ŁFN 27, M145, 20.XII.1920, LFN 27, 94, 17.V.1921.
6 LFN 143, employment records in twisting mill; ŁFN 144, employment records in spinning mill.
7 ŁFN 27, 6, 15.1.1920; ŁFN 27, M86, 24.IX.1920.
8 ŁFN 27, M, 6.VII.1920.
9 ŁFN 27, 66, 23.VII.1920; ŁFN 27, 70, 5.VIII.1920; ŁFN 27, 89, 1.X.1920.
10 ŁFN 27, M, 18.XI.1920
11 ŁFN 27, unnumbered, 'Minutes of a meeting held in Glasgow on 19th October 1920...'.
12 ŁFN 27, 11, 21.1.1921; ŁFN 27, 94, 17.V.1921.
13 ŁFN 27, M10, 30.V.1921.
14 ŁFN 27, M112, 21.VI.1921; ŁFN 28, 3.X.1921.
15 ŁFN 28, no. 6, 12.XI.1920; ŁFN 28, 37, 9.VII.1921 ff.; ŁFN 30, Ch. no. 4, 21.II.1922 ff.
16 WAPŁ, Zwiazek Przemysłu Włókienniczego 7, no. 52, p. 32.

17 ŁFN 28, 29.IV.1922.
18 ŁFN 28, 268, 5.X.1922 ff.; ŁFN 33, 309, 30.I.1923.
19 ŁFN 27, M16, 22.I.1921; ŁFN 27, M10, 30.V.1921; ŁFN 33, 369, 6.VII.1923; ŁFN 33, 373, 20.VII.1923.
20 FO 371–3936, 202703, 8.VI.1920, letter from W. H. Coats to Lord Curzon.
21 ŁFN 27, M111, 5.XI.1920.
22 CAW I.300.54.79; ŁFN 28, 170, 30.III.1922; CAW I.300.54. 77, LDG 48119/22V KM, 14.VI.1922; CAW I.300.54.132; ŁFN 33, 489, 6.VI.1924; ŁFN 33, 604, 2.X.1924.
23 CAW I.300.54.79, Dep. VII, Liczba 24251 KMV; CAW I.300. 54.79, Protokuł nr 30, Dep. VII, Komisja Mundurowa 15.III.1923.
24 ŁFN 28, 214, 16.VI.1922; CAW I.300.54.79, Dep. VII, Liczba 4130/OA, Eksp. 1-sza; CAW I.300.54.79, Dep. VII, Liczba 21273/23 KMV to SAA 21.III.1923; CAW I.300.54.79, SAA L6081/OA/WA/Tj. to Dep. VII.
25 CAW I.300.54.79, Dep. VII, Ldz. 12783/Zaop./23/ZP, 11.X.1923 to SAA.
26 ŁFN 30, 'Protokuł. W dniu 18-ego lutego 1924r....'
27 ŁFN 28. 231, 1.VII.1922; ŁFN 28, 134, 13.II.1922; ŁFN 28, 140, 22.II.1922; ŁFN 28, 261, 22.IX.1922; ŁFN 28, 262, 26.IX.1922; ŁFN 28, 277, 20.X.1922.
28 ŁFN 28, 130, 7.II.1922; ŁFN 28, 157, 18.III.1922; ŁFN 28, 184, 28.IV.1922; ŁFN 33, no. 537, 4.VIII.1924; ŁFN 33, no. 557, 29.VIII.1924; ŁFN 33, 424, 16.I.1924; ŁFN 33, 458, 14.IV.1924.
29 e.g. ŁFN 33, 468, 30.IV.1924; ŁFN 33, 462, 18.IV.1924.
30 ŁFN 33, 375, 27.VII.1923.
31 ŁFN 33, copy of letter from William George to company headquarters, 19.VIII.1923.
32 ŁFN 30, 'Protokuł. W dniu 18-ego lutego 1924r....'

13 Multinationals and the French electrical industry, *1889–1940*

PIERRE LANTHIER

The part played by multinational companies in a country's economy is often described in terms of dependence. If a nation is experiencing growth difficulties and has a weak market, almost inevitably that nation opens its doors to foreign companies, which, once they gain a foothold, tighten their grip. At first sight, this situation can be fairly convincingly applied to the French electricity industry. For France, in fact, had to rely on patents and capital from international groups in order to launch and maintain this sector. But a deeper analysis is needed, since these generalisations ignore the attitude of French business generally and attribute to all multinationals the same intentions and power, whereas there are important differences between them.

1880–1919: three waves of foreign investment

The French electricity industry was characterised by foreign investment. There was an American presence – most notably through the agencies of the Compagnie Continental Edison (CCE), Thomson–Houston and S. A. Westinghouse. The Swiss operated in France through Alioth and a French company – Compagnie Electro-Mécanique (CEM) – re-acquired by Brown Boveri. The German participation, although smaller, was felt mainly through the Société Française AEG and the Société d'Electricité de Crcil. Empain, Ericsson and Philips also owned French subsidiaries. But this sizeable foreign involvement in electricity did not necessarily imply domination of it. The earlier multinational companies arrived in France, the more they had to rely substantially on local assistance. To be precise three main waves of foreign investment can be traced: the first, during the 1880s, was in the area of electric lighting; the second, in the following decade, concentrated on the electrification of the tramways and the development of power stations; the last wave, after 1900, occurred when the French market appeared to be expanding.

The first of these waves was the most short-lived. The market was weak and the multinationals, still embryonic, had to ensure their own growth at home as much (if not more) than abroad. The majority of companies came to France through intermediaries, as was the case, in 1887, with International Thomson–Houston. Yet at the beginning of the 1880s the electrical lighting industry appeared to offer promise, and companies such as Swan, Maxim and Edison were encouraged to come directly. However, their arrival was not solely a result of foreign initiatives. French entrepreneurs themselves were aware of the opportunities; some wanted to take advantage of recent American research so as to exploit it throughout Europe. It was for this reason that Continental Edison was established in 1882, with French capital and American patents. However, the market proved to be deceptive. Edison, which mainly relied on the manufacture of incandescent light bulbs rapidly fell back on the metropolitan market of Paris, not so much because of the loss of other European markets but because of the weakness of the French national market. Before 1890 the majority of electricity companies in France seemed destined to remain small and to engage in competition without either side being able to change the situation. In these circumstances the first generation of foreign companies did not survive, with, for example, CCE becoming entirely French from 1886.

Specific conditions within the French market caused this stagnation. Populous towns have offered fertile ground for the electricity industry from its inception. Geographically concentrated markets have enabled prices per kilowatt hour to be lowered and outlets to be increased. Highly urbanised countries have advantages for electrification in comparison with others: in 1911 Germany and England each had more than forty towns with populations exceeding 100,000, while in France there were barely fifteen. As a result, both private and public electrical lighting, the various domestic applications of electricity and even telephones could not, in France, achieve comparable rates of growth. Power stations remained small with high prices which encouraged competition from the gas industry in Paris as in the provinces. To be sure, private companies could have looked for support to the banks and public authorities, as had happened elsewhere. However, from 1900 to 1905 private companies encountered strong mistrust so that the public authorities were not forthcoming with financial aid. Furthermore, fearing financial scandal and the monopolisation of a public service, the authorities instituted control mechanisms which constrained the way in which the companies were run. As for the banks, some unfortunate investments in horse-drawn tramways delayed their investment in electricity, while the narrowness of the market discouraged the raising of capital for building power stations.

To overcome this stalemate the electro-technical industry had to create and support its own market. For a decade after 1895 this strategy dominated the bulk of its financial efforts. And not until the market was likely to develop of its own accord could the electrical construction industry be expected to grow. Thus it was risky to invest in research and in large workshops, which explains why France resorted to foreign aid and patents. Many groups were invited: in New York businessmen like Nicolas Siry and Gabriel Chamon negotiated the establishment of a French Thomson–Houston. Similarly the Westinghouse group was approached in 1898 by the management of Compagnie Générale de Traction.

In this way a second generation of foreign companies arrived in France and, of our three waves of multinationals, this one experienced the most considerable development. However, the foreign element was not dominant within this wave. Empain was able to involve French capital. Thomson–Houston always remained in local control. Traction managed to keep its interests separate from those of Westinghouse through establishing a joint subsidiary – the Société Industrielle d'Electricité. But the most important factor was the almost general absence of foreign personnel within the highest ranks of management. At Thomson–Houston foreigners merely represented the mother company's interests. Empain had a mixture of French and Belgian staff – and avoided placing too many Belgians in posts of responsibility. In fact there was a need to gain investors' confidence and to regain the goodwill of the authorities, or at least encourage less rigidity. After 1895 it became increasingly common to recruit state engineers to key posts on boards of directors. This was not a question of the provision of sinecures but of employing those who were dynamic enough to change their professional universe. The risk of a career in private industry was preferred by many to a peaceful post in the public sector: this was the case with men like Gabriel Cordier, Albert Petsche, Henri Maréchal, Raynald Legouez and Ferdinand Meyer. Thanks to them the tensions between private industry and the state were eased.

The presence of state engineers diminished considerably the foreign nature of electrical companies. They were animated by precise intentions which they managed to impose on the multinationals. Far from giving in to adversity, they made every effort to provide France with an adequate electricity industry.

Before 1905 the most common strategy of the electricity companies was to establish holding companies as a protective screen between the investors and the companies. Such holding companies in fact offered investors on the one hand a guarantee of unquestionable technical competence and on the other a guarantee of greater financial stability to the companies. French Thomson–Houston, formed in 1893 to exploit the patents of the American group, transformed itself three years later into a holding of tramway and electricity production/distribution companies. From 1896 Empain, specialists in local railways, became interested in electric tramways and from 1903 in power stations. Investment banks such as Comptoir National d'Escompte de Paris and Paribas invested in these groups.

The tramways were the first to benefit from this strategy. The relative weakness of the urban network imposed a double constraint: on the one hand hard competition in the few promising towns; on the other the obligation to electrify less profitable lines elsewhere. In both cases heavy expenses would be incurred. The financial intervention of groups like Thomson–Houston, the Compagnie Générale de Traction and Empain, enabled this obstacle to be overcome. They even acted as banks to their subsidiaries by acquiring short- and medium-term credit for them. Some years later capital was directed equally towards electricity production. So Thomson–Houston invested in the formation of Energie Electrique du Littoral Méditerranéen (EELM) and Energie Electrique du Sud-Ouest (EESO). In the same way Empain helped in the formation of Société d'Electricité de Paris (SEP) and Electricité et Gaz du Nord (EGN). This support was not merely financial. In fact these groups were able to increase the output of power stations by finding a stable and significant market: their own subsidiaries. In Paris, for example, Empain entrusted SEP with the supply of electricity for the Metro, for a network of tramways and for a local supply circuit.

In this way many hundreds of millions of francs were directed to power stations and electric tramways. Good results, however, did not always proceed from this huge amount of capital. Générale de Traction, which had resorted to considerable bank loans, did not survive the crisis of 1902. Thomson–Houston also experienced problems, which were overcome solely because it was financed primarily with its own capital. Empain avoided the crisis, thanks to a network of self-supporting holdings and to a large number of tramway and railway concessions. All in all, it was a considerable effort which demanded a number of sacrifices, particularly on the export side.

However, the strategy behind holding companies did enable the cost per kilowatt hour to be reduced, which facilitated the electrification of industrial equipment in France, especially after 1904–5. If the French workshops had been too small until then, judged by the inadequate and unstable market, there followed after 1905 a process of consolidation. Empain acquired plants at Jeumont which it then proceeded to enlarge considerably. In 1908 Thomson–Houston ceased importing its heavy equipment from the United States and increased its productive capacity.

At the same time the third generation of foreign companies emerged. Some groups previously supplying importers now decided to build factories in France to avoid losing their share of the market. For example, CEM which since 1892 had been the agent for the Brown Boveri group built its first factory in 1900, at Le Bourget, with the aim of manufacturing turbines there.

Six years later it branched out into electrical appliances and, in 1911, having acquired Société Française Alioth embarked on the mass production of motors. The formation of the Société Anonyme Westinghouse (SAW) in 1902, after the disappointments of Traction, and of the Société des Téléphones Ericsson (STE) in 1911, offer examples of similar cases. The companies of this third generation were quite different from those preceding them. They had less capital, were no longer principally French, and foreign administrators had a far greater influence. They did not establish holdings and settled for specialised production. Only SAW sought to diversify its investments, but in 1907, after experiencing serious problems, reduced the range of its products.

After two waves of foreign companies retrieved by the French, did the third wave herald a more vigorous offensive?

The inter-war years

Several international groups invested in the French electrical industry in 1919–21 and 1927–30. General Electric contributed to the capital of Compagnie des Lampes and Alsthom. Ericsson advanced millions to its subsidiary. CEM received similar support from Brown-Boveri after the war. But this thrust was not followed through. Of the groups in the third generation, SAW had to sell its assets to CEM in 1920. The latter pursued an even path after it – but at the price of greater French financial and human investment. In many cases, moreover, the mother company experienced problems. Ericsson, for example, suffered considerably as a result of the Kreuger affair and in 1935 had to relinquish its majority holding in STE to French industrialists.

The 1930s crisis put paid to the financial expansion in France of other groups belonging to the second wave. Empain directed its new investments to Belgium and the Congo. American multinationals ceased their investments. Subsidiaries of these groups gradually took the shape of plain French companies. The most prestigious electrical bosses, August Detoeuf, Ernest Mercier, Marcel Ulrich and Aristide Antoine found themselves at the head of both subsidiaries of these groups and of French companies. The electricity industry was dominated by engineers: in the inter-war period, 82% of top managers had engineering diplomas and the Ecole Polytechnique surpassed other institutions with 60% of its graduates holding the highest positions in the industry by 1937–9. This domination is explained by the increasing complexity of the technology and of the supply networks – but only partly. It also resulted from the social and ideological concordance of this body of businessmen with public administration. After the war the two sides cooperated in national development to expand supply, as with the unification and electrification of the regional railways. This collaboration even led to an increase of financial participation by public authorities. The state invested several billion francs in telephones and rural electrification. After 1930 the Parisian authorities injected many hundreds of millions of francs into enlarging the Metro.

The lack of growth in foreign investments after the 1930 crisis did not of itself cause a disaster. In reality the French were gradually assured of their own financial autonomy, partly because of the arrival of investment firms specialising in the electricity industry. CCE fulfilled this role within the Empain Group; SCIE, Crédit Electrique, Société d'Applications Industrielles and Financière Electrique did the same for the Compagnie Générale d'Electricité (CGE) and Thomson–Houston. These investment firms replaced the holdings of the electrical manufacturers as the main shareholders in electricity companies. French stockbrokers were equally receptive to 'electrical' stocks and bonds being issued. Increasingly the banks invested directly in the industry, by way of either short-term loans or the placing of shares. Finally, the power stations became capable of self financing and even formed electrical transport and distribution subsidiaries.

All this allowed the electrical manufacturers to get on with their own development, to protect the market against foreign competition and to launch French firms of international status. In this context foreign firms belonging to the second generation did not prove to be different from their French counterparts. Some, like Thomson–Houston, even took the leader. Already before the war, but more decisively in the 1920s, efforts were made to contain German and Dutch control through international agreements, notably in the area of light bulbs and heavy equipment. Moreover, groups combined their interests in joint ventures of some considerable size. This process was aimed at simultaneously concentrating and rationalising firms. An example of this is Alsthom, which, as its trade name signifies, arose from the merger of two factories belonging originally to Alsacienne de Constructions Mécaniques and Thomson–Houston. In addition to these joint ventures, the groups adopted other strategies but with a similar aim. This was the case when groups absorbed small competitors, as in 1917 when Thomson–Houston purchased the workshops belonging to H. Pilon. It merged them with the Etablissements Gallot two years later and, in 1930, with Maison Ropiquet et Roycourt to form the Compagnie Générale de Radiologie (CGR). Similarly, a very large firm would be formed with foreign patents, but without multinational control. In 1928 Westinghouse came back to France in association with Schneider to float Le Material SW; but its investment was restricted to patents. Some of these firms even found significant outlets abroad; Empain and Thomson–Houston established subsidiaries in Spain. Others, like CGR and Lorraine de Charbons, were able to export profitably within Europe and even in North America. In this situation the roles of the groups were, in addition to protecting subsidiaries through agreements, to give financial support through short-term advances and, at times of crisis, to absorb any losses sustained by subsidiaries. When, in 1935–6 Alsthom, CGR and other manufacturing companies had to reduce their capital, the shock was absorbed by Thomson–Houston and its investment companies.

But these strategies did not, in the short term, achieve the desired result. Financial autonomy did not contribute to market growth and state investment did not generate substantial demand in France. In a country which was being urbanised slowly, rural electrification, while successful, was not sufficient to establish markets comparable in size to those in large towns. It was the same situation with telephones. The industry's problems arose from an industrialisation which was slow to intensify and domestic consumption which was underdeveloped. In addition, the electrical manufacturing industry had to make up for lost time. The war, far from concentrating production and leading to a renewal of research in electricity in the private sector, delayed the process. In 1920, in order to modernise its electro-technical industry, France had, all at once, to concentrate and rationalise. These two activities were accomplished successively elsewhere, especially in the US. The need to undertake these processes simultaneously in France required substantial capital which, in the short term, was not suitably rewarded. When the crisis of the 1930s came, it is easy to understand why the electrical manufacturing industry found itself unable to confront it and firms like Alsthom and Le Materiel SW felt the backlash of the crisis within a few years of their establishment.

In conclusion, the multinationals, far from dominating the French electricity industry, were, in fact instrumental to its development. In this way France benefited from the most up-to-date patents, as discussed earlier, and began to make up for lost time. To explain the multinationals' non-traditional role, it is necessary to understand that between them and the French market there was interposed a professional body which had an ideological and social cohesion arising from shared experience of the 'Grandes Ecoles' and public service – the state engineers.

The presence of these men is further explained when it is understood that the market could only develop with financial and organisational support from electro-technical holdings. Directors had to be recruited from among those who were technically and managerially competent and close to the state administration. This strategy became widespread. Thereafter, companies working in specialised and export-oriented areas, such as medical electricity, were favoured as well as enterprises of larger size active in several sectors and protected by agreements. However, in the short term this process demanded concentration and rationalisation simultaneously, which was expensive, especially in times of instability. But in the long run it bore fruit: after 1945 the industry profited from the nationalisation of electrical utilities and developed further, especially in the area of electric household appliances, and took up an important place in the French economy.

NOTE

This article was translated from the French by Maureen Cottrell. It is based entirely on the author's doctor's dissertation presented at the University of Paris X (Nanterre) entitled 'Le rôle des groupes internationaux dans la construction électrique française de 1880 à 1940'.

14　The Japanese cotton spinners' direct investments into China before the Second World War

TETSUYA KUWAHARA

Introduction

The Japanese cotton industry depended heavily on overseas markets for its growth since the beginning of its development. Japanese major cotton spinners exported about 40% of their total sales in 1914. The exports of Japanese cotton spinners were almost completely confined to the Chinese market before the First World War. They had established a dominant position there, especially in the area of cotton yarn and coarse cotton cloth. They exported 500,000 bales of cotton yarn (worth about 56.5 million yen) to China. This amounted to 55% of the total imported yarns to China in 1914. They also exported coarse cotton cloth (sheeting, drill and T-cloth) for a total of 24.7 million yen which was 57% of the total amount imported to China in 1913.

During the First World War the Chinese modern cotton industry began expansion of its production capacity on a large scale while imports from Lancashire decreased and the price of cotton goods rose considerably.[1] Then the Chinese market became self-sufficient in the areas of coarse cotton yarns (cotton yarns of 20 count and downward) and coarse cotton cloth. Imports of cotton yarns to China decreased from 901,000 bales in 1914 to 377,000 bales in 1918. Chinese imports of sheeting and drill decreased from 3,054,000 pieces and 1,759,000 pieces respectively in 1915 to 2,268,000 pieces and 952,000 pieces in 1918. This change in the Chinese coarse cotton goods markets had a serious impact on the Japanese cotton industry which had established a dominant position there. They continued to lose their market share of coarse cotton goods to the local cotton spinners during and after the First World War. Most major Japanese cotton spinners then embarked on building local mills.[2] At the same time the Japanese cotton spinners also had a chance of entering new overseas markets such as the fine cotton cloth markets in China and the cotton goods markets of other underdeveloped areas where these demands had been met previously with imported Lancashire cotton goods.

151

Table 14.1. *The four largest cotton firms* (*December 1918*)

	Total assets (1919) (thousand yen)	Spindles (December 1918) (thousand)	Looms (December 1918)
Toyo Cotton Spinning Company	84,316	512 (16%)	12,961 (32%)
Kanegafuchi Cotton Spinning Company	72,940	485 (15%)	7,323 (18%)
Dainippon Cotton Spinning Company	69,738	569 (18%)	3,561 (9%)
Fuji Gasu Cotton Spinning Company	48,525	298 (9%)	1,642 (4%)
Total	275,519	1,864 (58%)	25,487 (63%)
All Japan (43 companies in December 1918)	—	3,228 (100%)	40,391 (100%)

Source: Dainippon Boseki Rengokai (Japanese Cotton Spinners' Association) (ed.), *Menshi Boseki Jigo Sankusho* (*Reference Book for Japanese Cotton Spinning*) (Osaka, the second half of 1918).
K. Nakagawa *et al.* (eds.) *Nihon Keieishi no Kisochishiki* (*Basic Knowledge of Japanese Business History*) (Tokyo, 1974), p. 452.

This chapter examines the four largest Japanese cotton firms in terms of their assets at the end of 1918. They are the Toyo Cotton Spinning Company, the Kanegafuchi Cotton Spinning Company, the Dainippon Cotton Spinning Company and the Fuji Gasu Cotton Spinning Company (table 14.1) The number of spindles of these four was 1,864,000, which is 58% of all spindles installed in Japan.

The direct investments into China by these four Japanese cotton firms are analysed comparatively from the viewpoint of their product-market structures and their entrepreneurship. The product-market structure stands for the composition of products and their positions in markets, and is constructed through a series of strategies for corporate growth. When the environment changes, firms are required to formulate new strategies which result in new product-market structures. Entrepreneurship signifies the ability and energy of top management to recognise and respond to new external conditions by adopting the product-market structure.

Dainippon Cotton Spinning Company: no alternatives except for local production[3]

The Amagasaki Cotton Spinning Company (339,848 spindles, 2,703 looms) merged with the Settsu Cotton Spinning Company (214,000 spindles, 560 looms) in June 1918 and changed its name to Dainippon Cotton Spinning Company which made it the largest firm in terms of number of spindles. While Amagasaki was the largest producer of the middle count and high count cotton yarn, Settsu had specialised in coarse cotton yarn. Through this merger Dainippon became a major producer of coarse cotton yarn.

Settsu's growth had heavily depended on the Chinese coarse cotton yarn market, having been the second largest exporter of coarse cotton yarns to that market in the period from 1903 to 1910. Its proportion of exports to total production was as high as 60 % in 1914. This was based on high quality and productivity achieved by the company. Settsu's export increased to 72,123 bales (48 % of the total production) in 1914. During the First World War Settsu gradually lost its established share of the Chinese market. Its export decreased to 14,178 bales (18 % of the total production) during the first five months of 1918.

Dainippon Cotton Spinning Company inherited this formidable problem through the merger with Settsu. The president, Kikuchi, who had also taken up the presidency of Settsu in June, 1915, recognised changing needs, and immediately after the merger, Dainippon dispatched a mill manager to Tsingtao to investigate a prospective mill site. In October 1918, Dainippon considered buying a local cotton spinning mill, the Oriental Cotton Spinning Company in Shanghai. In March and April of 1919, Kikuchi travelled in Shanghai, Hankao and Tiengtao and other cities in China to search for placing direct investments there. While Dainippon was trying to acquire mill sites in Shanghai and Tsingtao, he announced a plan for investments in China at the general meeting of shareholders in June 1919. The Shanghai mill was late in beginning construction because of difficulties in the acquisition of a suitable site. Construction of the Tsingtao mill began in November 1919. The mill commenced partial operations in November 1921 and full operations with 58,000 spindles in the first half of 1923. The Shanghai mill was completed and began full operations in the latter half of 1923. Ninety per cent production capacity was applied to the manufacture of coarse cotton yarns and 10 % to that of middle count yarns. Through these two local mills the company defended its market position in China which had been established by the Settsu Cotton Spinning Company before the First World War.

Concomitant with the decrease in exports of coarse cotton yarns, the domestic spinning division suffered the problem of excess capacity. In order to increase the consumption of coarse cotton yarn within the company, the weaving section was enlarged. The number of looms was increased from 3,561 at the time of the merger to 9,504 by 1926. The weaving division had consumed 9 % of the total production of cotton yarns in 1918, but this rose to 26 % in 1926. Dainippon increased the output of coarse cotton cloth such as sheeting, most of which was exported to overseas markets.

The Kanegafuchi Cotton Spinning Company: some prejudice with regard to direct foreign investment[4]

Even before the First World War Kanegafuchi Cotton Spinning Company had built a diversified product-market structure as a result of the concatenation of preceding strategies. Kanegafuchi had grown to a big business by expanding the export of coarse cotton yarn to China after the Sino-Japanese War. It exported 78,065 bales (49 % of total production) mainly to China, which was equivalent to 25 % of the total of Japanese export to China in 1903. The rapid acquisition of a share in the Chinese market was based on the large-scale production facilities acquired by a series of mergers. For the purpose of more stability and growth, Kanegafuchi diversified its products to cotton cloth and fine yarns. While exporting sheeting to China after the Russo-Japanese War, Kanegafuchi took a leading role in import substitution of shirting in the domestic market. The product-market structure of 1914 is shown in table 14.2. In 1914 when Kanegafuchi's export of cotton yarn reached a peak of 93,688 bales, the estimated amount of coarse cotton yarn exported to China was 73,894 bales (25 % of the total production). The estimated amount of coarse cotton cloth exported to China was as high as 8.3 % of the total production in terms of cotton yarn consumed within the firm in 1914.

During the First World War, Kanegafuchi suffered badly, losing its established position in the Chinese market as the Chinese cotton industry began to develop rapidly on a large scale. Kanegafuchi exported only 12,007 bales of coarse cotton yarn in 1919 and 3,885 bales in 1921. Furthermore it began losing its established position in coarse cotton cloth in China.

On the other hand Kanegafuchi was given the opportunity of entry into new overseas markets where it replaced Lancashire goods. Also in the domestic market the demand for middle count cotton yarn increased. Due to the emergence of these new market opportunities, Kanegafuchi increased the production of middle count cotton yarn and fine cotton cloth. The output of middle count cotton yarn increased from 54,036 bales (19 % of the total production of cotton yarn) in 1914 to 124,194 bales (44 %) in 1919. And the production of thin cloth of Kanegafuchi's total production rose from 7 % to 20 % in the same period. This was executed not only by building new mills but also by utilising excess capacity arising from the decline in exports of coarse cotton goods to China. Kanegafuchi, moreover, constructed dying,

Table 14.2. *Product-market structure of Kanegafuchi Cotton Spinning Company in 1914*

Product / Market	Coarse cotton yarn (20 count and downward)	Middle count cotton yarn (higher than 20 count)	Total
Within the company	41,736 bales (14%)	16,554 bales (6%)	58,290 (20%)
Domestic market	114,494 (39%)	24,375 (8%)	138,869 (47%)
Foreign market	81,203 (28%)	12,485 (4%)	93,688 (32%)
Total	237,433 (82%)	53,414 (18%)	290,847 (100%)

Note: The bales of cotton yarn consumed within the firm are estimated on a basis of production volume of coarse and fine cotton cloth.
Source: Dainippon Boseki Rengokai (Japanese Cotton Spinners' Association) (ed.), *Dainippon Boseki Rengokai Geppo* (*Monthly Report of Japanese Cotton Spinners' Association*) (Osaka), February 1914–January 1915.
Dainippon Boseki Rengokai (ed.), *Menshi Boseki Jijo Sankusho* (*Reference book for Japanese cotton spinning*), 1914.

bleaching and printing mills on a large scale in Osaka to increase its outlets for the cotton cloth. The mill began dying operations in 1917, bleaching in the latter half of 1919, and printing in April 1924. The cotton cloth thus produced was exported.

Even if Kanegafuchi was successfully acquiring new market opportunities, it was still necessary to defend their established share in China for the sake of their corporate growth. But Kanegafuchi was slow to respond. Sanji Muto, the managing director of Kanegafuchi, believed that direct foreign investment was detrimental to the Japanese economy, because he thought it would result in the elimination of employment opportunities, in the decline of related industries, and in the decay of local communities. Muto thus could not accept direct investment into China as a legitimate policy. Meanwhile his Japanese competitors embarked on the construction of local cotton spinning mills in China. Muto finally recognised the need to emulate these competitors and to defend Kanegafuchi's share against them. Kanegafuchi thus broke new ground for a cotton spinning mill in Shanghai in March 1921. The first mill in Shanghai with 20,000 spindles for coarse cotton yarn was completed in October 1922, the second with 18,000 spindles for 42 count doubling cotton yarn in November 1923. A Tsingtao mill was completed with 40,536 spindles for coarse cotton yarn and 860 looms for sheeting in March 1925.

Kanegafuchi, moreover, purchased the Lao Kom Mow Cotton Spinning and Weaving Company and thus acquired 45,000 spindles and 850 looms in Shanghai in May 1925. At the end of 1925, Kanegafuchi held 131,576 spindles and 1,527 looms in China. This was the largest share among the local firms established by the Japanese cotton spinners during and after the First World War.

Toyo Cotton Spinning Company: preference for export to local production[5]

While Settsu and Kanegafuchi had been the largest exporters of coarse cotton yarn to China, the Toyo Cotton Spinning Company had established a major position in the Chinese market of coarse cotton cloth such as sheeting and drill. The Toyo Cotton Spinning Company had been reorganised as a new company through the merger of the Osaka Cotton Spinning Company and the Mie Cotton Spinning Company. Toyo held 10,136 looms (40% of the total Japanese looms owned by spinning firms) and 441,796 spindles (17%). Both companies had pioneered the export of Japanese coarse cotton cloth to North China, Manchuria and Korea. They took over the market share which had been held by Lancashire and American cotton goods, and established a leading position there after the Russo-Japanese War. Besides the export of cotton cloth, Osaka and Mie increased their export of coarse cotton yarn from about 1911 onwards. The export peak of 60.7 thousand bales (17% of the total production of cotton yarn) was reached in 1914.

During the First World War Toyo suffered a sharp decrease in its exports of coarse cotton cloth and yarns to China, while the Chinese output of machine woven cotton cloth increased from 58 million square yards in 1905-7 to 354 million square yards in 1923, and the hand woven cotton cloth rose from 375 million square yards to 1,591 million square yards in the same years. This increase of production of coarse cotton cloth was based on the development of the spinning industry there. Then Japanese export of sheetings and drills to China decreased respectively from 3,356,000 pieces in 1913 to 1,856,000 pieces in 1920, and 1,667,000 pieces to 433,000 pieces in the same years. As a response to the impact on the weaving division, Toyo shifted the export market from China to South East Asia, the Middle East and Africa where there were large markets for coarse cotton cloth. Thus the major destination for the export of Japanese coarse cotton cloth changed to areas outside China after the First World War. Seventy-two per cent of the total export of Japanese sheeting was destined for markets outside China in 1921. For the Chinese market Toyo increased exports of fine cotton cloth such as shirting and jeans.[6]

On the other hand, there was no export market for cotton yarn outside

China. Thus Toyo's spinning division had no alternative for maintaining its overseas market share but to produce locally in China. The strategic need to build mills there was recognised by Toyo's managers, but Toyo did not take positive action towards local production when faced initially with the loss of its share in China. This can be explained by the fact that cotton yarn did not play such an important role in Toyo's exports as it did in the product-market structure of other major cotton spinner. Even at the peak year of Toyo's exports to China, cotton yarn was equivalent to only 8 % of its sales, while the export of cotton cloth to China amounted to 19 % of Toyo's total sales. The export of cotton yarn of Toyo was 17 % which was the lowest among the major cotton spinners. The average for exports of all Japanese cotton spinners was 34 % in 1914.

But when the Japanese competitors began the construction of local mills in China, Toyo felt that its competitive position was threatened. This threat generated a galvanising force in Toyo to take action in China. The Toyo Cotton Spinning Company began to construct a local spinning mill in Shanghai in October 1921, when the Dainippon Cotton Spinning Company had already begun trial operations in their local mill in Tsingtao. The Shanghai mill was completed with 45,600 spindles for coarse cotton yarn in the latter half of 1923.

The Fuji Gasu Cotton Spinning Company: mobilised on the standpoint of national interests[7]

Fuji Gasu Cotton Spinning Company which had established a position in the middle count cotton yarn market in the Kanto (Tokyo) district through merging with the Tokyo Gasu Cotton Spinning Company (Tokyo Gasu Boseki Kaisha), the largest producer of gassed yarn in Japan in 1906. It then became the third largest cotton spinning company in Japan. Fuji Gasu had a 39 % market share in gassed yarn, 17 % in middle count doubling yarn and 11 % in middle count yarn in the domestic market in 1909. When some major cotton spinners which had specialised in coarse cotton yarns entered into the high and medium count cotton yarn markets in the Kanto area, Fuji Gasu entered into the coarse cotton yarn market on a large scale as a countervailing response to these competitors. Fuji Gasu completed the Koyama No. 4 Mill in 1910, and increased production of coarse cotton yarn steadily. The coarse cotton yarns which were mostly sold in the domestic market totalled 58 % of the production of the firm in 1917.

Through establishing a position as a major firm in the domestic markets, Fuji Gasu developed managerial skills which allowed it to be not only domestically but also internationally competitive with such resources as blending techniques for raw cotton, combining processes of spinning and weaving facilities and labour management.

Fuji Gasu accomplished these achievements under the leadership of its managing director, Toyoharu Wada. After the remarkable success of Fuji Gasu, Wada began a wider engagement in business activities around 1910. He assisted in organising new companies and reorganising failing ones in a variety of industrial fields. He helped form the Nihon Kogyo Club (Industrial Club) in March 1917. He believed himself to be a leader in the Japanese cotton spinning industry and expected to play a role in protecting and promoting the national interest.

As soon as the Chinese cotton spinning and weaving industry began to make great progress during the First World War, Wada perceived the possibility of losing the established position of Japanese cotton spinners there. He saw the new situation as a symptom of decline of the Japanese cotton spinning industry with a consequent depression of the Japanese economy. As a result he recognised the need to have local plants in order to defend their established position. Motivated by the national interest, he worked on several projects with local cotton spinning and weaving businesses in China. In October and November 1916, for example, he inspected the Soy Chee Cotton Spinning Company of Shanghai for sale on the spot. He also organised the Sina Sen-i Kogyo Kumiai, an association for Chinese textile industries concerned with the cotton growing, spinning and weaving businesses in China; he organised Nikka Boshoku Kaisha (Japan China Cotton Mill) in Shanghai in July 1918; he invested in Nisshi Boshoku Kaisha, the Japan China Cotton Spinning and Weaving Company formed in Shanghai in November 1919; and he assisted in concluding three loan agreements between Toa Kogyo Kaisha (a Japanese investment company for Chinese industries) and three Chinese cotton mills in 1921–2. Nikka Boshoku Kaisha was the first local production base which the Japanese established during and after the First World War. The company was organised mainly through the capital of cotton merchants in Osaka, starting with a factory which had previously been bought by a Japanese merchant. For the reorganisation of the mill Wada not only gave directions himself but also sent engineers and technicians of the Fuji Gasu Cotton Spinning Company and other Japanese spinning firms with which he was concerned to the local mill.

In the process of channelling Japanese investment into the Chinese cotton industry, he mobilised the managerial resources of Fuji Gasu Cotton Spinning Company. Fuji Gasu began the mill construction in Tsingtao in October 1921. The mill was completed in April 1924; with 30,720 spindles it produced coarse cotton yarn. Fuji Gasu invested 30% of the total share capital in Manshu Boseki Kaisha (Manchuria Cotton Spinning Company) in March 1923. Their mill opened in the first half of 1925, with 31,000 spindles and 504 looms for coarse cotton yarn and sheeting. Through these local mills in China, Fuji Gasu entered the Chinese coarse cotton yarn and cloth market, a market to which it had previously paid little attention.

Conclusion

Most of the major Japanese cotton spinners established local production bases in China in order to defend their market shares, which they had acquired through exporting.[8] Most of the local mills produced coarse cotton yarns. Large Japanese export companies established larger mills than smaller exporters. Only a few local mills produced coarse cotton cloth. While the export of coarse cotton yarns could only be possible to the Chinese market, Japanese coarse cotton cloth could find alternative markets overseas outside China. Thus the coarse cotton cloth exporters were able to shift their market from China to more distant areas.

Beside them, a few Japanese cotton spinners such as Fuji Gasu Cotton Spinning Company built local production bases in China to secure their market for cotton goods there. Fuji Gasu mobilised its managerial resources aggressively in order to acquire a share there.

While proceeding to invest directly in China, most Japanese cotton spinners at the same time diversified their products for the home market. This solved the problem of excess capacity which arose as a result of the loss of the Chinese market. They increased their own weaving looms to increase consumption of coarse cotton yarn within the company. Also, production of middle count yarns was increased, replacing output of coarse cotton yarns. Thus the product-market structures of Japanese cotton spinners became more diversified.

To compete successfully with the Chinese cotton spinners, Japanese-owned local mills were required to have some advantages over them. Managerial resources transferred to the local mills were expected to carry this additional advantage even after compensating for the cost of operations abroad. Having the competitive managerial resources such as the technological expertise for cotton blending, for repair and maintenance of spinning and weaving machinery, and the organisational capability of labour management, these local mills could stay ahead of the Chinese owned mills in cost and quality. The sales agencies and distribution networks that had been established in China by Japanese merchants were also favourable to the local mills.

The different strategies in the investment behaviour of Japanese cotton spinners in China was also influenced by the varying quality of entrepreneurship of each firm. Kanegafuchi's slow response to the needs for establishing production units abroad can be traced to the managing director Muto's prejudice towards direct foreign investments overseas, whereas president

Table 14.3. *Processes of Japanese cotton spinners' direct investments into China*

| Names of firms | Relations with the Chinese markets prior to the local production | | Entrepreneurship |
	Coarse cotton yarn exported to China in 1914 (proportion of it to total production)[a]	Coarse cotton cloth exported to China in 1914 (proportion of it to total production)[a]	
Dainippon Cotton Spinning Company	Settsu only: 65,600 bales (44%) total of Settsu and Amagasaki: 66,300 bales (32%)	Settsu only: none total of Settsu and Amagasaki: 1,100 bales (0.5%)	Recognition of almost no alternatives except for local production
Kanegafuchi Cotton Spinning Company	73,900 bales (25%)	24,200 bales (8%)	Muto Sanji's partial prejudice on direct foreign investments
Toyo Cotton Spinning Company	23,700 bales (7%)	54,800 bales (16%)	Preference for export to direct investment
Fuji Gasu Cotton Spinning Company	800 bales (0.9%)	4,600 bales (5%)	Toyoji Wada's aggressive mobilisation of managerial resources on the standpoint of national interests

Notes: The data source is the author's papers cited in this chapter.

[a] The volume is estimated by the following method in cases of Dainippon, Kanegafuchi and Fuji Gasu:

– coarse cotton yarn export = each firm's export volume of coarse cotton yarn × 91%; 91% is the proportion of the Japanese export to China to Japan's total export of cotton yarn.

– coarse cotton cloth export = total production volume (converted into cotton yarns) × 2/3 × 87%; 2/3 is the export ratio of width coarse cotton cloth; 87% is the proportion of Japanese sheeting export to China to Japan's total export of sheeting in 1914.

Direct investments into China after the First World War

Motive	Location and year of commencement of construction	Mill size and product lines[b]	New strategies of the domestic division during and after the First World War
Defending the market position of its major export item	Tsingtao, November 1919 Shanghai, April 1921	120 thousand spindles – 90% of them for coarse cotton yarn and 10% for middle count yarn	Downward integration into the weaving section for increased consumption of coarse cotton yarn within the mills. The weaving looms increased from 3,561 in June 1918 to 9,504 in 1926.
Defending the market position of its major export item	Shanghai, March 1921 Tsingtao, May 1922 Shanghai, May 1925 (purchased)	124 thousand spindles and 1,295 looms – 51% of spindles for coarse cotton yarn, 23% for middle count cotton yarn, and 27% of spindles and looms for coarse cotton cloth (on a basis of 79 thousand spindles and 860 looms at March 1925)	Shift of product lines from coarse cotton yarn and cloth to middle count yarn and to fine cotton cloth such as shirtings. Proportion of middle count and high count yarn of total production increased from 19% in 1914 to 52% in 1924.
Defending the market position of its minor export item	Shanghai, October 1921	46 thousand spindles for coarse cotton yarn	Shift of export markets for coarse cotton cloth from China to the other undeveloped areas – from coarse cotton yarn to middle count yarn and to fine cotton cloth. The production of fine cloth (shirtings, jeans, calico) increased from 43 million yards in 1915 to 84 million yards in 1919.
New entry into the local market	Tsingtao, October 1921 Liao Yang, Manchuria, 1923 (a mill to be constructed by Manchuria Cotton Spinning Company)	41 thousand spindles and 168 looms[c] for coarse cotton yarn and cloth	

[b] The proportion of volume of product lines is obtained on a basis of the production facility.

[c] The total of Tsingtao mill and 30% of the production facilities of Manchuria Cotton Spinning Company.

Source: Yokohama Shi (ed., 'Yokohama Shi Shi' (History of Yokohama City), *Shiryo Hen* (Book of Statistical Data), vol. 2, 1962.

Export volume of Toyo Cotton Spinning Company is estimated on a basis of value amount.

Wada mobilised Fuji Gasu's managerial resources for acquiring local mills in China because of his own understanding of what was best for national interests.

NOTES

1 Tetsuya Kuwahara, 'The business strategy of Japanese cotton spinners: overseas operations 1890–1931' in Akio Okochi and Shin-ichi Yonekawa (eds.), *Textile industry and its business climate: Proceedings of the Fuji Conference*, (Tokyo, January 1982), in English.

2 The investment amount of Japanese-owned cotton spinning and weaving industry in China was 300 million yen whose proportion to total Japanese investments into China except for Manchuria was 36 per cent in 1936. Naosuke Takamura, *Kindai Nihon Mengyo to Chugoku (The modern Japanese cotton industry and China)* (Tokyo, 1982), p. i.

3 For more details refer to the following paper: Tetsuya Kuwahara, 'Zaika Bosekogyo no Seisei: Dainippon Boseki Kaisha no Jirei o chushin to shite' ('Formation of Japanese owned cotton spinning firms in China: case of Dainippon Cotton Spinning Company) *Keizai Keiei Ronso (Review of Economics and Business Administration)*, 16: 3, Kyoto Sangyo University, 1981.

4 Tetsuya Kuwahara, 'Senzen ni okeru Nihon Boseki Kigyo no Kaigai Katsudo: Kanegafuchi Boseki Kaisha no Jirei' (Overseas operations of Japanese cotton spinners in the pre-Second World War period: case of Kanegafuchi Cotton Spinning Company), *Roddokai Ronshu (Rokkodai Review)*, 22: 1 (Kobe University Graduate School, April 1975). Also see Tetsuya Kuwahara, 'Zajka Bosekigyo no Seisei: Kanegafuchi boseki Kaisha no Jirei' ('Japanese cotton spinners' direct investments into China: case of Kanegafuchi Cotton Spinning Company'), unpublished.

5 Tetsuya Kuwahara, 'Senzen ni okeru Nihon Bosekikigyo no Kaigai Sijo Senryaku: Toyo Boseki Kaisha no Jirei' ('Overseas market strategies of Japanese cotton spinners in the pre-Second World War period: case of Toyo Cotton Spinning Company'), *Keizai Keiei Ronso*, 17: 3, (Kyoto Sangyo University, December 1982). *Toyo Boseki Kaisha (Toyo Cotton Spinning Company)*. *Toyo Boseki Hyaku Nen Shi (One Hundred Years of Toyo Cotton Spinning Company)*, (Osaka, 1986), vol. 1, pp. 216–227.

6 The numerous values in this paragraph are from the following sources. N. Takamura, *Kindai Nihon Mengyo to Chugoku (Modern Japanese cotton industry and China)* (Tokyo, 1982), p. 127. Yokohama Shi (ed.), *Yokohama Shi Shi (History of Yokohama City)*, *Book of Statistical Data*, vol. 2 (Yokohama City, 1962), p. 174. Statistics of the Chinese Maritime Customs quoted in M. Yasuhara, *Shina no Kogyo to Genryo (Manufacturing industries and raw materials in China)* (*Shanghai*, 1919), vol. 1, 19, chapter 4, section 1, and Ki-ichi Nishikawa, *Menkogyo to Menshi Menpu (Cotton industry and cotton yarns and cloth)* (Shanghai, 1924), pp. 259–61.

7 Tetsuya Kuwahara, 'Zaika Bosekigyo no Seisei n: Kansuru Seihin Sijo Kozotek Kigyosha Seinoteki Bunseki: Fuji Gasu. Boseki Kaisha c Toyoj Wada' ('Japanese cotton spinners' direct investment into China Before the Second World War: Fuji Gasu Cotton Spinning Company and Toyoji Wada'), *Kyoto Sangyo Daigaku Ronshu, International relations series*, no. 12, (Kyoto Sangyo University, March 1985).

8 The processes of Japanese cotton spinners' direct investments into China are summarised in table 14.3.

15 Mitsui Bussan during the 1920s

HIROAKI YAMAZAKI

Introduction

The decade of the 1920s was an era of great difficulties for trading companies in Japan. A number of large trading firms became insolvent: Mogi Shōten, Furukawa Shōji and Kuhara Shōji during the crisis of 1920; Takada Shōkai in 1925; and Suzuki Shōten during the financial panic of 1927 were representatives. Moreover, even those trading firms which barely escaped bankruptcy often suffered severely from widely fluctuating incomes which accompanied losses in the worst situation or from stagnating at low income levels as shown for the firms excluding Mitsui Bussan in table 15.1. However, in what was a period of hardships for most trading firms, Mitsui Bussan performed exceptionally well, continuously attaining high profit rates. Its profit rate, as shown in table 15.1, remained almost constant at around 15%, and stood out in sharp contrast to the movement and the level of other traders' profit rates. The purpose of this chapter is to look into the factors behind the superb managerial performance of Mitsui Bussan during the 1920s.

The characteristic features of Mitsui Bussan's commodity transactions

1. The close relationship between its commodity transactions and key industries

Mitsui Bussan was not a mere trading company but also was active in sideline businesses such as marine transportation, shipbuilding, agencies for ocean transport and insurance, and was rapidly taking on the characteristics of a holding company at this time. Nevertheless, commodity transactions continued to account for a predominant share of its profits as shown in table 15.2.

At this point, the statistics for gross earnings from commodities during the period from 1922 to 1929 enable us to identify the particular commodities

Table 15.1. *The ratio of profit to paid-up capital for major trading firms*

Unit: %

Year and biannual term	Mitsui Bussan	Mitsubishi Shōji	Nichimen	Itō-Man	Tazuki	Iwai Shōten	Ataka Shōkai
1924, I	14.0	17.6	22.3	26.9	5.3	10.5	3.1
II	14.4	9.0	27.0	52.5		6.2	18.6
1925, I	16.1	1.8	25.5	3.4	0.8	3.7	1.1
II	16.3	10.9	25.9	20.4		2.9	10.2
1926, I	17.6	11.9	16.8	11.2	4.1	3.4	5.3
II	16.0	4.5	2.0	22.3		1.5	6.3
1927, I	15.2	8.6	17.1	26.0	5.8	4.2	9.7
II	16.0	15.9	16.9	25.6		4.3	3.1
1928, I	18.0	16.2	16.2	15.0	10.5	3.7	6.5
II	17.3	22.7	11.6	17.5		6.6	5.8
1929, I	17.6	3.2	13.6	10.6	1.7	2.5	0.8
II	17.5	2.0	297.7	8.5		0.3	7.7

Sources: Matsui Kiyoshi (ed), *Kindai Nihon Bōeki-shi* (*History of modern Japanese trade*) 1963, vol. 3, pp. 258–9; and appended statistics in *Iwai Hyakunen-shi* (*One hundred years of Iwai & Co.*), (Tokyo, Osaka, 1964), and *Ataka Sangyo 60-nen-shi* (*Sixty years of Ataka & Co.*) (Osaka, 1968).

that contributed to its lucrative transactions. Our calculations show that five commodities were of special importance. These were, in order of percentages shared by each commodity in total gross profits, coal (20.6), machinery (16.1), raw silk (9.6), sugar (6.6) and metals (6.0). They outdistance timber (4.3) by a considerable margin. Together they accounted for 58.9% of the company's commodity transactions.[1]

In addition to these five items, Toyō Menka, which was established in 1920 as a wholly-owned subsidiary of Mitsui Bussan, dealt in cotton products such as raw cotton, cotton yarn and cotton cloth, and its gross earnings exceeded those earned by Mitsui Bussan's metals and sugar trades.[2]

On the other hand, table 15.3 shows the key Japanese industries in terms of production value or revenue in 1926. An examination of the correspondence between the above-mentioned six main commodities which Mitsui Bussan dealt in directly or indirectly and these key industries shows us the following picture.

Coal corresponds to coal mining, raw silk corresponds to silk reeling, sugar corresponds to sugar manufacturing and cotton corresponds to cotton spinning and weaving. Metals which the company handled consisted of iron and steel as well as non-ferrous metals. The former involved the products manufactured by both the government-operated Steel Mill and private companies. Therefore metals correspond to iron and steel produced by the

Table 15.2. *The breakdown of Mitsui Bussan's earnings by origin*

Units: 1,000 yen & %[1]

Year and biannual term[2]		Earnings						Costs	Current net profit
		Commodities trade	Ship-building	Trans-portation	Agential business	Miscella-neous accounts	Total earnings		
1919,	I	15,922 (64.4)	—	4,265 (17.3)	971 (3.9)	3,566 (14.4)	24,724 (100.0)	15,071	9,653
	II	24,488 (87.3)	—	1,033 (3.7)	1,108 (4.0)	1,421 (5.1)	28,050 (100.0)	17,839	10,211
1920,	I	20,829 (68.4)	—	1,252 (4.1)	1,185 (3.9)	7,206 (23.6)	30,472 (100.0)	19,149	11,323
	II	5,409 (29.2)	—	2,850 (15.4)	735 (4.0)	9,520 (51.4)	18,514 (100.0)	13,442	5,072
1921,	I	9,510 (51.3)	—	826 (4.5)	701 (3.8)	7,507 (40.5)	18,544 (100.0)	14,462	4,080
	II	10,273 (76.0)	484 (3.6)	550 (4.1)	694 (5.1)	1,522 (11.3)	13,523 (100.0)	10,885	2,638
1922,	I	12,545 (74.7)	403 (2.4)	712 (4.2)	708 (4.2)	2,430 (14.5)	16,798 (100.0)	11,723	5,075
	II	14,630 (83.5)	123 (0.7)	403 (2.3)	453 (2.6)	1,912 (10.9)	17,521 (100.0)	11,475	6,046
1923,	I	16,934 (94.5)	37 (0.2)	339 (1.9)	535 (3.0)	75 (0.4)	17,918 (100.0)	11,765	6,153
	II	14,651 (96.6)	379 (2.5)	489 (3.2)	418 (2.8)	776 (5.1)	15,161 (100.0)	11,150	4,011
1924,	I	14,611 (75.9)	479 (2.5)	796 (4.1)	640 (3.3)	2,713 (14.1)	19,239 (100.0)	12,262	6,977
	II	14,189 (72.4)	260 (1.3)	868 (4.4)	564 (2.9)	3,716 (19.0)	19,597 (100.0)	12,397	7,200
1925,	I	14,239 (71.9)	205 (1.0)	677 (3.4)	610 (3.1)	4,078 (20.6)	19,809 (100.0)	11,755	8,052
	II	14,611 (69.5)	233 (1.1)	617 (2.9)	590 (2.8)	4,984 (23.7)	21,035 (100.0)	12,861	8,174
1926,	I	14,739 (73.3)	385 (1.9)	789 (3.9)	602 (3.0)	3,605 (17.9)	20,120 (100.0)	11,330	8,790
	II	13,525 (57,4)	318 (1.3)	531 (2.3)	528 (2.2)	8,663 (36.8)	23,565 (100.0)	15,589	7,976
1927,	I	13,258 (66.1)	281 (1.4)	373 (1.9)	594 (3.0)	5,545 (27.7)	20,051 (100.0)	12,469	7,582
	II	13,764 (71.7)	275 (1.4)	770 (4.0)	563 (2.9)	3,816 (19.9)	19,188 (100.0)	11,197	7,991
1928,	I	15,282 (71.8)	302 (1.4)	789 (3.7)	622 (2.9)	4,277 (20.1)	21,272 (100.0)	12,291	8,981
	II	14,615 (72.9)	315 (1.6)	730 (3.6)	557 (2.8)	3,828 (19.1)	20,045 (100.0)	11,374	8,671
1929,	I	14,455 (67.7)	315 (1.5)	747 (3.5)	649 (3.0)	5,196 (24.3)	21,362 (100.0)	12,565	8,797
	II	13,200	338	848	595	4,899	19,880	11,119	8,761

Notes: [1] The percentage in parenthesis is relative to total earnings. [2] The first and second half-yearly accounting terms of the company end on the last days of April and October, respectively.

Source: Computed on the basis of various issues of Mitsui Bussan, *Jigyo Hokoku-sho* (Report on business).

Table 15.3. *An overview of Japanese industrial structure in 1926* (*Production value or sales revenue of each industry*)

Industry	Output (¥000)		
	Over 500,000	300,000–500,000	100,000–300,000
I Mining			Coal (223,120) Non-ferrous metals (100, 648)
II Light manufacturing	Raw silk (793,219)		Broad silk fabrics (120,349) Narrow silk fabrics (126,146)
	Cotton yarns (660,822)	Broad cotton fabrics (482,123) Sake (313,420)	Narrow cotton fabrics (107,837) Wool fabrics (172,756) Lumber (120,802) Printing (158,052) Paper (179,630) Sugar (199,252) Flour milling (134,895)
III Heavy/chemical manufacturing			Steel products (112,407)
	Electrical power (566,859)		Government-operated Steel Mill (185,261) Military ordnance (190,884)
IV Transportation	Railroads (683,182)	Marine transportation (279,280)	

Source: The Ministry of International Trade and Industry, Kogyo Tokei 50 Nenshi; Shiryo Hen 2 (50 Years History of the Census of Manufacture; a volume of materials 2) 1962, Shinohara Miyohei, Chōki Keizai Tōkei 10; Kōkōgyo (Long-term Economic Statistics 10; Mining and Manufacturing), 1972, Minami Ryoshin, Chōki Keizai Tōkei 12 Tetsudō to Denryoku (Long-term Economic Statistics 12 Railroad and Electric Power Industry), 1966, Zenkoku Keizai Chōsa Kikan Rengōkai (The National Federation of Organizations for Economic Research ed., Nihon Keizai no Saikin Jyūnen (Recent Ten Years of Japanese Economy), 1930.

government-operated Steel Mill and by private companies, and to non-ferrous metals. Machinery which the company handled consisted mainly of electric machinery, cotton-spinning and weaving machinery and the manu-factured goods for railroads such as rail and rollingstock. So machinery

Table 15.4. *Mitsui Bussan's branch network in 1926*

	Headquarters	Branches	Sub-branches
Japan	Tokyo	Otaru	
		Yokohama	
		Nagoya	
		Kobe	
		Osaka	
		Moji	
			Wakamatsu
		Nagasaki	
		Miike	
Formosa		Taipei	
		Tainan	
Korea		Seoul	
China (Northeast)		Dairen	
			Newchawang
			Mukden
			Harbin
China (Mainland)		Tientsin	
			Chefoo
		Tsingtao	
		Shanghai	
		Hankou	
			Amoy
		Hong Kong	
			Kuantung
Asia		Bangkok	
			Rangoon
		Singapore	
		Surabaja	
		Manila	
		Bombay	
		Calcutta	
Oceania		Sydney	
Europe		London	
		(Germany)	
		(France)	
USA		New York	San Francisco
			Seattle

Note: In Germany and France, German Mitsui Bussan and French Mitsui Bussan were established as its local subsidiaries.

Table 15.5. *Major trading firms' capital composition, as of the second half-yearly term, 1925*

Unit: 1,000 yen

Company	Equity capital	Loans payable	Major liabilities Advance borrowing on exports	Notes payable	B.E. accepted	Total liabilities
Mitsui Bussan	141,635	30,051	—	97,538	—	127,589
Suzuki Shōten	65,930	18,898	9,591	37,976	31,817	98,282
Nihon Menka	49,684	—	—	85,768		85,768
Mitsubishi Shōji	19,614	10,671	—	40,857	—	51,528
Ohkura Shōji	11,809	—	—	—	2,211	2,211
Iwai Shōten	8,891	—	—	14,132	—	14,132
Itō Chū Shōji	8,137	4,185	—	—	3,420	7,605
Itō Man Shōten	7,842	1,483	—	—	—	1,483

Note: Mitsui Bussan's reserve fund is the net sum of reserves for the maintenance of ships and for insurance.
Source: Tokyo Koshinjo, *Ginko Kaisha Yoroku* (*Directory of banks and companies*), 30th edn (Tokyo, 1926).

corresponds to electric power industry, cotton-spinning and weaving industry and railroad industry. Moreover the shipping department, which was a sideline business for this company, corresponds to marine transportation.

In sum, Mitsui Bussan handled mainly the commodities which corresponded closely to the key Japanese industries during the 1920s and could take advantage of the economy of scale. Of course other trading companies also handled some of these commodities but only Mitsui Bussan diversified into almost all commodities which corresponded closely to the key industries of this period.

2. *An abundance of talented employees and capital resources*

Mitsui Bussan had a worldwide branch network as shown in table 15.4. But this was not a characteristic peculiar to Mitsui Bussan. Its strongest competitors, for example Suzuki Shōten and Mitsubishi Shōji, also had networks of a similar scale.

But in terms of its abundance of talented employees and capital resources, Mitsui Bussan far surpassed its competitors. According to the valuable survey by Professor Yonekawa Shinichi, it is clear that Mitsui Bussan had 731 university graduates in 1914, far more than its competitors, of which Takada Shōkai had 151, Okuragumi had 85 and Suzuki Shōten had only

72.[3] In terms of capital resources, table 15.5 shows that Mitsui Bussan's equity capital far surpassed that of its competitors and it was larger than its total liabilities, while in most other cases except those of Itō Chū and Itō Man, whose capital scale was very small, equity capital was smaller than total liabilities.

In short, a large number of talented and well-trained employees enabled Mitsui Bussan to utilise effectively a large amount of information collected through its world-wide branch network and its abundant financial resources assisted its operations in many commodity markets. Therefore in so far as Mitsui Bussan's headquarters could control the operations of all its departments and branches, its possibility of success in market operations was very high.

3. *The characteristic strategy in five staple commodities transactions*

In addition to the above-mentioned advantages which Mitsui Bussan enjoyed, it adopted a characteristic strategy in every one of the five staple commodities, a strategy that increasingly strengthened its advantageous position.

The monopolistic transactions with the manufacturing companies which belonged to Mitsui Zaibatsu

In all of these five staple commodities there were the manufacturing companies which belonged to Mitsui Zaibatsu and occupied an advantageous position in each field. Mitsui Bussan had the sole rights both to sell the products manufactured by these companies and to buy the raw materials which they required. The correspondence of the commodities to the companies are as follows. The figures in parenthesis show the ranking of the production volume and the market share in terms of production volume or sales volume at around the mid-1920s.

Coal – Mitsui Kōzan (1, 15.2%), Hokkaidō Tankō Kisen (3, 9.5%), Matsushima Tankō(1.0%), Taiheiyō Tankō (0.9%), Kiirun Tankō (No. 1 in Formosa).[4]
Raw silk – Gunze Seishi (2, 4.1%)[5]
Machinery, electric machinery – Shibaura Seisakusho (1); cotton spinning and weaving machinery – Toyoda Shokki Seisakucho (1)[6]
Metals – Kamaishi Kōzan (pig iron; 7, 20%: steel bar; 3, 9.4%), Wanishi Seitetsusho (pig iron; 3, 16.7%)[7]
Sugar – Taiwan Seitō (refined sugar 3, 14.9%; raw sugar produced in Formosa 1, 26.9%; raw sugar from Java 1, 35.2%)[8]

Table 15.6. *Mitsui Bussan's machinery sales for companies with agential arrangements, 1924–5*

Units: 1,000 yen & %

Company with agential arrangements	Values of machines sold	% of total	Major items sold
International General Electric Co., Inc.	22,616	14.8	Electric machinery
Burmeister & Wain Ltd	13,463	8.8	Diesel engines
Platt & Brothers & Co., Ltd	4,773	3.1	Cotton and wool weaving and spinning machines; Looms
General Motor Export Co.	4,553	3.0	Automobiles
Mother & Platt Ltd	2,258	1.5	Sprinklers; Spinning, weaving and finishing machines
Sykes Brothers T.	1,994	1.3	Textile machine parts
R. Hae & Co.	1,413	0.9	Printing machines
Sullivan Machinery Co.	974	0.6	Mining equipment
Shibaura Seisakusho	7,623	5.0	Electric machinery
Nakajima Hikoki	6,607	4.3	Aircraft; Motors
Toyodashiki Shokki	3,326	2.2	Spinning, weaving and finishing machines
Dainippon Mokkan	2,568	1.7	
Yuasa Chikudenchi	2,556	1.7	
Tokyo Keiki Seisakusho	1,604	1.1	Search lights; Gyro-compasses
Sumitomo Seikohsho	1,162	0.8	
Fujikura Densen	912	0.6	
Other manufacturers with agential arrangements	14,973	9.8	
Sub-total of machines sold through agential arrangements	93,375	61.2	
Sub-total of sales of other machines	59,145	38.3	
Total machinery sales	152,520	100.0	

Source: Mitsui Bussan, *Dai 9-kai Shitenchō Kaigi Kikai-bu Ippan Hōkoku-sho* (General report submitted by the Machinery Department to the ninth branch managers' meeting), 1926.

Generally speaking, Mitsui Bussan could secure an advantageous position in each market by obtaining the sole rights to deal with these companies, which themselves occupied dominant positions in the market.

The exclusive agency for leading foreign manufacturers

Mitsui Bussan also was an exclusive agent for leading foreign manufacturers. In the case of machinery, approximately 60% of the machines the company sold in the period from 1919 to 1926 were imported from abroad. Also as shown in table 15.6, it is clear that more than 60% of the machinery the company handled in 1924–5 was sold through agential arrangements. Sales for foreign manufacturers, whose share amounted to 34.0% were far larger than those for domestic manufacturers, whose share amounted to 16.4%, as far as the companies whose names were listed on the table were concerned.[9] It seems safe to conclude that the company dealt in machinery imported from leading manufacturers for whom it acted as the exclusive Japanese distributor.

In the case of coal, Mitsui Bussan had the sole agency for Hongay coal in Vietnam and Fushun coal in Northeast China for export.[10]

Money lending to domestic leading manufacturers

Moreover, Mitsui Bussan often lent money to domestic leading manufacturers to procure higher quality goods, or to obtain the sole agency for their products. In the case of raw silk, the company lent a large amount of money to the leading silk reelers or silk merchants to acquire the higher quality goods every year.[11] Also, in the case of coal, the company lent money to some coal producers and in 1926, 15.1% of the coal with which the company was dealing was from mines for which the company was acting as sole distributor through loan arrangements.[12] In the case of iron and steel, Mitsui Bussan had given financial support to Kamaishi Kōzan which had fallen into difficulties after the 1920 crisis. In the long run Mitsui Kōzan which belonged to Mitsui Zaibatsu together with Mitsui Bussan came to hold the controlling power over this company and Mitsui Bussan held the exclusive agency for its products.

The advantageous position in each market

The above-mentioned factors enabled Mitsui Bussan to occupy an advantageous position in each commodity transaction.

1 *Coal.* Table 15.7 shows that Mitsui Bussan accounted for 33.2% of all coal transactions handled inside Japanese territory at that time. This figure was by far the largest and even surpassed the combined shares of the five other largest coal dealers. In addition to this the company succeeded in controlling the import of coal from Northeast China through becoming

Table 15.7 *Coal output and major trading firms' shares, 1925*

Unit: 1,000 ton

Trading firm	Total output	Share (%)	Coal output in Kyushu	Coal output in Honshu	Coal output in Hokkaido	Coal output in the outer territories*
Mitsui	10,282	33.2	5,341	341	3,348	1,252
Mitsubishi	4,753	15.4	3,588	—	1,135	30
Kaijima	1,725	5.6	1,725	—	—	—
Yasukawa	1,336	4.3	1,280	—	—	56
Furukawa	977	3.2	918	59	—	—
Yamashita	476	1.5	124	83	269	—
Teitan	1,222	4.0	958	150	—	114
Asoh	649	2.1	649	—	—	—
Sumitomo	442	1.4	429	—	13	—
Asano	1,096	3.5	—	1,096	—	—
Others	6,513	21.1	2,657	2,442	549	865
Sub-total	29,471	95.3	17,669	4,171	5,314	2,317
Steel works & Navy	1,455	4.7	1,360	—	—	95
Total	30,926	100.0	19,029	4,171	5,314	2,412

*The 'outer territories' here include Taiwan, Yaeyama, Korea and Sakhalin.
Source: Coal Department, Mitsui Bussan, *Shitencho Kaigi Sekitan-bu Hokoku-sho* (Report of the Coal Department to the branch managers' meeting), 1926, Table 12.

one of the major shareholders of Bujuntan Hanbai Gaisha (Fushun Coal Distributing Company) which was the sole agent for the Fushun coal mine. Furthermore the company occupied the dominant position in major Asian coal markets as shown in Table 15.8.

2. *Raw silk.* Misui Bussan was the leading exporter of Japanese raw silk, with a 22.9% share. A considerable gap separated it from Asahi Silk, which ranked second with 15.5%; Nihon Kiito (Japan Raw Silk) of the Mitsubishi group ranked third with 14.6%.[13] Moreover, the company ranked third among the handlers of raw silk exports from Shanghai following Madier Ribet and Jardine Matheson; it ranked fourth among traders of raw silk exports from Kuantung, following Madier Ribet, Paskille, and Griffith, and among exporters of silk fabrics from Japan, it enjoyed the top place with a 6.0% share.[14]

3. *Machinery.* Although statistics are not complete enough to provide an accurate picture of the relative strength of Mitsui Bussan's machinery transaction in Japan, the following two sets of data give us a general idea. First, in 1921, Mitsui Bussan accounted for an extremely large 43.7% of

Table 15.8. *Mitsui Bussan's share of the Japanese and major Asian coal markets, 1925*

Market	Total amount sold* (ton)	Amount sold by Mitsui Bussan (ton)	Ranking	Share (%)	Shares held by major competitors (%)
Japan	30,926,000	10,282,000	First	33.2	Mitsubishi, 15.4; Kaijima, 5.6; Yasukawa, 4.3; Teitan, 4.0; Asano, 3.5; Furukawa, 3.2; Asoh, 2.1; Yamashita, 1.5; Sumitomo, 1.4
Shanghai		967,116	First	32.4	Kairan (K'ai-luan), 19.1; Mitsubishi, 8.9; Kiyohara, 8.2
Hong Kong & Kuangtung		500,340	First	38.1	Mitsubishi, 10.9; Kairan (K'ai-luan), 7.7; Yamashita, 6.5
Manila		171,403	Second	34.6	Madrigal, 60.7
Singapore		132,352	First	20.4	McAlister & Co., 10.4; Bousted & Co., 7.9; A. Gifillian, 4.6; P.S., 3.8

Note: * The 'total amount sold' in the case of Japan is inclusive of the amounts of coal sold in Korea and Taiwan, while in the case of other markets, this stands for the amount of coal imported into the market concerned.
Source: Coal Department, Mitsui Bussan, *Shitencho Kaigi Sekitan-bu Hokoku*, 1924, pp. 43–5, Table 12.

the total value of imported machinery.[15] The second set of data compares Mitsui Bussan's machinery transaction with those of its leading competitors. In 1925, Suzuki Shōten's Machine and Iron Department was doing an annual business of between 60–70 million yen and Mitsubishi Shōji sold approximately 20 million yen worth of machinery, against Mitsui Bussan's 68 million yen.[16] But assuming that machines accounted for approximately half of Suzuki's sales, this means that the volume of Mitsui Bussan's machinery transaction was approximately twice as large as that of Suzuki and more than three times that of Mitsubishi Shōji.

4. *Metals.* Mitsui Bussan's metal business was roughly classified into two areas: iron and steel, and non-ferrous metals. The iron and steel business

Table 15.9. *Amounts of Javanese sugar purchased by major trading firms*

Trading firm	1920 (long ton)	1922 (long ton)	1924 (1,000 Javanese ton)	1927 (1,000 Javanese ton)	1930 (1,000 Javanese ton)
Mitsui Bussan	153,100	86,800	3,659	4,046	1,039
Suzuki Shohten	117,000	187,800	2,855	4,195	—
Mitsubishi Shoji	—	43,400	1,696	3,701	1,998
Arima Yokoh	26,000	14,500	1,057	1,398	138
Senda Shohkai	1,000	34,500	305	—	5
Nihon Satoh Boeki	—	51,300	568	929	—
Yuasa	17,500	10,000	—	—	—
Masuda	66,000	—	—	—	—
Nichi-ran Boeki	—	—	247	—	—
Java Boeki	—	—	—	329	—
Nangoku Sangyo	—	—	—	—	49
Total incl. others	395,600	446,300	10,387	14,599	3,228

Sources: The figures for 1920 and 1922 are taken from *Gendai Nihon Sangyo Hattatsu-sui, Shokuhin* (*Contemporary history of Japanese industrial development: the food processing industry*) (Tokyo, 1967), p. 154, and those for 1924, 1927 and 1929 are taken from Kohno Shinji, *Nihon Tohgyo Hattatsu-shi, Shohi-hen* (*History of Japanese sugar processing industry: consumption*) (Tokyo, 1931), p. 248.

was threefold, and included: (1) sales of products produced by the government-operated Steel Mill as its designated agent; (2) exclusive marketing of pig iron produced by the Kamaishi Kōzan and the Wanishi Steel Mill, and of steel products manufactured by the Kamaishi Kōzan; (3) marketing of iron and steel imported from abroad or manufactured by other iron and steel mills in Japan. As far as the products of the government-operated Steel Mill were concerned, Mitsui Bussan accounted for 33% of its sales and secured the top position after Suzuki Shōten failed.[17] In the case of bar steel, which was one of the most important steel products at that time, the Kamaishi Kōzan accounted for 16.7% of its sales, excluding bar steel sales of the government operated Steel Mill, and ranked second next to Nippon Kōkan (Japan Steel Tubes).[18] The company's non-ferrous metal business was two-fold: (1) the exclusive marketing of lead and zinc from the Mitsui Kōzan (Mining); (2) the dealings in copper, lead, zinc and tin imported from abroad or manufactured domestically. According to the statement of the director of the Metal Department at the 1931 branch managers' meeting, aside from copper, Mitsui Bussan held 'in most of the non-ferrous metal trades, a quite superior position' relative to the competitors.[19]

5. *Sugar*. Mitsui Bussan's sugar business consisted of two kinds of transactions: (1) the purchase of Java sugar for importation into Japan; (2) the exclusive sales of the products of the Taiwan Seitō (Formosa Sugar Refining). Of these, as is evident from Table 15.9 with respect to the purchase of Java sugar, it engaged in a tough competition for leadership with Suzuki Shōten and Mitsubishi Shōji. Between 1922 and 1931, Taiwan Seitō consistently dominated the market for raw sugar manufactured in Formosa, maintaining a share that fluctuated between 23% and 31%. In the domestic refined sugar market, its share fluctuated between 15% and 23%, and followed those of the Dai Nippon Seitō (Great Japan Sugar Refining) and of the Meiji Seitō (Meiji Sugar Refining).[20] When we combine its trades in Java sugar, Formosa sugar and domestic refined sugar, we can imagine that Mitsui Bussan stood side by side with Mitsubishi Shōji as the leading sugar trader in Japan.

Conclusion

Mitsui Bussan's commodity transactions during the 1920s were characterised by its transactions mainly in staple commodities which corresponded closely to key industries, and its ability to hold the dominant share in each of the commodity markets. Strong ties through sole agency contracts with the leading manufacturing companies both in Japan and abroad contributed largely to this share. As a result of the combined effect of these characteristics, the company enjoyed an economy of scale to the maximum degree and maintained a position of strength over its competitors. Moreover, its large number of talented employees and abundance of capital resources which it had accumulated by that time, along with its above-mentioned dominant share in each commodity market, heightened its possibilities for success in its operations in each market. The stable and high level profits of Mitsui Bussan came as the result of the interaction of these factors.

NOTES

1 Computed on the basis of table 2 which is attached to his paper, in Kasuga Yutaka, 'Nendai ni okeru Mitsui Bussan Kaisha no Tenkai Katei Jō' ('The development of Mitsui Bussan in the 1930s', volume 1), *Mitsui Bunko Ronsō* (*The Journal of Mitsui Library*), 16 (1982), pp. 190–3.

2 Toyō Menka's gross earnings from commodity transactions amounted to a total of 4,791,000 yen for the two years from 1928 to 1929. In contrast to this, Mitsui Bussan's gross earnings from commodities for the same period were as follows: (in thousands of yen): coal (12,149), machinery (8.082), raw silk (5,326), metal (3,930) and sugar (2,882) (computed on the basis of Toyō Menka's Eigyō Hōkokusho (Annual Reports) and the above-mentioned attached table 2, listed in Kasuga's paper).

3 Yonekawa Shinichi, 'University graduates in Japanese enterprises before the Second World War', *Business History,* 25: 2, (1984), *pp.* 196, 197.
4 Computed on the basis of Kōzan Konwa-kai (ed). *Nihon Kōgvō hattatsushi* (*History of the development of the Japanese mining industry*), vol. 2 (Tokyo, 1932), pp. 174 and p. 174 and pp. 230–3.
5 The Ministry of Agriculture and Forestry, *Zenkoku seishikōzyō chōsahyō Dai jyū ji* (*An investigation of silk-reeling mills in Japan*, vol. 10) (Tokyo, 1926).
6 There are no materials to show the market shares of each company in the machine industry. The estimated ranking is based on the numbers of employees of each factory.
7 Hashimoto Jvurō and Takeda Haruto (eds.), *Ryō taisenkaki Nihon no karuteru* (*Japanese cartels during the inter-war period*) (Tokyo, 1985), pp. 41, 98. Kamaishi's ranking and market share of steel bars are based on the figures which include the production from the government-operated Steel Mill. If we exclude this figure, Kamaishi's ranking and its share rise to second and 16.7%.
8 Nakajima Tsuneo, *Gendai Nihon Sangyō hattatsu shi, shokuhin-hen* (*History of contemporary Japanese industrial development; the food processing industry*) (Tokyo, 1967), p. 170. Kōno Shinji, *Nihon tōgyō hattatsu shi, syōhi-hen* (*history of Japanese sugar processing industry: consumption*) (Tokyo, 1931), p. 248.
9 Computed on the basis of various issues of Mitsui Bussan, *Jigyō hōkoku-syo* (Business reports).
10 Mitsui Bussan, *Dai 9-kai Shitenchō kaigi gijiroku, Taisyō 15-nen* (Proceedings of the ninth branch managers' meeting, 1926), p. 95.
11 Mitsui Bussan, *Torishimariyaku kaigi gijiroku* (Minutes of the meetings of the board of directors), Proposition No. 1121.
12 *Gijiroku*, 9th meeting, 1926, p. 95.
13 Mitsui Bussan, Director of the Raw Silk Department in Yokohama, *Kiito-bu gaiyōhōkoku* (*The summary report of the Raw Silk Department*), submitted to the branch managers' meeting in 1926.
14 *Ibid.*
15 Mitsui Bussan, *Dai 9-kai Shitenchō kaigi Kikai-bu Ippan Hōkoku-sho* (General report of the Machinery Department to the ninth branch managers' meeting), 1926, table 2.
16 *Ibid.*, p. 11. Mitsubishi Shōji, *Ritsugyō bōeki roku* (*A History of Mitsubishi Shōji*) (Tokyo, 1958), p. 185.
17 Ataka Sangyō, Inc., *Ataka Sangyō 60 nenshi* (*Sixty years history of Ataka Sangyō*) (Osaka, 1963), p. 167.
18 See note 7.
19 *Gijiroku*, 8th meeting, 1921, p. 105.
20 Nakajima, p. 170.

16 Japanese business in the United States before the Second World War: the case of Mitsui and Mitsubishi

NOBUO KAWABE

Introduction

General trading companies (*sogo shosha*) have begun to attract the interest of scholars because of their unique role and importance in the Japanese economy. The general trading company is a very unique economic institution. It is called a general trading company, not simply a trading company. There are various kinds of definitions of the general trading company. One example is that of Yoshio Togai who defines the general trading company as an economic institution that has the following characteristics:[1]

1. Having a wide variety of product lines.
2. Having a lot of domestic and overseas branches as well as engaging in domestic trade, export, import, and trade between countries other than Japan.
3. Having a large transaction volume.
4. Having to play the role of organiser of industry, on the one hand, by supplying machinery, technology, and materials, and on the other hand, by developing markets for its final products.
5. Having the nature of holding companies which have a lot of subsidiary and affiliated companies.

There are no comparable economic institutions in the Western world. By the time of the Second World War some of the trading companies had already assumed the characteristics of general trading companies.

Recently, several scholars have studied general trading companies, stressing the importance of the overseas activities of these companies. But, in spite of the critical importance of general trading companies, no systematic study has been done relating to the activities and roles of their foreign branches. There are several questions related to the activities of overseas branches of general trading companies: (1) What general forms do these overseas operations adopt? (2) Why, how, when, and what specific forms do these overseas operations adopt, that is, establishing branch offices, overseas affiliated firms or subsidiaries? (3) How are the opening of overseas branch offices and establishment of local affiliated firms related to the growth strategies of general trading companies such as diversification of business and merchandise handling? (4) What are the functions and activities of overseas operational arms of these trading companies? (5) How are these overseas operational arms related to the corporate headquarters and how are they managed and controlled? (6) What problems do these overseas operations arms face and how are they countered?

The objective of this chapter is to answer these and related questions. In doing so, we will base our analysis on actual data obtained from mainly the cases of Mitsui and Mitsubishi trading companies' branches on the West Coast of the United States before the Second World War.

Japanese business in the United States before the Second World War[2]

This chapter is about the activities and development of the San Francisco and Seattle Branches of Mitsui Bussan Kaisha and Mitsubishi Shoji Kaisha. However, to facilitate our understanding of these firms, we will examine the general background of general trading companies so that we may grasp more clearly the nature and characteristics of these branches. We will view direct investments as a whole. We will study what types of companies had direct investments in the United States and what they were doing, in order to know the position of Mitsui and Mitsubishi.

In 1941, just before the Second World War, Japanese direct investments in the United States totalled $35.1 million. More than half of the investments were in the finance sector; the second largest investments were in the distribution sector. Some investments were in the shipping sector. The types of investments of Japanese companies were simple. They arose in connection with the establishment of foreign branches to market the products of Japanese companies and in turn to buy American raw materials and products for Japanese companies. The trading companies were the main factors of this business. Other companies such as banking, insurance, and shipping supported the operations of the trading companies. However, Japanese manufacturers were not developed sufficiently to compete with their American counterparts in the United States.

Most big Japanese trading companies had branches mainly in New York, California, and Washington, and they did basically four types of transactions: exports to Japan, imports from Japan, trade between countries other than Japan, and domestic trade in the United States. For example, Mitsui, which was the largest trading company before the Second World War, opened its New York Branch in 1878 in order to import Japanese silk. (As Mitsui failed in its silk transactions, it closed its operation. It began exporting silk again, and re-opened its New York Branch in 1896.) The New York Branch imported Japanese cotton products as well as silk to the United States, and exported American machinery, railroad products, and raw cotton to Japan. In turn, it exported American raw cotton to England and machinery to Manchuria, particularly for the Southern Manchurian Railroad.

Mitsubishi, Asano Bussan Kaisha, and Okura Shoji Kaisha had branches in New York, San Francisco, and Los Angeles. These companies were also handling a wide variety of product lines, and doing similar transactions. Before 1927, Suzuki & Company had been playing an important role as *sogo shosha* in the trade between the United States and Japan, having branches in New York, Seattle, Portland, Houston, and Fort Worth.

In addition to these biggest *sogo shosha*, there were many relatively specialised trading companies. Some dealt with silk, cotton, and textiles. Some specialised in the iron and steel business while others handled mainly canned food and miscellaneous goods. Yamanaka Shoten, which had three wholly-owned subsidiaries in Boston, Chicago, and New York, sold oriental art and antiques in the United States.

Yamanaka Shoten was not alone in establishing subsidiaries in the United States. Subsidiaries allowed Japanese firms to enjoy privileges, comparable to those received by American competitors, in the trade of raw cotton. Mitsui established its Southern Products Company in Houston in 1911 (it was moved to Dallas in 1912). Nippon Menk Kaisha established its Japan Cotton Company in Fort Worth in 1910. Gosho Company established its Crowford Gosho Company in San Antonio in 1913, and in 1918 it also established its Gosho Corporation in New York for the silk business.

In sum, Japanese direct investments concentrated on banking, trading, and shipping in New York, California, Texas, Washington, and Hawaii. The main business was the trade between the United States and Japan. Before the Second World War, Japanese direct investments were limited to the branch operations of trade related companies. This type of Japanese investment differed very much from that in China, where many manufacturers invested and general trading companies were also involved in manufacturing.

The operations of Mitsui and Mitsubishi on the West Coast of the United States[3]

1. *The first period (prior to 1918)*

Branches of general trading companies played a very important role in the trade between Japan and the United States. Mitsui and Mitsubishi were leading companies in this period. Mitsui's business activities on the West Coast began with the opening of the San Francisco Representative under the jurisdiction of the headquarters in 1903. They also opened their Portland Representative Office under the jurisdiction of the San Francisco office in 1906. We do not know about the early operations of these offices. By the outbreak of the First World War, the Portland office was handling wheat, wheat flour, pine wood, and pulp. In 1915, the San Francisco office handled sulphur, rice, feed and cereals, matches, oil and fat, bags and cloth, coffee, and other commodities. In 1916, the Seattle office was established in order to handle wheat, pulp, wheat flour, rice and lumber.

In 1914, the San Francisco office opened their Vancouver office to handle wheat and wheat flour, pine trees, salt herring and salmon, and Japanese rice for the Japanese community. However, during the First World War, as they suffered from space shortage and the demands of war, they could not develop transactions and therefore closed the Vancouver office in 1920. In the same year, they opened an office in Havana to handle rice, but they closed this office three years later. The business of these offices was not limited to the transactions of products. They did some subsidiary functions of trade. They not only acted as the agent for the Steamship Department, but they also received commissions from the department. They further attended to the transhipment and other shipping details for the imports and exports through Pacific Coast ports for the account of the New York Branch and sub-departments in the United States.

In 1918, Mitsubishi Goshi Kaisha opened its Seattle office mainly to supply iron and steel to Japan for the construction of cargo vessels for the United States Shipping Board. We know very little of its early history. After the creation of Mitsubishi Shoji Kaisha, Seattle became the representative office of the New York Branch in March 1921. Transactions of wheat, flour, and lumber became an important business following the 1918 armistice. Few transactions were in metals, machinery, and provisions.

2. *The second period* (*1919–31*)

In the early 1920s both Mitsui and Mitsubishi adopted a new strategy which influenced the development of their San Francisco offices. This strategy was closely related to technological changes. It was also the beginning of transactions in oil. In the early part of this century, military and civilian demand for petroleum as a fuel increased rapidly. Japan was not an exception to this trend. Therefore, Japanese businessmen and government planners thought mostly in terms of acquiring fuel oil for ocean steamships.

Mitsui, which had begun its operation of oil business in 1877, tried to go into the competitive oil market by importing foreign oil products. In September 1921, the San Francisco office succeeded in making a contract with the General Petroleum Corporation in California. In September 1922, headquarters set up the Section of Diesel Oil in the Coal Department. Mitsubishi also set up the Fuel Department in 1923, and made a sole agent contract with the Associated Oil Company of California. Both companies chose Californian oil companies as their suppliers because it was less costly to transport oil to Japan and because the transfer from coal to oil as fuel was most advanced in California. Moreover, Mitsubishi established Mitsubishi Sekiyu Kaisha in 1932, as a joint venture with Mitsubishi Goshi Kaisha, Mitsubishi Mining, and Associated. This move was to meet the changing structure of import from final products to materials so as to be competitive with Shell and Socony, and also to get higher profits in refining. Mitsui also tried to create a new refining company with the Standard Vacuum Oil Company. However, since both parties insisted on 51% ownership, this project did not materialise.

The Trade Department of Goshi Kaisha and, later, Mitsubishi Shoji established its basis as *sogo shosha* by diversifying product lines and developing an overseas branch system. During the First World War, the world market was open to Japanese companies. Mitsui opened new offices in the United States, Europe and Asia. It exported Japanese miscellaneous goods through branches in these areas where imports from Europe had stopped. By the time Mitsubishi Shoji was established in 1918, it handled many product lines – coal, metal, machinery, produce, oil and fat, marine products, textiles, chemicals, and miscellaneous goods in Europe, the United States, and Asia. Mitsui, which started its operations earlier, led this diversification while simultaneously increasing the number of its branch offices.

This uncontrolled rapid development caused problems in the recession after the First World War. For example, the value of products handled by Mitsui in San Francisco decreased from 20 million yen in 1919 to 10 million yen in the 1920s. (It did not again reach 20 million yen until 1934.) It became necessary for both companies to attain the orderly development of a company as a whole, avoiding the competition among departments and branches. In the case of Mitsubishi, except in special cases, all profits and losses were to be calculated only by the *motoatsukaiten* (original accounting office), or by the selling office for certain merchandise transactions, for which the *motoatsukaiten* was not provided, and the other *atsukaiten* (accounting office) attended to transactions without any profit or commission. By this system the branches did not compete with one another in the transactions. In Mitsui the conflict between department and branch appeared earlier. In 1897 the Cotton Department introduced a common accounting system, with which the headquarters controlled the profits and losses of transactions of a particular item at branches. In 1911, they developed the departmental system along product lines, by which they entrusted departments and main branches with a particular product. In order to control the company as a whole they developed the main sub-department system about 1914, and, for example, the Cotton Department created its sub-department in the New York Branch.

In transactions, the activities of branches were completely controlled by the department concerned at headquarters. However, they could not solve the problem of authority of personnel management. The main other control means was to limit credit. They also developed communication and reporting systems to attain an effective control of diversified activities of the branches. Managers of branches submitted various reports regularly.

3. The third period (1931–5)

The World Depression and the Manchurian Incident influenced the activities of offices of Japanese trading companies in the United States. In order to retain the increase of operating cost and to acquire foreign exchange, it became important for these offices to diversify their product lines. The oil business became very important to the San Francisco offices of Mitsui and Mitsubishi. Mitsubishi's San Francisco office added product lines, and each staff member came to deal with a few lines. With the increase of operations, the San Francisco office came to transact directly with each branch to avoid the increase of cost and overlapping transactions. Finally, it became a branch in May 1931 which increased its independence.

This development occurred during a time when Japanese industries were suffering from depression-induced overproduction. In addition, after the outbreak of the Manchurian Incident, some Japanese industries found it difficult to produce products for the domestic market because of tight foreign exchange controls and control of materials. American branches of both Mitsui and Mitsubishi tried to find outlets for their products in the overseas market. They began aggressively importing from Japan such goods as canned crabmeat, fertilizer, clothing, pottery, and other consumer goods. Japanese manufacturers always asked Mitsui and Mitsubishi to pay attention to the possibility of export. As a result, Mitsubishi's headquarters in Japan came to direct branches in the United States to export products of such Japanese companies as Asahi Glass Company (window glass), Nippon Optical Company (optical products), and Yokogawa Electric Company (electric meters), whose products were able to compete with Western companies.

Tokyo Rubber Chemical Company, which was a joint venture of Mitsui with Nettai Sangyo, could not manufacture their products for the domestic market. They tried to secure the overseas market through Mitsui. Mitsui stressed the exploration of foreign markets for products of medium- and small-sized companies. Because Mitsui's transactions concentrated on the silk business, this accounted for 70% of all their transactions. Coal, sugar, silk clothing, flour, and camphor accounted for 15%. Except for these products, Mitsui's total exports were really small. Therefore they wanted to establish their position in the exports of miscellaneous goods by using their accumulated experience and world-wide network.

Branches in the United States played important roles in spearheading attempts to find markets for Japanese products. They provided manufacturers with various kinds of marketing information. They first tested marketing with a small consignment. When they found that Japanese products could not penetrate the market because of their questionable quality, they conveyed information to manufacturers regarding the taste and need of the market, prices, and competition to enable them to overcome these problems.

Besides simply finding a market for Japanese manufacturers, Mitsui and Mitsubishi worked to organise entire industries. They wanted 'to lead promoting trade and control domestic manufacturers or co-operate with them'. Both companies played an important role particularly in the export of such consumer commodities as cotton textile products and canned crabmeat. Each company in these industries was very small and had no ability to find its own overseas market. They competed harshly by cutting prices. They could not benefit from economies of scale, in the absence of co-operative organisation among the manufacturers. It was necessary for Mitsui and Mitsubishi to decrease these weak points by establishing close relations with domestic manufacturers, directing and controlling them, and encouraging shipping companies to pursue a proper freight policy. Export finance by trading companies was important in controlling them. Mitsubishi and Mitsui co-ordinated the flow of products from production to marketing. Overseas branches played an important role integrating these functions by giving necessary marketing information to manufacturers. For example, branches in the United States made efforts to integrate the flow of canned crabmeat from producers to consumers by developing a new distribution system and informing consumers by aggressive advertising.

Although San Francisco Branches developed the transactions of miscellaneous goods, Seattle offices did not because they did not have a large market and they did not have export goods. Only trade with lumber was active. In the case of Mitsubishi the weight of San Francisco and Seattle Branches reversed by the end of this period. Mitsui closed the Vancouver office in 1932, which had been re-opened in 1919 to handle wheat for the Nippon Flour Company, because by this time they had established the basis of business in Vancouver and because American agents and Canadian companies had established their offices in Vancouver and Seattle. As a result, it became easier to handle Canadian goods.

4. *The fourth period (1936–42)*

Since the outbreak of the Manchurian Incident, Japan had been developing a wartime economy. After the outbreak of the Sino-Japanese War, this trend became clear, and the general relationship between Japan and the United States worsened. The result for business was tightened foreign exchange controls. Competition among trading companies intensified, and they all suffered shipping shortages.

Activities of branches in the United States were influenced by these movements inside and outside of the companies. As Japan developed a war economy, the trade patterns of the branches rapidly changed. The export of war related materials, like oil and scrap iron, increased, while imports from Japan decreased. The reasons for decreased Japanese exports to the United States were: shortages of materials for Japanese industries to produce export goods; continued depression in the United States market; and the export control by the Japanese government of products such as fertilizers.

These trends helped the development of transactions by the San Francisco Branch, but the Seattle Branch showed a decline in transactions and inefficiency. For example, after 1938 the Seattle office of Mitsui could not develop wheat and lumber transactions although they increased the exports of lumber to China somewhat because of its location. In the case of the Seattle Branch of Mitsubishi, in addition, communication between the headquarters and the Seattle Branch worsened after an American took the position of acting manager. He could not understand either Japanese or the intentions of headquarters. Judging the situation, the manager of the San Francisco Branch concluded, 'It is unreasonable to give an American the post which represents the branch as a whole.' In the transactions, they left the daily operations to *yoin* (employees hired locally) to avoid the various kinds of problems caused by the lack of knowledge about the local transactions and culture of Japanese staff members. On the other hand, Japanese became chiefs of sections controlling the *yoin* to solve the communication gap between Japan and the United States and not to bring this communication gap into the transactions between the headquarters and branches and between branches. Thus, Mitsui and Mitsubishi transformed the transactions from international transactions on the market to these within the company.

Responding to the changing environment and business organisation, Mitsui and Mitsubishi developed new strategies. The first strategy was to develop transactions with countries other than Japan and the domestic transactions to compensate the decrease of imports from Japan. Both Mitsui and Mitsubishi tried to develop transactions with Mexico. In 1936 Mitsui sent a representative to Mexico City and Mitsubishi opened a representative office in 1940. After the war broke out in Europe, European trade with Mexico stopped, forcing the Mexicans to begin trade with Japan. On the Japanese side, the abrogation of the Japan–United States Commerce and Navigation Treaty increased the desirability of trade with Mexico. The primary goods handled by Japanese trading companies were rayon and mercury.

As Los Angeles developed as a centre of business on the West Coast, both Mitsui and Mitsubishi became interested in establishing offices there. Mitsui opened their Los Angeles office in 1933 and Mitsubishi in 1939. They expected to develop transactions in petroleum, metals, machinery, foods, chemicals, lumber, fertilizer, and miscellaneous goods. Hosting Japanese visitors to obtain business was another important task of the Los Angeles offices. Although they had high expectations, they could not develop their business because of the further worsening international situation.

The second strategy was the co-operation with other companies. This was caused by two factors: increasing competition between Mitsui and Mitsubishi and tightening control of foreign exchange and business activities by the Japanese government. For example, Mitsubishi, which had been suffering from the high rate and lack of shipping space, made a special contract with Nippon Yusen Kaisha to obtain a special rate and space. Mitsubishi also tried to build a brewery with Kirin Beer Company in Hawaii in order to compete against the joint venture between Mitsui and Dai-Nippon Beer Company. Their plan was to produce beer in Manila where they could advantageously export beer to Hawaii and the West Coast. Although Mitsubishi could not realise this project because of the tight control of the foreign exchange, this type of joint venture among *sogo shosha*, manufacturer, and local interest became very popular after the Second World War. Tight control of foreign exchange led Mitsubishi, Toyo Steel Plate, and Toyo Can Company to create a new system of financing; thereby when Mitsubishi sold canned products using materials imported by Mitsubishi, the sales turnover was pooled at both New York and London Branches to pay for the materials.

In spite of these actions, Mitsui and Mitsubishi could not avoid a difficult situation. Since the outbreak of the Sino-Japanese War, anti-Japanese feeling had been increasing, particularly among labour and citizen organisations. In 1938, the export of weapons to Japan was banned, and in January 1940, the Japan–United States Commerce Treaty was abrogated, and the export of American products to Japan was placed under a licence system. As a result, even American businessmen began having difficulty in doing business with Japanese trading companies. They began to refuse loans and credit to Japanese trading companies. Further, after the outbreak of war in Europe the shortage of shipping space intensified, causing the activities of branches in the United States to decrease.

However, the San Francisco Branches of Mitsui and Mitsubishi were active with emergency buying, expecting the restriction of oil exports. The San Francisco office of Mitsubishi recorded their largest transactions in the second half of 1940 and Mitsui in the first half of 1941. By March 1941, the permission for oil exports ceased. And by May 1941, both branches were involved in business transactions where no trade came in through the open door.

Finally, in July 1941, the United States government froze Japanese assets in the United States, placing all the assets of Japanese companies under its control. Thus, without permission from the United States government, Japanese companies could not do anything and transactions by branches of Mitsui and Mitsubishi ceased.

Conclusion

It is impossible to reconstruct the full story of all the important activities of Mitsui and Mitsubishi on the West Coast of the United States. Nevertheless this endeavour enlarges our understanding of Mitsui and Mitsubishi in particular, and of the trading companies in general.

To understand the development of the general trading companies, it is essential to keep in mind the nature of *zaibatsu*. Mitsubishi and Mitsui were part of a family of companies. General trading companies performed the integrative functions, importation of raw materials and exporting products. Japanese trading companies worked as the procurement and sales department of member industrial companies of *zaibatsu*. Therefore, for example, Mitsubishi did not impose limitations on the transactions with member companies in the *zaibatsu*. Their fate was Mitsubishi Shoji's fate. With this consciousness, member companies left these functions to their member trading companies, without the necessity of controlling the flow of products on their own.

Because of the scarcity of raw materials and its limited market, Japanese general trading companies had to find overseas supply sources and markets for member companies. As a result, the diversification of product lines was closely related with the development of overseas branches. For example, Mitsubishi opened its Seattle Branch to sell iron to Japanese ship building companies, particularly Mitsubishi Ship Building Company. It also opened its San Francisco Branch to handle oil products for the Japanese Navy, which was a large and secure market in Japan. Mitsui opened its Vancouver office to procure wheat for Nippon Flour Company.

By increasing the number of overseas branches while increasing diversification, Mitsui and Mitsubishi internalised some functions of international trade that traditionally importers and exporters of host countries had performed. By internalising international trade, both companies were able to do business without the difficulties caused by communication and cultural gaps. International transactions became those either between headquarters and branches (export and import), or between overseas branches (trade between countries other than Japan). They could decrease risk in international transactions by leaving daily operations to *yoin*, and Japanese *seiin* controlled their activities.

Once this internalised transactions system was established, theoretically trading companies could increase their product lines and overseas branches without any limitation. They could find the cheapest raw materials and the most profitable markets all over the world. However, there actually appeared many problems which prevented further development of general trading companies. For example, there was a possibility that these branches and departments might compete with one another as independent operating units, with Mitsui and Mitsubishi experiencing diseconomy of scale. They had to overcome these problems to grow continuously. They developed a new organisational structure and management system. They developed a decentralised, divisional structure along product lines (line departments) and geographical areas (overseas branches). By this organisation top management could concentrate its effort on long-range, strategic problems, and department and branch managers had responsibility for the daily operations of their departments and branches. In order to avoid competition among departments and branches, Mitsubishi induced the *motoatsukaiten* and *atsukaiten* system, and Mitsui created a common accounting system as well as other systems.

In order to control overseas branches and the firms effectively, Mitsui and Mitsubishi set limits on transactions and credit. Each branch could transact only within these limits. They also continuously improved their communication and reporting system by which headquarters could know and coordinate the activities of branches. It was one of the most important things for a trading company to collect the right information as soon as possible to coordinate the activities of branches.

A stable and regular flow of products was necessary to control the internalised transactions effectively. It is said these trading companies handled various kinds of products, 'from noodles to missiles'. We have the impression that they handled an unlimited variety of products. However, careful study shows that the products they handled were limited to those for which they could effectively control their flow from suppliers to customers. In order to attain a stable and regular flow of products, the general trading companies had to perform various kinds of subsidiary functions.

The main products Mitsui and Mitsubishi handled were: (1) raw materials from large suppliers to large customers; (2) highly mechanised, expensive products, particularly machinery; and (3) undifferentiated, unperishable miscellaneous goods that were sold through many channels. In the first category, oil which was the main item of the San Francisco Branches was a good example. In order to secure the supply of oil they had to make a sole agency contract with the Associated Oil Company and General Petroleum

Corporation. In this kind of business, there were few marketing problems because of the nature of the products and the market.

In the second category of products, Mitsui and Mitsubishi handled mainly advanced Western machinery and technology for the member companies of *zaibatsu*. In these transactions, trading companies seem to have given supplementary service to them. They did preliminary negotiations, collecting information on both products and export business affairs.

The third category of products, undifferentiated, unperishable miscellaneous goods, were many export items to the American market. Canned crabmeat was one of them. The canned crabmeat industry was very competitive and unstable with many small canneries. Mitsubishi particularly tried to secure the supply of products in several ways. By supplying them with funds for fishing or export financing, they could control the suppliers. They played the role of promoter in the consolidation of small manufacturers into a large company. They integrated the small amount of products of small producers into a large transaction unit, and sold them to American brokers and Japanese importers, who, in turn, sold through various channels. This decreased the transaction cost and risk. It was necessary to control distribution in the United States in order to increase the efficiency of the internalised transactions and stable flow of the products, so Mitsubishi aggressively developed advertising. By appealing to consumers directly, they could keep their supremacy over distributors, and controlled the flow of the products from production to consumption.

In the process of adding product lines and overseas branches, general trading companies internalised the international transactions in its own organisation. Therefore the management of Mitsubishi and Mitsui had to co-ordinate and control their departments and branches effectively in order to attain efficient transactions. They developed a new decentralised organisation with strong centralised control. In order to attain profit in transactions, it was necessary to control the flow of products they handled. Mitsubishi did this by supplying funds, making sole agency contracts, and investing in suppliers. They also performed other functions, such as scheduling shipping, collecting market information, and hosting visitors from Japan. Once an effective transaction system was established, Mitsubishi did not want this disturbed by competitors, and competition among trading companies, particularly with Mitsui, was intensive because they wanted to keep their established flow of products and their transactions system intact. By this effective system of internalised transactions, Japanese large trading companies controlled the American–Japanese trade before the Second World War, in spite of the fact they faced restrictions by the United States government and strong competition from established American and European business interests.

NOTES

1 Yoshio Togai, 'Saisho ni Shutsugen shita Sogo Shosha' (The first general trading company), in Mataji Miyamoto, Yoshio Togai and Yasuo Mishima, (eds.), *Sogo Shosha no Keieishi (History of general trading companies)* (Tokyo, 1976), pp. 81–2.
2 On the Japanese investment in the United States, see Mira Wilkins, 'American–Japanese direct foreign investment relationship, 1930–1952', *Business History Review*, 52 (Winter, 1982), pp. 497–518, and Bureau of Administration, Ministry of Finance, *Nipponjin no Kaigai Katsudo ni kansuru Rekishiteki Chosa (A study on the overseas activities of the Japanese)* (Tokyo, 1948), volume on Europe and the United States.
3 This study basically draws upon the materials of Mitsui and Mitsubishi at the National Record Center in Suitland, Maryland. On the operations of Mitsubishi, see Nobuo Kawabe, *Sogo Shosha no Kenkyu (A study of Sogo Shosha)* (Tokyo, 1982) and Mitsubishi Shoji Kaisha, *Ritsugyo Boeki-roku (A history of Mitsubishi Shoji Kaisha)* (Tokyo, 1958). On the operations of Mitsui, Nihon Keieishi Kenkyusho, *Kohon Mitsui Bussan 100 Nenshi (Draft 100-History of Mitsui Bussan)* (Tokyo, 1978) is useful.

17 The state and private enterprise in United States–Latin American oil policy

STEPHEN J. RANDALL

In a comparatively brief analysis it is clearly not feasible to provide detailed historical discussion of each national area in which the United States following the First World War established petroleum relations. The extant literature on inter-American relations in those years is now sufficiently well established, however, to provide an opportunity to assess the general nature of American oil policy and of the state-private sector relationship in particular.[1]

This literature enables us to explore the state–private sector relationship on several levels; firstly, the relative importance of the two sectors in the formulation of policy; secondly, whether that relationship altered significantly during the period in question; thirdly, whether or not policy itself altered. On an entirely distinct level, one might examine the nature of United States policymakers' attitudes toward the involvement of the Latin American states in indigenous oil development. Finally, the historical record enables us to consider the extent to which United States policy influenced the role of the Latin American state in the oil industry. The answers that are offered here to these questions are suggestive only. The analysis is historical in nature, intended to explore ideology, political developments, and international relations rather than to evaluate in economic terms the actual importance of the oil industry to host societies, the private companies, or to the United States.

The most frequently advanced interpretations of state-private sector relations in foreign policy are the statist, instrumentalist, and various versions of the pluralist model of decision making. Each has its strengths and weaknesses. The statist model fails to provide adequate explanation for the important contribution that various segments of the private sector make to the formulation of foreign policies. The instrumentalist interpretation, with its emphasis on the state apparatus as a mere appendage of a ruling elite, is not adequate to explain the frequency and severity of disagreement among state officials, the executive of the major companies, spokesmen for the independent oil producers, and often Congressmen over specific oil policy that the evidence suggests characterised the post-First World War years. The pluralist explanation fails, in my view, because it postulates a private sector that is considerably more unorganised than was the reality in the oil industry and a state that was less autonomous than was the case. The interpretation that has gained increasing credibility in the past decade is the idea of the associational state. Its appeal is that it draws the best insights from each of the other models and enables us to understand how and why the state and private sectors often firmly disagreed not only on specific policy but also on long-term objectives, yet generally shared common assumptions about what was in the long-term best interest of the United States.[2]

The control and direction of United States foreign oil policy in Latin America in the more than two decades encompassed in this chapter resided in the Department of State. At various times other federal departments and agencies made significant contributions. Such was the case with the Department of Commerce in the 1920s when Herbert Hoover was secretary; with the Department of the Interior in the late 1930s and war years when Harold Ickes was secretary and petroleum administrator for war. The Departments of Navy and War made an ongoing but lesser contribution to the debate with the possible exception of the war years when the immediacy of the supply problem made essential their involvement in short-and long-term planning. Such federal agencies as the Federal Oil Conservation Board, established by President Coolidge, and the United States Geological Survey made timely contributions to the concern over possible exhaustion of United States domestic oil supply in the 1920s.

With rare exceptions state officials supported an entirely free enterprise approach to United States involvement in foreign oil development, with those exceptions occurring in the 1920s and during the Second World War. Even the exceptions, however, did not pertain to Latin America but rather to the Middle East, in particular during the short life span of the Petroleum Reserves Corporation (PRC) under Harold Ickes. In this regard there appears to have been no fundamental disagreement between state officials and the private sector. Those who supported a considerably expanded role for the government in foreign oil development were influenced by the experience of the First World War and the fear of post-war scarcity, such as the petroleum geologist Mark Requa, director in 1919 of the United States Fuel Administration Harry Garfield, George Otis Smith of the Geological Survey, and Van H. Manning of the American Petroleum Institute. By 1919 they were advocating the formation of an international oil company financed by United States capital and supervised by the United States government, an arrangement that, had it materialised, would clearly not have challenged the principle of free enterprise but strengthened state–private sector relations. The proposal of California Democratic Senator James Phelan in 1920 to form a United States oil corporation along the lines of the US Shipping

Board's Emergency Fleet Corporation certainly went further toward expanding state influence, but it died in Congressional committee.[3] Objections in Congress and in the State Department were that other governments would be unwilling to grant concessions to any company that was controlled or believed to be controlled by a foreign power. The formation of the Export Petroleum Association in the late 1920s under the provisions of the Webb–Pomerene Act provided one instance of the state attempting to facilitate the ability of American corporations to combine to compete more effectively in international markets, but this project also stopped short of any challenge to the freedom of the private sector. It is important to emphasise that in each instance it was not private sector opposition but a broad consensus that defeated these initiatives in the expansion of state power. Not until the Second World War and the formation of the Petroleum Reserves Corporation under Harold Ickes was there another significant effort to inject state control into overseas American oil development, and the PRC was directed toward the Middle East rather than Latin America.

Since no consensus could be reached in support of a state oil enterprise that would advance American strategic interests, the private sector remained the vehicle through which American oil interests expanded in Latin America following the First World War.[4] The state provided diplomatic support for that expansion, and the weight of American economic, technological, entrepreneurial and potentially military power provided a competitive edge for American enterprise. The State Department exercised its good offices with Latin American governments in order to deflect what was considered legislation unfavourable to American corporations in exploration, development, and marketing activities. The Department arranged for United States specialists in petroleum legislation and legal experts to serve as intermediaries between the United States and Latin American governments. Such was the case with H. Foster Bain, former official of the US Department of Mines, J. W. Steel of the US Geological Survey, and George Rublee, a prominent Washington attorney. In the late 1920s and early 1930s they participated in drafting revised oil legislation for the Colombian government in an effort to remove more nationalistic and, from the American perspective, unacceptable provisions from original drafts. Such efforts were successful in the main areas of petroleum development in the 1920s and early 1930s, which were Colombia, Mexico and Venezuela, with the last gaining substantially on the others in importance. The main thrust of American policy was directed toward counteracting nationalism and ensuring a place for private American firms in the foreign oil industry. This meant that Latin American state enterprises as well as European competitors in Latin America, such as the Anglo-Persian Oil Company, were not acceptable to American policymakers.

The issues that confronted American policymakers and companies in

Mexico and Chile in the 1920s and early 1930s were somewhat different, although they both derived from the growth of nationalist sentiment in Latin America with the corresponding desire to gain more effective control over mineral resource development. The main concern of United States officials in both instances was with the threat of possible nationalisation of foreign properties. In mid-1930, the Chilean government introduced legislation proposing nationalisation of the oil industry and the establishment of a government monopoly for refining and distribution. The draft legislation authorised the president to establish refineries and to grant exploration and development concessions to national or foreign firms, which would function in partnership with the state. The actual ownership of mineral resources and industrial plant would rest with the state.[5]

Although there was little initial American reaction, in large part one suspects because American holdings in Chilean oil were minor, the Latin American division of the State Department emphasised that the objective should be to ensure the payment of indemnity for any property expropriated. At the same time, however, some officials perceived the larger issue as the main concern, which was to counteract any trend toward the creation of state monopolies under foreign control in the extractive resource industries. Company officials were even more adamant in their opposition. Standard Oil of New Jersey's local manager indicated in late 1931 that the company would discontinue its operations in Chile if such restrictive legislation passed because the company was not prepared to work with a government monopoly. The State Department lent official endorsement to that position in June 1932 when it informed the Chilean government that the United States would insist on 'full and effective compensation' if American companies were forced out of business. This pressure did not prevent Chile from enacting legislation in 1934 creating the Chilean Petroleum Company to market oil products, but it is reasonable to assume that Chile was restrained from more radical action by the American position.

Although the developments in Chilean–American oil relations during the Hoover administration are an accurate indice of the direction of United States policy, they were also comparatively minor aspects of United States foreign policy. The events of the later 1930s and early 1940s assumed greater significance. During the pre-Second World War years of the Franklin Roosevelt administration, the United States faced two nationalisations of American oil properties, the first in Bolivia in 1937, and the second and more important in Mexico the following year. In addition, Venezuela for the first time began to assert its desire for a larger control of its now substantial oil industry, and lesser producers such as Colombia continued to legislate to protect national labour, to ensure adequate royalty payments from the companies, and to promote actual development of the oil fields. The response of the Roosevelt administration to these issues indicated continued commitment to the equality of access for American capital, security for that capital, and a strong preference for private enterprise over state enterprise in oil development abroad. Throughout the crises in Bolivia, Mexico and Venezuela between 1937 and 1942 United States objectives were hemispheric solidarity and the security of oil supply. At the same time, the evidence suggests that policymakers in the course of the crises gained a more subtle understanding of the nature of Latin American nationalism and greater appreciation of the need for American enterprise abroad to adopt policies that strengthened their relations with host societies. To a substantial extent State Department pressure on the companies to improve their image combined with the extended and often unsuccessful negotiations with Bolivia and Mexico over the expropriation of oil properties to strain relations between the Roosevelt administration and the companies, but the larger consensus on the need for private sector control of foreign oil resources with strong diplomatic support from the government held firm.

The Bolivian expropriation of Standard Oil's Bolivian subsidiary in March 1937 was complicated by the fact that Bolivian authorities justified the action on the grounds that the company had been illegally selling oil during the war between Paraguay and Bolivia, and was thus not entitled to compensation.[6] In addition, Bolivian officials noted that the company had not been actively engaged in exploration for several years and was not promoting oil development. It had not drilled a new well in five years, and at the time of the expropriation was discussing a possible sale to the Bolivian state company, YPFB (Yacimientos Petroliferos Fiscales Bolivianos). The inclusion of a Calvo clause in the original contract between the government and company, binding the company to restrict its efforts to achieve legal redress within Bolivian courts only further complicated the diplomatic dimensions of the question, because the company refused to be restricted by the clause.

A second consideration that muted State Department enthusiasm for a stronger stand against Bolivia was the comparative unimportance of Bolivia as an oil producer and its significance for supplies of other vital raw materials, in particular tin, tungsten, lead and zinc. The United States was anxious that such raw materials not come under European control. That concern was greatly exacerbated by the outbreak of war in Europe in September 1939. When there was an attempted coup in Bolivia in 1941, in which the German minister was implicated, the United States intensified its efforts to resolve the oil dispute by holding out to Bolivia the possibility of financial credits through the Export-Import Bank. It was consequently made clear to Bolivian officials that loans depended on across the board reciprocity, and Bolivia responded in 1942 with an agreement to pay $1.5 million to Standard Oil, well below the company's estimate of its worth.

The basic area of difference between the company and the State

Department during the negotiations was over the degree of state involvement in and responsibility for achieving a settlement. The Department insisted, as it did later with Mexico and Venezuela, that any agreement was a private one between Bolivia and the company. Such an approach was to senior Standard Oil officials unfortunate, as one suggested, because it might 'indicate that a foreign government in confiscating American property does not violate international law'. Undersecretary of State Sumner Welles, on the other hand, was of the firm opinion by 1941 that to press the Bolivian case would 'lead to blowing up the political situation ... As I see it, the Bolivian situation should be handled in much the same way as we are attempting to handle the Mexican situation.' This more moderate stance, rather than that favoured by some company officials, was the one that prevailed.[7]

Throughout the Bolivian dispute, it was the situation in Mexico that was of primary concern to American policymakers. Mexican expropriation of the properties of most of the foreign oil companies operating in the country in early 1938 precipitated the crisis of the late 1930s in Mexican–American relations, but the underlying issue of resource control had been an area of dispute since the First World War. Article 27 of the 1917 Mexican constitution had vested in the nation ownership of land and the right to regulate the use of all natural resources; the article reserved the right to acquire mineral concessions to Mexican nationals or corporations and provided for the right of expropriation, with compensation, for reasons of public utility. Those provisions were also incorporated into a general petroleum bill in 1921 which contributed to several years of dispute in the following decade.[8]

The Mexican nationalisation was coloured by the long historical relationship between the two nations, the geographic proximity to the United States, the greater symbolic importance of Mexico among Latin American states, the higher level of United States and British investment in the Mexican oil industry relative to that in Bolivia, and, as in the Bolivian and Venezuelan situations, the strategic considerations occasioned by the war.[9]

Even more than in the Bolivian expropriation, the Mexican case severely strained state–company relations, in part because so much appeared to be at stake and because there were more companies with a higher degree of political influence. For both the companies and the state, differences transcended narrow profit and even strategic considerations. What was at stake in part was whether the United States would recognise the rights of foreign nations to determine the direction and control of their natural resource development. The Roosevelt administration moved further toward accepting that approach than any administration had previously. It recognised the need to contain nationalism and channel it along lines that would not threaten the broader strategic, economic, and political objectives of the United States. Many corporate officials found this posture difficult to reconcile with their own perception of what was at risk, which was the sanctity of the free enterprise model. From the state perspective, the administration from the outset recognised the right of a foreign power to nationalise with adequate compensation. At the same time, administration officials were cautious not to drive Mexico into the German or Italian orbit. In essence the question was never whether or not the state should play a role in the dispute but what the nature of the intervention should be.

During the pre-war and wartime negotiations there was a distinct preference on the part of US policymakers that the companies effect their own agreement with Mexico in order to protect the non-interventionist image that the Roosevelt administration wished to foster in the hemisphere. Private negotiations continued to founder on the corporate inability to accept a compromise on the issue of subsoil ownership and the total valuation of American properties held at the time of the nationalisation. What might only loosely be considered a private settlement thus consistently involved various forms of state intervention from the State Department through the presidency. The administration worked to keep negotiations active, worked closely with company and Mexican officials, and used economic leverage by discouraging purchases of Mexican oil and by forcing down the price of silver to pressure the already hard hit Mexican economy. The agreement that broke the impasse in 1941 was one prepared by State Department officials and addressed a broad range of outstanding issues in Mexican–American relations, including past agrarian claims, defaulted Mexican bonds, Mexican currency and silver, as well as the oil question. The timing of the settlement was clearly tied to wartime exigencies. The United States sought the use of air and naval bases in Mexico, an objective that was realized in 1942 with the creation of a joint defense commission.[10]

There was a high degree of continuity between the wartime and post-war state–private sector relationship in United States oil policy towards Mexico.[11] Early in the conflict, Cordell Hull had indicated that nothing 'except the exigencies of war should be permitted to interfere with the sound and orderly re-establishment of the oil industry in Mexico'. From the company and American government perspective 'orderly re-establishment' meant private initiative and ownership. The Truman administration was firm in its position from 1945 on that the United States would not extend credit to Mexico for oil development if that development were to be under the control of Pemex; in part this position reflected opposition to foreign state enterprise in the oil industry but it was also based on the belief that Pemex was not capable of developing Mexican resources in an efficient and profitable manner. The companies' attitude to operations in Mexico was just as dramatic. By 1948, of the major international firms only Gulf Oil was still operating in Mexico; in the same year Pemex acquired 40 % of its operations, and two years later the remainder.

To return to our original questions, the evidence suggests a relatively high degree of continuity in policy objectives over a thirty-year period. Although there may have been a hardening of state officials' attitudes toward the companies and a more explicit desire to have the companies contribute to the development of a positive image for the United States in Latin America, on the whole the state remained wedded firmly to the preference for a private enterprise model, a high degree of state support for the industry in gaining concessions, developing them, and ensuring security of supply for the United States, without the state acquiring financial or management responsibilities in oil industry development abroad. The same preference applied to the approach the United States sought to have Latin American states pursue in oil development. Venezuela remained the ideal for much of this period. There was no effective state control over the industry and no sustained effort to develop a state enterprise that would either compete with or absorb the foreign companies as transpired in Mexico, although it appeared in the early 1940s that Venezuela would adopt a much harder stance in its relations with the foreign sector. It is very difficult to assess the extent to which United States policy shaped the pattern of oil development in Latin America. Certainly even if it preferred the free enterprise model, it was not able to prevent the formation of state oil companies throughout the hemisphere, Ecopetrol in Colombia, Pemex in Mexico, YPF in Argentina, YPFB in Bolivia. In some cases those state companies co-existed with the private sector. In general, what tended to determine the history of inter-American oil relations in these years was the economic and political power of the companies and of the nation which perceived them as an instrument of United States foreign economic policy.

NOTES

1 The main literature in the area includes the following: Robert F. Smith, *The United States and revolutionary nationalism in Mexico, 1916–1932* (Chicago, 1972); Stephen Rabe, *The road to OPEC: United States relations with Venezuela, 1919–1976* (Austin, Texas, 1980); Joseph Tulchin, *The aftermath of war: World War I and United States policy toward Latin America* (New York, 1971); Clayton Koppes, 'The Good Neighbor Policy and the nationalization of Mexican oil: a reinterpretation', *Journal of American History*, 69 (June 1982); S. J. Randall, *The diplomacy of modernization: Colombian–American relations, 1920–1940* (Toronto, 1977); Randall, *United States foreign oil policy, 1919–1948: for profits and security* (Montreal, 1985).
2 The most persuasive of the statist literature in the area of foreign raw materials policy is Stephen D. Krasner, *Defending the national interest: raw materials investments and US foreign policy* (Princeton, 1978). The most prominent work in the instrumentalist area has been Gabriel Kolko, *The roots of American foreign policy: An analysis of power and purpose* (Boston, 1969); *The politics of war: The world and United States foreign policy, 1943–1945* (New York, 1968); with Joyce Kolko, *The limits of power: the world and United States foreign policy, 1945–1954*

(New York, 1972). The most perceptive of the work which advances the idea of the associational state includes Michael Hogan, *Informal Entente: The private structure of cooperation in Anglo-American economic diplomacy, 1918–1928* (Columbia, Missouri, 1977), and Joan Hoff Wilson, *American business and foreign policy, 1921–1933* (Lexington, Kentucky 1971). The pluralist approach to United States–Latin American relations in the 1930s and 1940s is represented by Bryce Wood, *The making of the Good Neighbor policy* (New York, 1967), and Irwin F. Gellman, *Good Neighbor diplomacy: United States policies in Latin America* (Baltimore, 1979). A thoughtful review of interpretation for the 1920s is John Braeman, 'The New Left and American foreign policy during the Age of Normalcy', *Business History Review*, 57 (Spring 1983).

3 For the position of Requa, Garfield, Smith, and Manning see their memorandum of 28 February 1919, Fuel Administration file, box 518, Josephus Daniels Papers, Library of Congress (hereafter cited as LC). For the Phelan proposal see US Congress, Senate, Senate document no. 97, 66th Congress, 2nd session (1920); *Congressional Record*, 17 May 1920, 7144; 17 January 1920, 1491. See as well the State Department discussion of the idea, DS 811.6363/25/46/328 (all references to Department of State records are to decimal files in Record Group 59, US National Archives, unless otherwise indicated). For a discussion of the Export Petroleum Association see Mira Wilkins, *The maturing of multinational enterprise: American enterprise abroad from 1914 to 1970* (Cambridge, Mass. 1970). For a thorough discussion of the Petroleum Reserves Corporation during the Second World War see M. Stoff, *Oil, war and American security: The search for a national policy on foreign oil, 1941–1947* (New Haven, 1980) and I. Anderson, *Aramco, the United States and Saudi Arabia* (Princeton, 1981).

4 On this early period, in particular on Colombia, Venezuela, and Mexico, see Smith, *The United States and revolutionary nationalism in Mexico*; Rabe, *Road to OPEC*; and Randall, *The diplomacy of modernization*.

5 For Chilean developments see the following: Stuart Gruman, Latin American Division, to Edwin C. Wilson, chief of division, 10 November 1931, DS 825.6363/90 1/2; J. Stinson, Latin American Division, to Wilson, 15 February 1932, DS 825.6363/93; memorandum of State Department meeting, 23 November 1931, DS 825.6363/82, /130, /150.

6 On the Bolivian expropriation see Herbert Klein, 'American oil companies in Latin America: the Bolivian experience', *Inter-American Economic Affairs*, 18 (Autumn, 1964); Wood, *Making of the Good Neighbor policy*; Gellman, *Good Neighbor diplomacy*. For state department positions see Cordell Hull memorandum of meeting, 11 April 1939, box 57, Hull Papers, LC; undated state department memorandum, DS 824.6363 ST 2/607; correspondence of 28 April 1937, DS 824.6363 ST 2/117.

7 Department of State memorandum, 28 April 1939, DS 824.6363 ST 2/375. Welles to E. Briggs (Division of American Republics), 19 April 1939, DS 824.6363 ST 2/373. See also box 85, petroleum file, Hull Papers, LC. T. Armstrong (Standard Oil) to Duggan (Division of American Republics), 16 January 1940, DS 824.6363 ST 2/432; Armstrong to Secretary of State, 13 November 1940; Welles to William Farish (Standard Oil), 13 December 1940, DS 824.6363 ST 2/495a; Welles to Bonsal (American Republics), 26 February 1941, DS 824.6363 ST 2/526; Farish to Bonsal, 19 February 1941; Bonsal to Daniels, 8 March 1941, DS 824.6363 ST 2/536/538. Bonsal to Duggan, 18 September 1941, DS 824.6363/197.

8 On the early years of the dispute, see US Department of State, *Foreign Relations*

of the United States, 1921, II, 439–46 (hereafter cited as *FR*); A. C. Millspaugh (State Department) memorandum for delegates to the Washington Conference on the Limitation of Armament, 1921, folder 25, box 130, RG 43, NA; *FR*, 1928, III, 301–06.

9 For this phase of the dispute see Wood, *Making of the Good Neighbor policy*; Koppes, 'The nationalization of Mexican oil'; Gellman, *Good Neighbor diplomacy*; H. Stegmaier, 'From confrontation to co-operation: the United States and Mexico, 1938–1945' (Ph.D. dissertation, University of Michigan, 1970); J. Ring, 'American diplomacy and the Mexican oil controversy, 1938–1943' (Ph.D. dissertation, University of New Mexico, 1974); D. Baldridge, 'Mexican petroleum and United States – Mexican relations' (Ph.D. dissertation, University of Arizona, 1971); for the level of investment see Research and Analysis Branch Report no. 2099, 'Foreign investments in Latin America,' RG 59, NA.

10 See Welles to Daniels, 31 August 1939, Welles file, Box 106, Daniels Papers, LC; W. Farish to Secretary of State, 10 August 1939, box 80, Hull Papers, LC; Hull to George Messersmith, 6 August 1941, box 221, interior file, Ickes Papers, LC; Hull memorandum, 18 November 1942, box 60, Hull Papers, LC.

11 Department of State memorandum signed by President Truman, 13 October 1945, *FR*, 1945, IX, 1161; Dean Acheson to Walter Thurston (US Ambassador to Mexico), 27 August 1946, DS 812.6363/8-2746; Randall, *United States foreign oil policy*, p. 229.

18 Transnational corporations and the denationalisation of the Latin American cigarette industry

PHIL SHEPHERD

Introduction

The last thirty-five years have witnessed some extraordinary changes in the world tobacco industry. For example, the expansion abroad of US cigarette companies (which had been domestically oriented from 1911 to 1952) first led to the break-down of forty years of international co-operation among the major producers (a *de facto* cartel) in the 1960s and 1970s and, then, to the re-establishment of global 'equilibrium' in recent years. This, in turn, signified the emergence of a truly global, highly concentrated transnational cigarette industry.

Likewise other changes have had considerable impact on the industry. Medical research in the last three decades has increasingly revealed the lethal side of the industry, implicating smoking with a wide variety of illnesses, usually terminal: lung, mouth, throat and bladder cancers, emphysema, cardiovascular diseases and so forth (USDHEW, 1979). The development of the smoking and health issue in all the industrialised nations has caused stagnating and even declining cigarette sales in those nations, thus leading to a shift in growth to LDCs where, for a variety of reasons, the public health issue is much less salient. The major cigarette firms have therefore turned to LDC markets for future growth.

All these developments have been highly interrelated and linked to still others: (1) the ever-increasing predominance of cigarettes within the tobacco industry to the point where other products (cigars, chewing, etc.) have been completely overshadowed and the cigarette industry equals the tobacco industry in most nations; (2) dramatic changes in demand creation ('marketing') strategies and techniques which have enabled the major firms to hold onto older markets and expand new ones; (3) diversification into non-tobacco lines of business by the leading producers to cushion the impact of the smoking/health issue effects in home nations and make effective use of the large cash flow generated by cigarettes (a complementary strategy to expanding abroad in cigarettes); (4) considerable changes in the technology

201

of tobacco farming, marketing and cigarette manufacture in the direction of much more capital-intensive production; and (5) changes in the international trade of leaf tobacco and cigarettes, leading to the rise of LDCs as major leaf producers while DCs continue to dominate trade in manufactures.

I have reviewed these changes and the peculiar, often fascinating, history and structure of the industry elsewhere (Shepherd, 1979, 1983). In the present study, I will examine part of another interesting change that took place in many areas of the world and their replacement by a transnational corporate subsidiary (usually of Anglo-American parentage).

Specifically, this work focuses on the questions of how and why this process of 'denationalisation' took place in Latin America. It is worth emphasising that the focus here is less on what factors led cigarette firms in industrialised countries to expand abroad (thus becoming transnational enterprises) than on why and how these firms were able to penetrate Latin American cigarette markets once they had decided to do so. As discussed in the conclusion, this is a process that has been generally neglected in the literature on transnational corporations (TNCs).

Historical emergence of Latin American cigarette industries

In Latin America, tobacco often played an important part in the economic and political struggles of the colonial era. For example, the famous 'Comunero' rebellion in Socorro, Colombia in 1781, one of the precursors of the drive for Independence, was initially a protest against policies with respect to the growing and marketing of tobacco under the Crown tobacco monopoly (Leonard, 1951). The deeply-felt hatred of the colonial monopoly eventually led to the dismantling of most Latin American tobacco monopolies (Stein and Stein, 1970: 123–57; Harrison, 1952; McGreevey, 1971: pp. 111–8).

Under the onslaught of sentiment for free trade in the mid-nineteenth century, most Latin American tobacco industries thus became at least formally private. As Latin America was increasingly linked into the international system of trade, nations there experimented with various commodities in which they might enjoy some comparative advantage in order to finance increasing imports of manufactured and other goods from the more industrialised nations. Tobacco often figured as one of these primary products and various 'export booms' centred on tobacco took place. For example, tobacco became Colombia's most important export commodity in the mid-19th century, and was intimately involved in a number of very important political economic events there during the nineteenth century (Harrison, 1952; Sierra, 1972; McGreevey, 1971: pp. 97–183). Tobacco exports were also important at various times in Brazil, parts of Central America and the Caribbean, Peru, and, of course, Cuba. Domestically, tobacco production and consumption was a crucial factor in governments' revenue in virtually all Latin American nations both before and after independence (Stein and Stein, 1970; pp. 71–4 and 99–106).

Latin American tobacco industries were based on locally-grown, 'dark tobacco' (*tabaco negro*), largely used for cigars, snuff and chewing in the pre-cigarette era. 'Dark', air-cured tobaccos of this type were (and still are) traditionally favoured in areas of Spanish or Latin cultural influence. In the late nineteenth century, cigarettes were introduced after cigar-type leaf production was already well-established in Latin America. Thus, early Latin American cigarette producers found it natural to make cigarettes from cigar leaf cuttings (Brooks, 1952: pp. 257–8). This is the reason why Latin America traditionally had dark tobacco (*tabaco negro*) cigarettes prior to the entry of TNCs rather than light tobacco (*tabaco rubio*) cigarettes of the Anglo-American types of blends.[1]

Latin American tobacco firms often played important roles in the early stages of import substitution industrialisation (ISI) in the region. Most Latin American cigarette firms date from the early years of the twentieth century and some from the 1890s. Cigarette production and tobacco manufacture in general was a prime candidate for ISI efforts: tobacco products were a luxury to import; domestic raw materials in the form of leaf tobacco were readily available; some local familiarity with the industry was often present; the scale requirements were not large; the technology was not unduly difficult to acquire or adapt to local conditions; agricultural production of leaf was labour-intensive; cigarette manufacturing did not require much skilled labour, and so forth. The industry was thus ideally suited for import substitution industrialisation, as was the case with other agricultural processing sectors. It also had the added advantage of providing considerable tax revenues for the state (through cigarette taxes) and cutting down on 'non-essential' imports to ease balance of payments problems. Thus it is not surprising that the industry frequently received substantial (and early) effective tariff protection.

Nationally-owned tobacco firms grew rapidly in most Latin American nations after 1900 or so. Substantial local industries developed in protected markets all over Latin America, but particularly in Argentina, Mexico, Brazil, Colombia, Chile and Peru. In a variety of nations, including Cuba, Paraguay, Brazil and Colombia, leaf exports of tobacco were also important. Because of its relative importance in ISI and its role as a source of governmental revenue, the tobacco industry has played a key role in the political-economic history of a number of Latin American nations in the twentieth century.

In the largest markets of the region, such as Argentina, Brazil and Mexico, British-American Tobacco Ltd (BAT)[2] entered the industry fairly early (often just prior to or after the First World War), frequently acquiring a local firm. Agressively carving out large market shares, BAT often met with considerable opposition from owners of national firms, the national bourgoisie in general, and others who feared foreign penetration and control of the local economy. In some nations, such as Colombia, BAT was unable to gain a permanent foothold in the market (Shepherd, 1983: pp. 1448, 1460–3). However, BAT usually followed a low-profile, 'live and let live' strategy for dealing with economic nationalism, and substantial local firms grew up alongside BAT subsidiaries in some markets. Later on these locally owned firms made rather attractive targets for TNC acquisition. It was only with the wholesale take-over of these firms by other (largely US) TNCs in the 1960s that Latin American cigarette industries were effectively 'denationalised'.

The process of denationalisation

It is important to view the process of TNC expansion not only from the perspective of TNCs and the 'home' nations (as most of the literature on TNCs and direct foreign investment tends to), but also from the viewpoint of 'host' nations, local firms, and LDCs. Most theories of direct foreign investment and TNC expansion focus on characteristics of TNCs and their 'home' economies to explain how these things are important in the transformation of national firms into transnational firms. The idea that the causes and dynamics of TNC expansion abroad are to be located largely within the TNC itself and its immediate context of oligopolistic competition in the industrialised (home) nations is important. But it clearly neglects the broader context of action in which such expansion takes place. These theories do not examine the conditions under which 'host' nations are opened up to direct foreign investment or open themselves up; they tell us very little if anything about how, when, and why TNCs penetrate given national markets overseas. Rather, these theories implicitly assume – sometimes quite unjustifiably – that foreign nations' markets may be entered at will and at any time.

Moreover, TNCs are not merely passive actors responding to given market demands and developments, but have a substantial, though imperfect, ability to shape the context in which they operate. TNCs have often operated in the context of an international 'demonstration effect' which they themselves have partially created, nurtured and manipulated.

The patterns of consumption encouraged by TNCs and their effects on the international 'product cycle' can often be stated with considerable specificity. In the case of the cigarette industry, there has been a remarkable convergence of world-wide consumption trends and patterns towards TNC product forms developed in their home markets. This convergence is partly the result of prior TNC efforts at demand creation and partly the result of the diffusion

Table 18.1. *Cigarette sales[a] by type of tobacco blend, 1950–75* (in %)

	Nation						
	Argentina			Colombia		Peru	
	Light tobacco	Mixed light and dark	Dark tobacco	Light tobacco	Dark tobacco	Light tobacco	Dark tobacco
1950	36	—	64	Not available		Not available	
1955	50	—	50	Not available		5	95
1960	46	—	54	Not available		13	87
1965	52	—	48	Not available		19[b]	81[b]
1966	55	—	45	—	—	33	67
1967	60	—	40	—	—	50	50
1968	67	—	33	10	90	52	48
1969	71	3	26	11	89	55	45
1970	72	4	24	12	88	57	43
1971	72	6	23	16	84	56	44
1972	72	7	21	23	77	64	36
1973	72	10	19	24	76	67	33
1974	72	12	16	25	75	77	23
1975	75	12	13	—	—	—	—

Notes:
[a] By unit volume.
[b] 1964.
Sources: Argentina: Depto. de Tobaco, Secretaria de Estado de Agricultura y Ganaderia, *Estadistica Anual, 1950–1975.*
Colombia: Estimates from La Compania Colombiana de Tobacos, S.A.
Peru: 1952–1964: Instituto Nacional de Promocicion Industrial y Banco Industrial del Peru, *La Industria del tobaco en el Peru* (Lima, 1965), table 8, p. 29; 1966–74: Empresa Nacional de Tobaco, 'La Industria tabacalera nacional y la participacion del estado dentro de su desarrollo' (Lima, 1974), Anexo No. 1.

of contemporary industrialised nations 'life-styles', first to LDC élites, and then to broader portions of the population. These are both aspects of a single process, and consumption trends in the international tobacco industry over the past thirty years bear eloquent testimony to the degree to which TNCs are able to channel and bias consumption patterns in favourable directions for their continued success and profitability. In cigarettes, these have benefited US TNCs in particular.

There have been four major worldwide shifts in the consumption of tobacco products in the last thirty-five years, all of them considerably influenced by TNCs: (1) From all other tobacco products (cigars, chewing, pipe tobacco, etc.) to cigarettes; (2) from the consumption of 'dark' tobaccos to the consumption of 'light' tobaccos; (3) from the consumption of unfiltered cigarettes to the consumption of filtered cigarettes; and (4) from the consumption of short (70 mm) cigarettes to the consumption of longer cigarettes (85 mm, 100 mm, 120 mm). Hence, the trend has been strongly towards TNC product forms (e.g. longer-length, filtered, 'light' tobacco cigarettes) and away from shorter-length, non-filtered 'dark' tobacco products of national producers.

In particular, there has been a decisive worldwide shift to the consumption of 'American Blend' cigarettes (containing approximately 50–55 % 'flue-cured' tobaccos; 30–35 % burley, 10–15 % 'Oriental–Turkish' and 2–3 % Maryland), once culturally-specific only to the US. More comprehensive data than it is possible to present here clearly indicate these trends (Fidel *et al.*, 1977: pp. 3–17). For a long time, perhaps as long as fifty years, the battle lines in the Latin American cigarette industry have been drawn between domestic *tabaco negro* cigarettes made by national firms and foreign *tabaco rubio* cigarettes made by TNCs. The 'winners' are clearly evident in Table 18. 1.

The 'controlled' product cycle

To see why particular product forms have tended to give TNCs an advantage, it is necessary to understand that, in the course of attempting to create demand, TNCs have developed a vested interest in channelling demand into products with which they are already familiar. Rather than bother to ascertain the consumer's *existing* preferences, TNCs generally find it more profitable and efficient to attempt to stimulate in the consumer those responses which would lead him to prefer the products which TNCs already have and which they wish to establish in the market. This is particularly crucial just prior, during, and immediately after TNC entry. This channelling of demand into the well-worn grooves of the TNC's product-cycle is highly favourable to TNCs. It puts national firms at a severe disadvantage, especially those producing culturally-indigenous or idiosyncratic product forms.

Thus TNCs' efforts will be directed towards making sure that markets abroad do converge along lines already well-explored and for which rents may be had for product forms and brands already highly-depreciated in the domestic market. TNCs will therefore attempt at least three things: (1) to direct product development and consumption in these directions; (2) to ensure that local product form 'deviations' are not too dissimilar; and (3) that consumption does not remain at a qualitative and/or quantitative level that is less favourable to it in terms of appropriability (Magee, 1977). These attempts to direct consumption and production along a product-cycle path already well-explored will act to convey upon TNCs certain systematic advantages. These advantages are not enjoyed by local firms who have not already scouted these product-cycle paths to the degree TNCs have.

There is no *necessity* that these foreign markets will proceed along the linear, 'stage' path implied by the TNCs' product-cycles. The problem from the TNC's point of view is precisely in making sure that foreign markets will, in fact, converge along similar lines given the cultural, political, social and economic diversity which reigns abroad. In foreign markets, not only are products likely to be at an earlier 'stage' in terms of product forms mapped out in the home market, but they are also likely to be dependent on demand configurations which correspond to idiosyncratic factors not well-known by TNCs, at least at the outset. And not only will products be 'different' in the sense of response to local cultural factors, but also, particularly in LDCs, present in forms that are much simpler and less appropriable by the private TNC (Shepherd, 1983: chapter 6).

The answer here, and the great success of TNCs, lies in guiding production and consumption down the product-cycle path already traced out in the home market in earlier stages. Adaptations will be made to local conditions *if* they are relatively consistent with TNCs capacities and the requirements of appropriability. But the real trick is to move consumption and production into 'international' (that is, TNC home nations') patterns and away from local, national idiosyncracies which may reduce appropriability and/or give local firms the decisive advantage.

These 'international' consumption patterns form a milieu in which any given national market resides. This in itself creates an implicit demand for TNC product forms and brands. But what if the local national market is cut off and protected by ISI policies that prohibit the effective communication of these trends to consumer? What if the prohibition of importation of TNC cigarettes means that local, culturally-indigenous product forms are the only ones available and promoted?

Rarely, of course, has any market in the 'Free World' been entirely shut off from world trade and completely isolated. Where import substitution industrialisation policies have prohibited imports of cigarettes, some consumers may still be familiar with TNC products through prior acquaintance before these policies took effect. In LDCs, a small quantity of imported TNC cigarettes has often been permitted with high duties in an otherwise protected market. This is to offer what Hirschman called 'gold-plated service' for the 'capital-city' élite. These imports are not only for the élite's benefit; they also 'comfort' the local tobacco industry and reduce the demands on it for 'connoisseur goods' (Hirschman, 1970: pp. 48–60). This, too, creates a certain latent demand for TNC product forms and goods.

The role of contraband

More importantly, protected markets were often 'softened-up' prior to TNC entry by contraband cigarettes. Increased smuggling of cigarettes was strongly associated with TNC expansion, especially that of US cigarette firms during the late 1960s and early 1970s (table 18. 2).

Table 18.2. *Recorded world exports and recorded world imports of cigarettes compared, selected years, 1951–60[a] and 1967–76[b].*

Year	Recorded world exports	Recorded world imports	Percentage difference
1951	126,735	106,508	16.0
1952	115,324	95,732	17.0
1953	114,869	90,708	21.0
1954	108,317	91,939	15.1
1955	108,420	92,179	15.0
1956	109,717	85,379	22.2
1957	110,129	92,334	16.2
1958	110,484	93,208	15.6
1959	108,609	86,425	20.4
1960	110,428	84,162	23.8
1967–71[c] Average	136,356	92,058	32.5
1972	178,415	126,016	29.4
1973	191,938	133,306	30.5
1974	203,888	153,615	24.7
1975	222,659	170,778	23.2
1976	241,797	177,361	26.6

Notes:
[a] In thousands of pounds of cigarettes.
[b] In millions of cigarettes.
[c] Unfortunately, the United States Department of Agriculture discontinued publishing data on world trade in cigarettes after 1962 and did not resume its international cigarette trade series until 1976 in which the 1957–72 average was provided. It may be precisely because of the large disparity between recorded exports and recorded imports that USDA discontinued the data series since it appeared so unreliable as to be worthless during the 1960s.
Sources: US Department of Agriculture, *World tobacco analysis-consumer marketing*, February 1958; *Foreign agriculture circulars – tobacco* FT 5–60, FT 8–62, FT 3–76, FT 2–77 (July, 1960; May, 1962; July, 1976 and 1977)

Significant contraband trade in cigarettes is not only evident in Latin America, but in many regions and nations, including relatively developed ones such as Italy and Belgium. In the tobacco trade press there have been scores of articles dealing with the contraband problem since the mid-1960s.

(See, for example: 'Former government aide claims Italy underselling itself to multinational firms', 1975: p. 51; 'Malaysia: smuggling accord reached', 1977: p. 66; 'Philippines: cigarettes go up in smoke', 1977: p. 14; 'Bangladesh: increased production fails to check smuggling', 1986: p. 12; 'South Korea: ruling party wants to curb flow of US cigarettes', 1986: p. 16). In Italy, for example, it was estimated that up to 200,000 Italians were earning their living smuggling cigarettes, costing the government an estimated $560 million a year in lost revenue. The practice was so firmly entrenched that formal protests were not uncommon when police acted to curb operations ('Italy: smuggling on the rise', 1978: pp. 20, 26).

The pattern of smuggling is well-nigh universal. TNC cigarettes are first exported from the developed countries to small, intermediary 'free trade zone' nations (Hong Kong, Panama, Netherlands Antilles, Paraguay, Lebanon, Malaysia, Belgium/Luxembourg, Singapore, etc.). US cigarette exports to these destinations far outstrip the local potential for domestic consumption by a factor of five to ten, even at levels of *per capita* consumption characteristic of the US (the highest in the world). For example, the Netherlands Antilles, with a population of 200,000, imported 4,126 million cigarettes from the US in 1976. This figure equalled 20,630 cigarettes for every single man, woman and child in the Netherlands Antilles when the estimated annual *per capita* consumption in the US was only 2,816 in 1975!

Large quantities of these cigarettes are then re-exported illegally to their final market destination in protected markets close to these (entrepot) centres of distribution. These cigarettes thus make their way through illegal channels into surrounding protected markets: the Netherlands Antilles and Panama supply Colombia and the Caribbean; Hong Kong, Malaysia and Singapore supply the Philippines, Thailand and Indonesia; Paraguay supplies Brazil and Argentina; Lebanon much of the Middle East, etc. The dollar value of this trade is considerable, even at the tax-free and duty-free prices reported at exit from the US: $50 million for Hong Kong; $37 million for the Netherlands Antilles; $18 million for Lebanon; $110 million for Belgium, to cite a few of the main smuggling centres (Shepherd, 1979: tables 33 and 34). The actual retail value of the contraband once it reaches the consumer is probably about twice this.

A variation on the pattern of contraband distribution takes place when TNC brands are manufactured by local subsidiaries and/or licensees for clandestine export into neighbouring markets from these smaller nations. Much of the contraband into Italy, for example, comes from TNC subsidiaries in Switzerland. Other cases include cigarettes made in Hong Kong, the Canary Islands, and Belgium/Luxembourg.

Contraband provides an effective – if unorthodox and illegal – method of market penetration to gain a foothold in 'protected' foreign markets. The

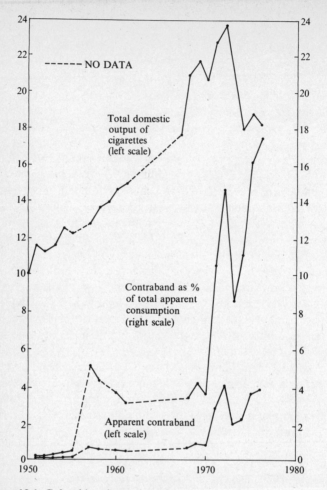

Figure 18.1 Colombia, domestic output of cigarettes, apparent contraband and contraband as a percentage of total apparent consumption of cigarettes, 1950–76.

Source: Shepherd, 1980 (based on USDA estimates of total domestic output, legal imports, US exports and Depto National de Planeacion data on contraband).

increase in the contraband cigarette trade of various nations is highly correlated with the battle to take over national cigarette industries. Usually smuggling reaches its peak just prior, during, and after TNC entry into a market through direct foreign investment or licensing. It may extend for a considerable period of time if resistance by locally-owned firms is prolonged, but after TNC entry and relative complete denationalisation, smuggling frequently declines.

The case of Colombia is illustrative (figure 18. 1). Colombia is one of the last wholly nationally-owned private cigarette industries with a fairly large market (above 20 billion cigarettes *per annum*). Until quite recently, it also produced and consumed almost exclusively 'dark tobacco' cigarettes, as was once the norm in most of Latin America (table 18. 1). As contraband climbed in the early 1970s, domestic manufacturers were hurt and domestic output declined significantly. In the early 1970s, two licensing agreements were signed between two locally-owned firms and TNCs to manufacture the two largest-selling contraband cigarette brands – Philip Morris' Marlboro and P. Lorillard's Kent.

This, however, was only the first stage of the process. Smuggling resumed as the domestic firms resolved to try to fight out the *tabaco rubio* versus *tabaco negro* battle (Perez Vasquez, 1975). Because Colombian firms resisted TNC direct foreign investment contraband continued at high levels in Colombia – approximately 4.5 billion cigarettes a year (Republica de Colombia, DNP, 1975: p. 6; Perez Vasquez, 1975). To gain some idea of the size of this trade in illicit cigarettes, it was nearly as large as *all* US exports of cigarettes to the EEC in the early 1970s (approximately 5.7 billion). The annual magnitude of contraband entering Colombia in the 1970s was larger than the total 1975 cigarette exports of either the American Tobacco Co. or Liggett & Myers, roughly one-half those of P. Lorillard; 31% of all exports of R. J. Reynolds, and 29% of those of Philip Morris. At early 1970s prices, this clandestine trade was worth in the neighbourhood of 40–50 million dollars (Shepherd, 1983: pp. 1487–8).

The entire process is revealed perhaps most clearly by the Argentine experience. Smuggling of cigarettes skyrocketed in the early 1960s (figure 18. 2). It then fell off momentarily in 1962 when legal imports were briefly permitted (with low duties) to combat the problem. This did not provide domestic firms with any respite, but only made their situation worse because effective protection had been lifted (as also took place in Colombia). To defend themselves, some national firms began to establish themselves as exclusive importers of TNCs' brands, thus beginning dependence on the TNCs. When legal imports were once again shut off, licensing arrangements were established for local manufacture of brands that had previously been imported. Quickly thereafter, in dire financial straits, all the nationally-owned firms were acquired at bargain prices by TNCs (Philip Morris-Massalin & Celasco; Liggett & Myers-Piccardo; Reemstma-Particulares and Imparciales) in 1966–7. This completed the denationalisation process. After the period of establishment of TNC brands, smuggling fell off rapidly back to 'normal', pre-1960 (unorganised?) levels (figure 18. 2).

Where were national governments in all this, given their interests as 'senior partners' in the cigarette industry through excise tax receipts? One study in Argentina estimated that some $28 million were lost in government revenue, and there was a balance of payments loss of $54 million in payments for

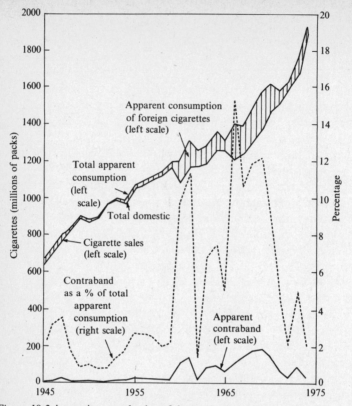

Figure 18.2 Argentina, total sales of domestic cigarettes, total apparent consumption, apparent contraband, apparent consumption of foreign cigarettes, and contraband as percentage of total apparent consumption, 1945–74

Source: Estudio Sur, *Estudio de la Demanda de Tabaco Nacional* (Buenos Aires, 1975 (mimeo)), Cuadro A-17, p. 24; Anexo C, Cuadro C-4, p. 81.

contraband cigarettes between 1961 and 1967, *after* deducting 35% to the smugglers who (presumably?) were Argentines (Oric, 1968: Anexo V: p. 5; 28). In fact, public policy towards the industry in both Colombia and Argentina (as well as many other Latin American nations) was extremely contradictory. It often made things worse for national firms even when governmental intent was otherwise.

It is truly remarkable how similar the basic outlines of this whole process have been – including Latin American governments' responses to these events. The political will to take decisive action on behalf of national firms was simply not forthcoming. Public policy tended to vacillate among various alternatives, none of them providing any real solution to the problem. Governments were totally incapable of eradicating political corruption and/

or incompetence in customs enforcement and in other crucial sectors of public administration such as the military. Although governments were losing untold millions of dollars in tax revenues, advertising for TNC brands that could only enter the countries illegally was blatantly apparent along public throughfares and in the mass media in both Colombia and Argentina (Perez Vasques, 1975: p. 31; Vilas, 1974; p. 12).

Government technocrats, reasoning on neo-classical economic grounds that legal imports with fairly low tariffs would cut smuggling and recoup government revenues, often experimented temporarily with lifting import bans and high tariffs on foreign cigarettes only to find that, while government revenue did recover somewhat, this served to consolidate, legitimise and expand TNC products' positions in the market. Since this did nothing to relieve TNC pressures on nationally-owned firms, the latter vehemently protested, not without reason, that they had willingly borne the brunt of high taxation on their products to help support the government and were therefore entitled to some support themselves. In fact, during periods of legal imports, the effective rate of taxation on nationally-owned firms' products was actually much *higher* than that levied on the TNC imported brands (Perez Vasquez, 1975: pp. 5–20). Thus temporary periods of legal imports alternated with increased smuggling when import bans and high tariffs were reimposed until national firms were sufficiently financially crippled to either sell out to TNCs or, at the minimum, sign licensing agreements for the local manufacture of the contraband TNC brands.[3]

Another factor in the vacillation of public policy appears to have been the protected status and quasi-monopolistic positions national cigarette firms had long held in their markets. Because of the long history of dominance and fairly significant political and economic power of these firms, lower sectors of the public administration (and some of the higher officials as well) were not sympathetic to their plight. Nationally-owned firms were sometimes able finally to get their way, but it often took Herculean pushing and shoving in national legislatures and the relevant bureaucracies. By that time it was often too late. Even when governmental support was forthcoming, action was taken not out of any great sympathy for the plight of nationally-owned firms, but rather out of concern for the effects on the economy as a whole and on tax revenues. Interviews with Latin American policy-makers confirm that many viewed national cigarette firms as predatory, oppressive monopolists finally getting a taste of their own medicine. Thus they tacitly encouraged TNC competition, legal or illegal (Shepherd, 1983: p. 1492).

Thus smuggling patterns strongly suggest that contraband has been an arm of TNC 'marketing' efforts to penetrate foreign cigarette industries.[4] The benefits of smuggling go considerably beyond the simple desire to export more cigarettes wherever and however they can. Contraband TNC cigarettes 'soften-up' prospective markets abroad for licensing and subsidiary operations later on by creating a demand for certain product forms and brands; by subtly changing consumer tastes through snob appeal and lower prices (smuggled cigarettes pay neither excise taxes nor import duties); and, they cripple the local competition which, if nationally-owned and relatively weak financially, can then be easily acquired. If TNCs are licensing their brands to local manufacturers, smuggling can also be employed to press for equity participation. If legal imports are temporarily permitted to combat smuggling, TNCs can switch to legal exports, contraband will still continue somewhat (because contraband pays neither excise taxes nor import duties), and, in any event, nationally-owned firms will *still* be hurt.

The smuggling problem in its entirety is simply too complex to be considered in any detail here (Shepherd, 1977: pp. 19–21; Shepherd, 1983: pp. 1492–1522). The exact nature of its causes is not sufficiently clear. 'Neo-classical' economists would point to relatively high taxes, high tariffs, and outright prohibitions on imports as the main sources of difficulty (Bhagwati, 1974). These are undoubtedly part of the problem. But the fact that contraband sometimes flourishes even where smuggled cigarettes are considerably *more* expensive than local products suggests that traditional economic theory is not very enlightening here – at least as a relatively complete explanation.

Because of the relatively large numbers of people involved in contraband distribution networks and the risk involved, margins on smuggled cigarettes tend to be rather high. So price differentials, in and of themselves, are not always that great or are even non-existent. They are certainly insufficient as a complete account of the problem, ignoring as they do the role of TNCs in influencing consumer choice. Other variables are clearly involved since many, if not most, LDC nations have ISI protectionism and high cigarette excise taxes. But only certain nations at certain times have had serious national smuggling problems with cigarettes. For example, Italy's state monopoly has serious problems but Japan's does not. Thus cigarette smuggling, as a general phenomenon, may be as closely related to TNC strategies and sociopolitical variables as to more narrowly economic ones (Shepherd, 1977: p. 21).

The role of TNCs in contraband also requires clarification. Smuggling has been an effective instrument of TNC market penetration in the cigarette industry *regardless* of the precise role of TNCs in contraband activities. Whether TNCs have been directly involved in the trade, whether they have indirectly encouraged it, or whether they have had no connection with smuggling activities whatsoever, TNCs have been the primary beneficiaries of contraband in cigarettes in Latin America (and probably elsewhere as well).

There is at least some (unfortunately confidential) evidence of direct TNC involvement in smuggling in both Argentina and Colombia.[5] There is also considerable circumstantial evidence implied in the basic outlines of these massive 'marketing' campaigns through smuggling: the blatant advertisement of TNC brands that can *only* be brought into a nation through *illegal* channels; the considerable financial dimensions of alternative contraband distribution networks; the rapidity with which they appear and disappear; the timing of contraband 'phases' in different nations; the fact that, while a variety of cigarette brands is usually available in contraband markets, certain brands (usually only two or three) are much more widely distributed and far outsell all others; the fact that it is precisely the manufacturers of these same brands that enter through licensing or direct foreign investment later on; and the fact that any self-respecting 'marketing' personnel in charge of cigarette exports in given regions would have to be blind not to realise where massive exports to countries like the Netherland Antilles finally end up.

Impact on industrial structure: foreign dominance and concentration

The process of denationalisation has largely entailed the expansion of US TNCs into the region since most of the BAT subsidiaries were established much earlier. But it was not exclusively a US TNC process – either in origin or in benefits. The West German firm Reemstma originally acquired two of the Argentine national firms, for example. And BAT may be the eventual beneficiary in Colombia since it assumed P. Lorillard's international operations.

There was a distinct, common pattern of denationalisation in Latin America. The same series of events – with some variation in the pattern and timing – took place in Brazil (1970s); Mexico (1960s); Peru (1960s); and Ecuador (1970s) as well as in many other smaller markets in Latin America. Only Venezuela, Chile, Uruguay, and Cuba have exhibited major differences. Venezuela largely escaped a major contraband assault because its oil wealth made it the largest (legal) importer of US cigarettes in the 1950s. US TNCs had already established a foothold in the market this way. This led to relatively early denationalisation at the outset of the formation of Venezuela's cigarette industry in the late 1950s and early 1960s. Chile seems to have deviated from the pattern somewhat because of the private, officially-sanctioned monopoly held by the local BAT subsidiary dating from the 1920s. A small market and depressed economic conditions during the 1970s evidently made it unattractive for other TNCs, although Philip Morris entered in 1982.

The case of Uruguay, which retained the only completely nationally-owned industry (without even licensing with TNCs) until as late as 1979 is not entirely clear. Depressed economic conditions there may have played some role as well as its small market and the disturbed political conditions characteristic of the late 1960s and early 1970s. However, Philip Morris acquired a locally-owned firm in 1979 and Uruguay may differ over the long

Table 18.3. *Multinational cigarette firms in Latin America: subsidiaries, licensing arrangements, and non-tobacco operations, c. 1976*

Nations	British-American %	Philip Morris %	R. J. Reynolds %	Liggett Group %	Rupert/ Rothman's Group %	Reemtsma %	Loew's %	Total output[1] 1976	Est MNC[2] Share %
Argentina	S-(42)NT	S-(22)		S-(17)		S-(19)	L	36,800	100
Barbados	S(100)	L					L	210	100
Bolivia		S-(5)	S-(11)	S-(NI)				1,700	NI
Brazil	S-(75)NT	L		S[3]		S[5]		117,000	91
Colombia		S-(16)		L			S[6]/L	18,300	3/15[12]
Costa Rica	S-(57)							2,300	75
Chile	S-(100)			L				8,800	100
Dom. Rep.		S-(NI)						3,200	NI
Ecuador		S-(60)	S-(40)					3,700	100
El Salvador	S-(76)	S-(15)						2,200	91
Guatemala		S-(45)NT					L	2,400	50
Guyana	S-(NI)							500	NI
Haiti		L						500	NI
Honduras	S-(100)							1,800	100
Jamaica	S-(27)				S-(70)			1,500	97
Mexico	S-(30)NT	S-(14)	S[7]/L(NI)	L			L	45,000	60
N. Antilles		L						NI	NI
Nicaragua	S-(96)							1,700	96
Panama	S-(55)	S-(43)					L	1,100	98
Paraguay	L	L[8]						700	NI
Peru	L		S-(NI)	S[9]/L			S[10]-(NI)	3,800	25
Puerto Rico		S[10]-(NI)						NI	100
Trinidad/Tabago		L						1,200	NI
Uruguay								3,500	0
Venezuela	S-(19)NT	S-(76)	S[11]-(2)					18,800	97

Notes:

1. In millions of cigarettes (not by value).
2. Estimates include cigarettes manufactured under licensing arrangements but *not* import/export sales (either illicit or legal).
3. Leaf exporting subsidiary only. Liggett closed its manufacturing subsidiary in 1972.
4. The Rupert/Rothman's Group (Martin Brinkman) sold this subsidiary (Lopes) to R. J. Reynolds in 1975.
5. Reemtsma sold this subsidiary (Fumos Santa Cruz) to Philip Morris in 1975.
6. Leaf tobacco production subsidiary to supply its licensee, Protabacos, S.A.
7. Reynolds sold its subsidiary (Baloyan) when the Mexican government forced divesture of majority MNC holdings after 1973.
8. Licensing agreement signed in 1978.
9. Liggett sold its subsidiary in 1975.
10. Apparently selling companies which do not manufacture in Puerto Rico.
11. May have been sold cff in 1976.
12. MNC sales are only approximately 3% not including contraband; approximately 15% including illicit imports of MNC brands.

Sources: United Nations Conference on Trade and Development, *Marketing and distribution of tobacco* (TD/B/C.1/205), June 16, 1978, Table 9, pp. 31–2; United States Department of Agriculture *Foreign agriculture circular-tobacco*, FT-2-77, July 1977 and estimates by the author based on various trade sources.

Key: S – (%); Subsidiary with significant (20%+) equity holdings. Market share (by volume) is given in parentheses.
L – Licensing agreement with a local company (either locally-owned or another MNC) in which no equity is held.
NI – No information available.
NT – Non-tobacco subsidiary operations are also present with significant (20%+) equity ownership.

run only in the relative tardiness of the denationalisation process ('Philip Morris invests in Uruguayan firm', 1979: p. 24).

'Denationalisation' is an apt term for the process of TNC entry into the Latin American cigarette industry over the past thirty-five years because it took place largely through the acquisition of *existing* nationally-owned firms. Nearly 80% of the traceable US TNC subsidiary operations in Latin America were acquisitions of this type (Shepherd, 1983: Appendix A). The complex reasons for this cannot be explored here, but several factors were at work in addition to the debilitating effects of contraband on national firms. First, the pressure of domestic market stagnation in TNCs' home cigarette sales dictated rapid entry into foreign markets while the large cash flow from domestic sales provided the necessary funds. Moreover, TNC cigarette firms' demand creation advantages logically implied a strategy of acquisition of existing national firms. This provided TNCs with some local marketing expertise, an easy entry into pre-existing distribution systems abroad and a 'national cloak' with which to deflect possible nationalist consumer rejection and adverse political reaction to aggressive competition based on 'artificial', 'unfair' demand creation techniques (Shepherd, 1977: pp. 14–15).

The process of denationalisation has been most aggressively pressed towards complete take-over in the largest, most attractive markets with considerable growth potential, such as Mexico, Argentina, Brazil and Venezuela. In many of the smaller, more sluggish markets, TNCs were content with licensing arrangements or with partial take-overs and minority equity positions as in Peru, Bolivia, Paraguay, etc. Nevertheless, by 1975 TNC market control in most markets in Latin America was quite high (table 18. 3).

The data in table 18. 3 are really rather striking: TNCs are present in one form or another in every single national market in the region and they are the dominating factor in most. Their market shares are quite large, giving them virtual control of most of the major Latin American cigarette industries. In the larger national markets of Brazil, Argentina, Mexico, Venezuela and Chile their dominance is obvious; but one should also note the degree of penetration in some of the smaller nations such as Ecuador, the Central American countries, and the Caribbean nations. In effect, nationally-owned cigarette industries survive in only very few nations – Uruguay, Peru, Colombia, and perhaps one or two more. Even these are tied to the TNCs by licensing arrangements and TNC influence is plainly on the rise. Perhaps the most disquieting thing about table 18. 3 is that, were it possible to assemble the same sort of information for, say, 1950 or even 1960, it would look very different. Apart from most of the BAT operations (and even then BAT market control was often much lower), Latin American cigarette industries were wholly national in ownership in 1950 or 1960. By the mid-

1970s, however, nationally-owned cigarette firms had become a thing of the past.

After TNC entry, a radical transformation of the contours of the industry frequently followed. After acquisition of local firms (or even, on occasion, after licensing began), a particular pattern tended to emerge, especially in the larger markets like Brazil, Argentina, and Mexico where denationalisation was almost total. Intense oligopolistic competition for a larger market share immediately broke out – which did not usually involve much durable price competition. There was a rather short (five-year) cycle of intense, more evenly divided competition in terms of market shares, followed by considerable market shake-up (firms with initially large market shares declined and vice versa), and then renewed concentration and consolidation. The Argentine experience after 1966 was typical of this pattern (Fidel *et al.*, 1977: pp. 21–39).

While there are a number of factors at work making for high levels of market concentration in Latin American cigarette industries, not all of them directly traceable to the impact of TNCs, TNC entry has done nothing to reverse these, and, on the contrary, has served to accentuate and accelerate high levels of concentration. Thus, although nationally-owned cigarette industries in the region have sometimes operated in conditions of tight oligopoly or quasi-monopoly historically, the entry of TNCs has further concentrated market structure.

For example, prior to TNC entry in Argentina in the mid-1960s, there had been five to nine major cigarette firms. Led by BAT's subsidiary with approximately 35–40 % of the market, for decades the rest of the market had been relatively evenly divided among locally-owned firms. After a short period of intense oligopolistic rivalry following TNC take-overs, however, successive mergers eventually reduced the industry to only *two* firms, a duopoly in the hands of BAT and Philip Morris. This transition from loose oligopoly to 'workable competition' and then to renewed concentration and consolidation under TNCs also took place in other Latin American markets, including Brazil, Mexico and Venezuela.

TNC expansion of demand

After TNC entry, markets were often 'turned around', as TNC managers describe it. This meant very rapid growth rates both in terms of total cigarette output and *per capita* consumption. In great contrast to the relatively stagnant aggregate market growth rates usually realised by nationally-owned firms, the newly-acquired TNC subsidiaries were able to expand primary demand (table 18. 4). The main method by which this was accomplished was a vast increase in demand creation efforts primarily

Table 18.4. *Sales of nationally-made cigarettes*[a] *in Argentina, 1950–75*

(in packs of 20)

Year	Packs (millions)	Index 1960 = 100	Packs *per capita* (number)	Index 1960 = 100	Packs *per capita* 17 yrs.	Index 1960 = 100
1950	876	81.0	51.1	97.3	77.6	97.2
1955	1,047	96.8	55.3	105.3	84.0	105.3
1960	1,082	100.0	52.5	100.0	79.8	100.0
1965	1,248	115.3	56.3	107.2	85.0	106.5
1966[b]	1,207	111.6	53.7	102.3	80.8	101.3
1967	1,241	114.7	54.4	103.6	81.7	102.4
1968	1,307	120.8	56.5	107.6	84.6	106.0
1969	1,376	127.2	58.7	111.8	87.7	109.9
1970	1,467	135.6	61.8	117.7	92.0	115.3
1971	1,509	139.5	62.7	119.4	93.2	116.8
1972	1,595	147.4	65.4	124.6	97.0	121.6
1973	1,676	154.9	67.8	129.1	100.4	125.8
1974	1,891	174.8	75.7	144.2	112.0	140.4
1975	1,905	176.1	73.5	140.0	108.6	136.1

[a] Does not include cigarette imports, either legal or illicit and hence is not a measure of actual consumption.

[b] 1966 is the year of entry of Philip Morris and Liggett and Myers as well as Reemtsma. It is the year usually given for the 'denationalization' of the Argentine cigarette industry, although the largest firm in the industry, Nobleza (BAT) was established in 1913.

Sources: Departamento de Tobaco, Secretaria de Estado de Agricultura y Ganaderia, and Instituto Nacional de Estadistica, Republica de Argentina.

advertising, but also through rationalisation of distribution systems, increased sales forces, and other promotional techniques.[6]

In Argentina, for example, there was a dramatic upsurge in advertising expenditures after TNC entry in 1966 (table 18. 5).[7] Once the industry 'shake-up' had taken place, new brands launched, and old ones repositioned or eliminated, advertising and other promotional expenditures declined in the 1970s. The increasingly dysfunctional advertising war led to a 'truce' in the form of a voluntary agreement to ban advertising in radio, TV and movie theaters between September 1969, and July 1972, ratified by the Argentine government (Fidel and Lucangeli, 1978: p. 11). Highly inflationary conditions coupled with governmental price controls caused a decline in the real price of cigarettes to consumers which aided in the effort to increase consumption and stimulate market growth. But in the context of an advertising war, this was a mixed blessing since it also seriously affected

Table 18.5. *Cigarette advertising expenditures in Argentina before and after entry of transnational cigarette firms, 1958–1976*

Year	Expenditure at constant prices[a] per 1,000 packs of cigarettes (1960 pesos)
1958	40.0
1959	16.0
1960	20.0
1961	45.0
1962	79.0
1963	80.0
1964	70.0
1965	83.0
1966 – Entry of TNC cigarette firms	73.0
1967	107.0
1968	312.0
1969	428.0
1970	249.0
1971	238.0
1972	197.0
1973	184.0
1974	133.0
1975	93.0
1976	118.0

[a] Deflated by the non-rural wholesale price index.
Source: Julio Fidel and Jorge Lucangeli, 'Cost-benefit of different technological options in the context of a differentiated oligopoly: the case of the Argentine cigarette industry', United Nations Economic Commission for Latin America and Inter-American Development Bank Research Program in Science and Technology, Working Paper No. 18, Buenos Aires, October 1978, Table 5, p. 18.

profit levels. Hence the advertising ban and the new, more settled equilibrium which evolved in the mid-1970s (table 18. 6).

TNC brand strategies after denationalisation in markets like Argentina, Brazil, and Mexico also demonstrate three important points: (1) the often tenuous nature of the advantage TNCs obtained over nationally-owned firms; (2) the full significance of the contraband phase to TNC take-overs; and (3) the important role acquisition of national firms played in TNC strategies.

Nationally-owned firms were not simply decisively defeated in a relative open, 'fair' game of commercial combat with TNCs. Often enough, nationally-owned firms were well-established, and their brands had accumulated a large stock of 'good-will' and market appeal. Most nationally-owned firms put up credible opposition to the entry of TNCs, both commercially and politically. They did not simply 'cave in' or sell out at the first hint of foreign competition. Without the debilitating effects of contraband and governmental vacillation, nationally-owned firms probably could have survived in many markets in Latin America.

Shortly after TNC entry and the acquisition of nationally-owned firms, TNCs heavily promoted their 'international' (read home market) brands, such as Marlboro, Kent, Winston, etc. This was necessary to gain market acceptance of locally-made versions of the 'international' brands formerly made available only through smuggling.[8] While these brands played a critical 'Trojan Horse' role prior to TNC entry, they became less important after the acquisition of national firms. National brands previously developed by local firms have remained popular and comprise a large, often major, portion of TNCs' subsidiaries' sales.[9] Although Marlboro alone accounted for more than one-third of Philip Morris' international sales (including exports) in 1976, about 60% of its volume abroad was in regional and national brands (Philip Morris, Inc., 1976: p. 6).

The continued popularity of national brands for the majority of consumers suggests that TNC footholds in the market with international brands during the contraband period were actually rather fragile and did not really provide the basis for long-term success. Hence, acquisition of national firms' brands was critical to TNC success. In the absence of the unique conditions of massive smuggling, public policy vacillation and so forth, nationally-owned firms probably could have continued as viable enterprises. Indeed, they had been quite successful for long periods of time in most Latin American markets prior to TNC assault.

Conclusion

This study examined part of the process of TNC expansion out of industrialised nations' economies into only one region (Latin America) in one industry (cigarettes) during a relatively short period of time (roughly 1950–80). Thus the general conclusions that can be drawn for the theory of TNC behaviour from this limited case study are inevitably rather circumscribed. Clearly post-war denationalisation in Latin American cigarette industries is only a very small piece of the larger puzzle that is the dynamic evolution of transnational capitalist organisation. While it is only a piece of the puzzle, it none the less remains an intriguing and important one for several reasons, briefly explored here as concluding remarks.

The attempt to describe and explain the denationalisation process is important and interesting in the first place because denationalisation of nationally-owned cigarette industries has not been confined to Latin America. As this case study showed, the takeover of national firms by TNCs was especially evident in Latin America. But it has also taken place to a surprising degree in Europe, Asia, Canada, Australia, and indeed wherever there were national cigarette firms to be acquired.

Even state-owned tobacco monopolies in highly industrialised countries like Japan, Italy and France have not been immune. For the past decade they have been under pressure by TNCs, both through commercial means and more 'political' bargaining process in trade talks, European Economic Community institutions and the like (for example, 'Former Government Aide', 1975; 'Japan: reorganizing to build markets', 1984; Japan: imports gain as domestic sales fall', 1985). Perhaps even more remarkable is the degree to which TNC cigarette firms have managed to penetrate Socialist Bloc nations. The licensing of TNC brands has been common throughout Eastern Europe for ten years and various joint ventures with TNCs have been set up in China ('Camels in China', 1980; 'China: the quest for better quality', 1986).

While it is unlikely that these state-owned cigarette industries will be denationalised in quite the same manner as in Latin America, these trends are indicative of TNC expansion around the world which has led to very high levels of industrial concentration. By the late 1970s the top six TNC cigarette firms accounted for well over 40 % of world-wide cigarette sales and nearly 85 % of cigarette sales in nations without state cigarette monopolies (Shepherd, 1979: pp. 34–6).

More importantly, denationalisation has not been unique to the cigarette industry. Evidence from other case studies strongly suggests that a similar process beset other industries and that this had a decisive impact on the structure of manufacturing in Latin America. Specifically, TNC denationalisation has affected pharmaceuticals, electrical machinery, and a wide variety of food and beverage industries (Gereffi, 1983; Newfarmer, 1980; Whiting, 1981). Greater attention to denationalisation would undoubtedly reveal that it has been more general than frequently acknowledged, especially in LDCs.

Secondly, denationalisation would not matter much if TNCs' conduct and performance were similar to those of national firms. However, denationalisation derives a major portion of its overall significance from the fact that TNC firms behave quite differently from national firms and their resulting performance is often worse by traditional industrial organisation criteria. For instance, explicitly comparing TNC firms' conduct and performance to that of national enterprises, I have shown elsewhere that TNCs differed substantially and that their performance was often socially adverse. This was true in a variety of areas such as: pricing behaviour, profitability, technology and employment, trade and balance of payments, linkage effects, income distribution, and product appropriateness, including the smoking/health issue (Shepherd, 1979: pp. 181–209). Moreover, these patterns of industrial conduct and performance by TNCs seem to be rather general (Newfarmer, 'Multinationals and marketplace magic', 1983).

Third, denationalisation of Latin American and other cigarette industries is an interesting phenomenon because it points to a peculiar area of industrial strength of British and US manufacturing firms. Whereas foreign competition from Japan, West Germany, France, Italy and even countries like Taiwan, South Korea and Brazil has severely eroded (and virtually eliminated in the British case) US/UK industrial leadership in a wide variety of industries, such as steel, autos, textiles, etc., in the world cigarette industry US and British dominance remains as strong as ever, perhaps more so. West Germany, Japan, Italy and France have made only a few inroads into Anglo-American strength (chiefly in manufacturing equipment and inputs) and seem unlikely to break into this condominium. Denationalisation and the world cigarette industry need further study if only to discover the source of this interesting deviation from world capitalist patterns of strength and weakness.

Finally, this study of denationalisation reveals a theoretical loophole in our understanding of TNC behaviour. Following new-classical theory, which assumes relatively open international trade and investment in a frictionless market flow of capital and goods, most theories of TNCs implicitly assume that overseas markets can be entered at any time. Indeed, some analysts, noting that host nations have often been eager to attract foreign investment, point to the ways in which nations have consciously manipulated tariffs and other policy instruments to induce foreign investment in their markets (Bergsten, Horst and Moran, 1978: pp. 290–3).

While this has undoubtedly been true, it tells only part of the story. In many cases, such as the Latin American cigarette industry, foreign investment was not originally welcome and import substitution industrialisation policies were designed to build up nationally-owned industrial structures. The oft-cited case of Japan also implies that TNC market penetration was not always accomplished at will or without problems.

Thus part of the historical experience has been obscured by the almost exclusive attention devoted to TNCs and industrial structures in home nations. We need a view 'from below' as well as 'from above', a theory of *entry into* host nations as well as theory of *exit from* home nations. The opening up of other nations to TNC operations seems indispensable – indeed tautologically so – to TNC expansion: TNCs only become TNCs by opening up other countries' markets and resources. Yet the conditions under which a nation is opened up or opens itself up to TNCs often reveal a complex process of political–economic interaction that appears rather industry – or nation – specific on the surface. A very different kind of theory is required here, one which has been slow in development.

NOTES

1 The terms refer to colour but also reflect smoking quality. Roughly, light tobaccos are associated with mildness and cigarette manufacture, dark tobaccos with strength and much more non-cigarette usage, as in cigars. See Shepherd, 1983, Appendix D.

2 British-American Tobacco was originally a joint venture of US and English tobacco firms (American Tobacco Co. and Imperial Tobacco Co.). Formed in 1903, with two-thirds US and one-third British holdings, BAT was the result of a cartel agreement whereby American Tobacco controlled the US market and Imperial the UK market while BAT served the rest of the world. In the aftermath of the 1911 anti-trust case (which broke up American Tobacco), control of BAT eventually shifted to British stockholders. Thus, since the early 1920s, BAT has been a British firm (a fact not usually known in Latin America). BAT is and has been for some time the world's largest tobacco firm with substantial holdings throughout the world, including Latin America (See Shepherd, 1979 and table 18. 3).

3 In Argentina, successive devaluations also had a disastrous effect on local firms by: (1) making it much more difficult for national firms to import badly-needed equipment to increase production efficiency and manufacture similar product forms; (2) making it difficult for national firms to pay royalties on TNC licences; and (3) inflating the buying power of foreign currencies, thus enabling TNCs to buy stock in the local firms at bargain rates (already depressed, of course, because of their difficulties with smuggling). All this also took place in the context of a general political-economic policy oriented towards the promotion of foreign investment by the Ongani regime (Vilas, 1974: pp. 13–15).

4 It is in this context that the significant upswing in US cigarette exports since the late 1960s should be interpreted. US cigarette exports were over 70 billion in 1978, valued at $692 million. This comprised over 10% of total US cigarette output, the largest percentage going abroad (other than to US Armed Services) since the year 1920. Cigarette exports from the US are now over 60% of the value of leaf tobacco exports, traditionally the most important US tobacco export commodity (Data from the US Department of Agriculture, 1978: pp. 4–5). While a number of factors have influenced increasing exports – oil exporting states' imports, the world-wide trend to 'American Blend' cigarettes, and the 'multiplier effect' of the presence of US TNCs' operations abroad that is claimed by the industry (Philip Morris, 1976: p. 7) – increased smuggling around the world is also a factor. Since US cigarette exports (legal or illegal) to any given national market normally fall off dramatically after the establishment of TNC operations in that market, continued high levels of exports will likely be dependent on the ability of US TNCs to 'roll over' from one market to another. Eventually, however, US exports are likely to fall off once overseas manufacturing facilities for these brands have been set up in most markets. There is still considerable potential for this kind of progressive market penetration, as markets in the Middle East, Africa and Asia become 'worthwhile', but one doubts that high levels of either legal or illegal exports can be sustained for a long period of time.

5 Names, dates and places cannot be cited, but the basic outline of the TNC links to smuggling can be revealed. Apparently one common pattern has been the employment of local, 'national advertising/publicity/marketing agencies' to run interference with local smugglers. It is understood that part of the local marketing agency's job is to deal with the kingpins of contraband in the general area (say,

Netherlands Antilles and Panama for Colombia, or Paraguay for Argentina). The primary TNC interest is to make sure that the company's brands are 'well represented' – perhaps overwhelmingly so – in smuggling networks and distribution channels. 'Seed money' needed for developing or maintaining contraband distribution systems and the appropriate bribes to local smugglers can also be transferred indirectly through these 'marketing' personnel using the local advertising/promotion budget. Not only is money thereby channelled to local smuggling rings, but, similarly, payoffs to customs officials and other governmental personnel can be made in this manner without any direct involvement by corporate employees.

6 It is of some interest to see precisely how this market growth took place. The demand creation efforts were successfully directed at three basic groups: women and young non-smokers as well as older smokers of the more idiosyncratic domestic product form (in Latin America these are usually cheaper, short (70 mm), non-filter, dark tobacco brands). The basic idea underlying demand creation campaigns aimed at women and adolescents is obvious: to create primary demand growth where the marginal efficiency of demand creation techniques is often highest. This also has the appealing feature of providing a 'positive-sum' game for the firms. The strategy behind demand creation techniques aimed at established smokers of the older domestic product forms is more complex. The effort to move these smokers towards more expensive, 'sophisticated' product forms (although often still 'national' brands) was designed to eliminate relatively cheap, unprofitable brands where appropriability is much lower (as are, incidentally, the barriers to entry to new competition). The strategy of 'converting' established smokers to more 'advanced', more expensive product forms even involved the creation of a new 'hybrid' product form in Argentina – the 'mixed' light and dark tobacco cigarette (table 18. 1). By using revised versions of some of the older brand names, and by mixing dark tobacco with light tobacco in longer, filtered product forms, these smokers could be more easily weaned from the older, cheaper products.

7 Reported advertising expenditures were actually larger than reported earning (108 %) for Philip Morris' Massalin y Celasco subsidiary in 1967. High levels of advertising also produced reported losses for three of the five TNC subsidiaries in Argentina during the years 1967–70.

8 Domestic versions of the 'international brands' made 'under licence' are frequently considerably different from the original brand manufactured and sold in the home market. This is not simply because of local governmental requirements mandating the usage of some minimum proportion of locally-grown tobacco either. One example may serve to illustrate the point. In Argentina, the locally-made KENT is a large seller and is clearly advertised as employing the 'Famous Micronite Filter' (the phrase even appears across the front of the pack itself). Technically, however, this is simply not true. The 'Micronite Filter' is an identifiably different filter rod patented in the US (as are many other filter materials). But the filter used in Kents in Argentina is in fact indistinguishable from the filter rod materials used in most of the other filter cigarettes in Argentina, and is definitely *not* a 'Micronite Filter'.

9 Even at the height of international brand popularity in Argentina during 1975 (because the combination of governmental price controls and extreme rates of inflation had made the more expensive 'international brands' relatively cheap), these brands accounted for only some 32.7% of the Argentine cigarette market by volume of sales (data from Camara de la Industria del Cigarrillo, 1976).

REFERENCES

'Bangladesh: increased production fails to check smuggling', *Tobacco Reporter* (1986), 12.

Bergsten, C. Fred, Thomas Horst and Theodore H. Moran, *American multinational and American interests* (Washington, D.C, 1978).

Bhagwati, Jagdish N. (ed.), *Illegal transactions in international trade* (Amsterdam, 1974).

Brooks, Jerome E., *The Mighty Leaf: tobacco through the centuries* (Boston, 1952).

Camara de la Industria del Cigarrillo, *Sintesis estadistica anual, 1975* (Buenos Aires, 1976), mimeo.

'Camels in China', *Tobacco Reporter* (May 1980), 58–9.

'China: the quest for better quality', *Tobacco Reporter* (March 1986), 26–30.

Departmento de Tabaco, Secretaria de Estado de Agricultura y Ganaderia, *Estadistica Anual* (Buenos Aires, 1950–75).

Empresa Nacional de Tabaco, 'La industria tabacalera nacional y la participacion del estado dentro de su desarrollo', (Lima, 1974).

Estudio Sur, *Estudio de la demanda de tabaco nacional* (Buenos Aires, 1975), mimeo.

Fidel, Julio and Jorge Lucangeli, 'Cost-benefit of different technological options in the context of a differentiated oligopoly: the case of the Argentine cigarette industry', (Buenos Aires, 1978).

Fidel, Julio, Jorge Lucangeli, and Phil Shepherd, 'Perfil y comportamiento tecnologico de la industria del cigarrillo en la Argentina', Programa BIC/CEPAL de Investigaciones en Temas de Ciencia y Tecnologia, Monografia de Trabajo No. 7, (Buenos Aires, 1977).

'Former government aide claims Italy underselling itself to multinational firms', *Tobacco Reporter* (October 1975), 51–2.

Gereffi, Gary, *The pharmaceutical industry and dependency in the Third World* (Princeton, 1983).

Harrison, John P., 'The evolution of the Colombian tobacco trade to 1875', *Hispanic American History Review* 33 (June 1952), 163–74.

Hirschman, Albert O., *Exit, voice, and loyalty: responses to decline in firms, organizations, and states* (Cambridge, Mass., 1970).

Instituto Nacional de Promocion Industrial y Banco Industrial del Peru, *La industria del tabaco en el Peru* (Lima, 1965).

'Italy: smuggling on the rise', *Tobacco Reporter* (February 1978), 20, 26.

'Japan: reorganizing to build markets', *Tobacco Reporter* (September 1984), 46–50.

'Japan: imports gain as domestic sales fall', *Tobacco Reporter* (September 1985), 48–54.

Leonard, David P., *The Comunero Rebellion of New Granada in 1781: A chapter in the Spanish quest for social justice* (Ann Arbor, Michigan, 1951).

Magee, Stephen P., 'Information and the multinational corporation: an appropriability theory of direct foreign investment', pp. 317–41 in Jagdish N. Bhagwati (ed.), *The new international economic order* (Cambridge, Mass., 1977).

'Malaysia: smuggling accord reached', *Tobacco Reporter* (October 1977), 66.

McGreevey, William P., *An economic history of Colombia, 1845–1930* (Cambridge, 1971).

Newfarmer, Richard S., *Transnational conglomerates and the economics of dependent development* (Greenwich, 1980).

'Multinationals and marketplace magic in the 1980s', in C. Kindleberger and D. Audretsch (eds.) *Multinationals in the 1980s* (Cambridge, Mass., 1983).

Oficina de Relaciones Industriales del Cigarrillo, *La industria del cigarrillo en la Argentina* (Buenos Aires, 1968), mimeo.

Perez Vasquez, Jorge. 'Comentarios sobre el estudio denominando "Consumo de cigarrillos rubios nacionales y extranjeros?" (Medellin: Compania Colombiana de Tabaco, S.A., 1975), mimeo.

Philip Morris Co., Inc. *Annual Report* (1976).

'Philip Morris invests in Uruguayan firm', *Tobacco Reporter* (September 1979), 24.

'Philippines: cigarettes go up in smoke', *Tobacco Reporter* (June 1977), 14.

Republica de Colombia, Departamento Nacional de Planeacion 'Consumo de cigarrillos rubios nacionales y extranjeros' (Bogota, 1975), mimeo.

Shepherd, Philip L., 'Toward a synthesis of product-cycle and demand creation theories of multinational corporate expansion: some introductory notes and comments', Paper presented to a meeting of the Working Group on Latin America and the International System: Multinational Corporations in Latin America, Social Science Research Council (New York, 16 December 1977).

'The dynamics of the international cigarette oligopoly', Discussion Paper for the Working Group on Transnational Corporations, Social Science Research Council (September 1979).

'Soooold American!!! – a study of the development of the foreign operations of the American cigarette industry', unpublished Ph.D. dissertation (Vanderbilt University, 1983).

Sierra, Luis F., *El tabaco en la economia colombiana del siglo XIX* (Bogota, 1972).

'South Korea: ruling party wants to curb flow of US cigarettes', *Tobacco Reporter* (April 1986), 16.

Stein, Stanley J. and Barbara H. Stein, *The colonial heritage of Latin America: essays on economic dependence in perspective* (New York, 1970).

United Nations Conference on Trade and Development (UNCTAD), Trade and Development Board. *Marketing and distribution of tobacco.* (TD/B/C.1/205) June 16, 1978. UN Publication Sales No. E.78.II.14.

United States Department of Agriculture. Foreign Agricultural Service. *Foreign agriculture circular-tobacco.* FT 2-77 (Washington, D.C., July 1977).

United States Department of Health, Education and Welfare, Public Health Service. *Smoking and health: a report of the Surgeon General* (Washington, D.C., 1979).

Vilas, Carlos M. 'Estructura de la propiedad y control en el mercado argentino de cigarrillos', Trabajo inedito (Buenos Aires, 1974), mimeo.

Whiting Jr, Van R. 'Transnational enterprise and the state in Mexico', Ph.D. dissertation (Harvard University, 1981).

19 Summary:
Reflections on the papers and the debate on multinational enterprise: international finance, markets and governments in the twentieth century

CHARLES P. KINDLEBERGER

The papers already published in Teichova, Lévy-Leboyer and Nussbaum (eds.), *Multinational enterprise in historical perspective* (1986), and those now gathered in this volume, are too varied, wide-ranging and rich in fact and analysis to summarise. Perhaps I might, however, be allowed to comment on three issues that strike me as not without intellectual importance. I have in mind the role of technology in the multinational enterprise, the variety of forms of doing international business, and the fact that the choice among exporting, licensing technology, forming cartels, entering contracts, joint ventures, and forming a wholly-owned foreign subsidiary is often a very close one.

As Fieldhouse's useful summary reminds us (1986), we learn from Hymer that business operating away from its home base is always at a disadvantage, because of long lines of communication, operations in a culture which varies in degrees from that at home, at least slightly and perhaps very widely, and the agency problem that perhaps applies to all business and is usefully discussed by Nicholas (1986) – the difficulty at a distance of ensuring that the agent does what the principal has contracted with him to do, rather than operating in his own differing interest. To overcome these disadvantages, such a business must have a large advantage. Chandler (1986) finds this in large size, economies of scale, direct marketing rather than reliance on middlemen, and capital intensity, plus – a point bearing on technology – attention to research and development. But these advantages, it seems to me, start late rather than early in the course of foreign direct investment.

A number of the contributions seem to think that the multinational enterprise came into being, or at least prominence, primarily in the 1960s. One can surely detect embryos of such creatures in foreign direct investment much earlier. Already in the 1930s there was a literature on the subject, if one not so flourishing as that today (Southard, 1931; Phelps, 1936; Marshall, Southard and Taylor, 1936). If we leave out the Vatican as an international business organisation of some antiquity, and such banks as the Medici, Fuggers, Hope and Co., the Rothschilds, Barings, Brown Brothers, Morgans,

Seligmanns, and the like, one can find direct investment as early as 1850, or even 1837 (Kindleberger, 1974, reprinted 1984). Several contributors to the two volumes mention that Siemens, founded in 1847, established a subsidiary in Russia in 1847 and one in Britain in 1858. Most of these early investments in manufacturing were based on new goods or new processes – in the American case labour-saving innovations such as the reaper, sewing machine, cash register, or the Colt method of producing rifles with interchangeable parts. In the German case, the innovation lay in the military application of the telegraph. Henry George, who thought of the United States as an exporter of agricultural products and raw materials and importer of manufactures, waxed ironic about American agencies for selling manufactures abroad – 'curiosity shops' he called them – expecting them to wither away (1886, p. 185). In the nineteenth century the product cycle, which Fieldhouse (1986, p. 22) says is based primarily on the evidence of recent investment overseas, took a long time to lead to such withering. Direct investment not only proceeds from large firms with economies of scale and efficient management, attention to marketing, and so on. It also leads small firms to grow large.

Other points about technology in the early stages of foreign direct investment are worth making. Standardised commodities have qualities which are well understood by purchasers, and can be bought and sold in markets at arms length with no contact between seller and buyer. Hohenberg may have been somewhat parochial in suggesting that software – instruction to the buyer how to use the product – grew up in the chemical industry he was studying (1967). It is none the less clear that with complex manufactured products – fertilizers, farm machinery, electrical appliances, machine tools, and the like – it was necessary to supply the buyer with instruction at a minimum, and in frequent cases demonstrations, spare parts, repair facilities, even in the more complex instances, products specially designed for special needs. In an essay on Swedish multinationals, Sune Carlson emphasises that with a need for software, companies engaged in exporting must establish distributors, spare parts depots, repair instruction and similar facilities, that easily lead from modest beginnings to local manufacture, especially of market-oriented processes such as assembly, or supply-oriented stages such as the manufacture of heavy components. He claims that Volvo, Ericsson and other Swedish companies manufacturing advanced technical products went abroad piecemeal in this fashion, rather than growing large at home and ultimately reaching a stage when they invested overseas in a complete operation. In a vivid metaphor he suggests that most passenger airplanes flying at a given time will have several Swedish sales engineers on board travelling between Stockholm, Göteborg or Malmö and Swedish subsidiaries in the corners of the earth to assist the latter's customers in the design of hardware to their specific needs (1977).

The other technological point is dynamic rather than static. In the same volume with Carlson's essay is an exploration by Jürg Niehans of five Swiss multinationals – Nestlé, Brown Boveri, Ciba-Geigy, Alusuisse and Swiss Reinsurance. Niehans is a theorist and econometrician, but in presenting his paper he said that the best technique for penetrating the nature of the multinational corporation is that of the economic historian. The varied firms he studied make mostly final products which are built up from raw materials and go through a number of intermediate stages. A company producing at one stage only is likely to be afraid of being cut off from a supply of inputs or from markets for outputs. For locational reasons, stages may readily be located in separate countries. But the fear of bilateral monopoly and the need to assure access to inputs and markets leads to vertical integration, as Niehans sees it. The reasoning applies *a fortiori* to perishable products, like bananas, or those with continuous production processes in which interruption of the flow of inputs or the dispatch of outputs is costly, and inputs and outputs are difficult to store in inventories – petroleum, for example, or bauxite, phosphates, or iron ore. In such cases vertical integration enables the head office better to co-ordinate the flow from raw materials in one country to final distribution in others.

The new Japanese groups go further and include with their manufacturing and trading companies an insurance company and a bank so as not to get caught needing credit and unable to get it in a crunch or because of rationing by an outside bank. Moreover the new Japanese method of reducing inventories to a minimum to save capital costs – the so-called 'on time delivery of components' puts a high premium on vertical integration for fear of market failure.

There is a dynamic dimension to vertical integration relating to technical change that is especially illuminating. It is another instance of market failure, that can also be described as involving high transactions costs. I encountered it first in trying to explain, with Thorstein Veblen (1915) and Marvin Frankel (1957), why English railway coal cars remained small when those of other countries were enlarged to a more efficient size, or why English grain farms in East Anglia did not switch to dairy products and meat when the price of wheat fell after 1880 as did especially the farms in Denmark. The market failure arises when different stages in a vertical process are owned by different interests. In the railroads, the coal cars and sidings were owned by the mines, the locomotives and the right of way by the railway companies. Co-ordinate investments were required – in cars and sidings by the mines, and in switches and couplings by the railways – and the profits of the gain in efficiency had to be divided. The market was unable to perform these tasks. In farming, a system of separate landlords and tenant farmer was highly efficient in static conditions, but blocked change that required co-ordinated investment in buildings, tools and stock and division of the efficiency gains (Kindleberger,

1974, pp. 141–7, 247). On a more general level, the problem recalls Paul Rosenstein-Rodan's famous 1943 article on economic development, emphasising external economies in innovation and expansion that can be internalised with planning that coordinates growth in consecutive stages of production in balanced fashion. In this connection, to be sure, one must keep in mind the Hirschman doubts that the market cannot achieve such co-ordination by cheapening outputs and increasing the demand for inputs of industries that grow independently (1958). These examples are, of course, domestic.

For the multinational corporation, Chandler is, of course, correct in emphasising marketing as a function that needs to be taken away from outside wholesalers and jobbers and brought into the firm as scale grows, to convert co-ordination from a market to a management question. But there is more. Technological change at one level in the production chain may require co-ordinated changes at another, that separately-owned levels may find it impossible to achieve. William Lever created his own shipping line, after first chartering ships for his exclusive use, because the Elder-Dempster Line of Liverpool was slow, reluctant or unwilling to substitute tanks for drums in hauling palm oil from West Africa to Britain, or to provide special loading facilities for the tanks (Leubuscher, 1963, p. 48). The most striking example, however, comes from the contrasting changes in the transport of oil, which moved from small T-2 tankers in the Second World War to bigger and bigger ships, limited only by the draft depths at harbours. In 1930, I worked as an ordinary seaman on the MV *Australia* which, at 10,000 tons, was then the largest tanker in the world. Today's standard for unspecialised uses is 200,000 to 300,000 tons, and one ship has gone to 560,000 tons. Much of this shipping is company owned, more when tankerage is tight than when it is in excess. In coal, on the other hand, with separate ownership of mines, railroads, harbour facilities, ships and distribution, the size of ships carrying coal – mostly tramps – is small, while in bauxite and iron ore, bulk carriers have gotten bigger as in oil. A recent development in Hampton Roads, Virginia has been a public investment by the city of Hampton Roads in large-scale loading facilities, and an associated initiative by the Norfolk and Southern Railroad, taking the lead, in a specialised ship for topping up bulk carriers at sea, outside the Chesapeake tunnel at 55 foot draft, that prevents large carriers from getting into the harbour. In consequence after many years of transporting this bulk cargo in retail carriers, mainly liberty ships, the size of coal carriers is growing (Kindleberger, 1985).

Fear of bilateral monopoly and the need for co-ordination of technical change are not unrelated. The critical question is reliability. Can a company count on the market reliably to deliver the appropriate inputs, or to absorb outputs, and can they rely on the demanders and/or suppliers to make the necessary investments in technically-improved facilities when it has an opportunity to gain from a substantial investment in technical change in its own unit?

Unit or agglomeration, and alternate forms of international business

In reading *Multinational enterprise in historical perspective*, I was struck by the phrase 'free-standing corporation' in McKay's essay, for example, and further by the fact that some essays in that book and the present volume treat of cartels as an alternative to the multinational enterprise. Other alternatives to be sure are exporting, licensing technology, joint ventures, and, of increasing interest as it may make possible achieving the same economic end without the objectionable political overtones, the long-term contract. Varied institutional arrangements for international business inspire two lines of thought: one comparing arrangements for doing business across national lines with those in political administration between regions or countries: the empire, unitary state, union, united—, as in the United Provinces of Holland, community, federation, confederation, entente, alliance and so on; second, deriving from a book by a macro-biologist some years ago (Haskins, 1951), suggesting that some species are organised into agglomerations, like flocks of birds, and others into interdependent units, such as a beehive, with queen, drones, workers, and among workers those collecting pollen, nectar, guarding the entrance and assisting the circulation of air in the hive. The question may be put whether the multinational corporation is a unit like a non-decomposable matrix, or simply an agglomeration that can be expanded or cut down without drastic change of function? What is controlled from the centre – assuming there is a recognised centre – new products, capital budgets, top management of the subsidiaries, dividend policy, perhaps exporting by the subsidiary? Are joint costs so large in the system – including the cost of the head office, of advertising to establish brand names, of research and development – that it is impossible to calculate the costs and profits of each unit separately? Does the corporation indulge in a great deal of 'defensive investment', i.e. in units that do not earn a normal return on their own but are created to protect the profits of other units, for example, branches of service companies established to create a presence in out of-the-way localities that may be wanted by clients dealing mainly with the head office or another branch?

The issue has many ramifications. Was the Bhopal disaster the responsibility of the head office of Union Carbide in Connecticut as the Indian government claims or of the Indian unit that allegedly failed to follow out instructions? Should each unit be taxed on the basis of local profits, with intracompany transactions priced on the basis of arm's length competitive prices, or can a case be made for the unitary tax that would tax the subsidiary of a foreign company located in an American state on notional income, calculated as a proportion of the company's world income, with the proportion derived from a simple average of the shares of the company's assets, employees and sales in that state. The unitary tax is bitterly opposed by many corporations and by such organisations as the International Chamber of Commerce and BIAC (the Business and Industry Advisory Committee to the Organisation of Economic Co-operation and Development). The opposition is based on various grounds: it is said to involve double taxation where one jurisdiction taxes on one basis, another on a different one; and especially, it would penalise companies that tolerated losses, or less than normal profits, in a given tax jurisdiction because of defensive investment on the one hand, or in order to break into a new market on the other. American states assert broad principles to the effect that the multinational company is a unit, but often are merely rationalising their own pecuniary interest. Thus New York state, with primarily gasoline distribution, applied the tax to oil companies which try to shelter their profits where crude oil is produced to take advantage of depletion allowances, while Alaska levied it on all companies except those producing oil, in order not to lose taxes on the latter. In the same fashion, companies tend to claim to be agglomerations, with each subsidiary responsible for its actions as a profit centre, especially when disaster occurs as in the Bhopal instance, but sometimes behave as units. In the latter connection, Citicorp asserts control over the assets of all branches from New York, and Exxon and Shell apply zero-based budgeting to capital expenditures, i.e. each year notionally stripping every subsidiary of its cash flow – profit, depreciation and depletion – and rebuilding the subsidiary on a maintained or expanded basis only if it is justified by profit prospects.

The issue is further related to a number of problems raised by the papers in the two volumes. In the electrical industry, for example, the strength of such technocrats as August Detoeuf and Ernst Mercier kept the French subsidiaries of foreign electrical companies quasi-independent, as in an agglomeration (Lanthier, this volume). German fears concerning *Überfremdung* (overforeignisation) discussed by Feldman (this volume) were based on the view of the permanence of such investment, related to the theory of the multinational corporation as a unit, whereas when the advantage held by a foreign direct investor was lost after some time, a considerable part of the investment was undone – in accordance with the agglomeration concept. The recent experience of American multinationals selling off major European subsidiaries to offset losses in the United States and to carry out restructuring – Singer its sewing machine units, ITT those in telecommunications and Chrysler its producing companies – further support the agglomeration unit.

Parenthetically in relation to *Überfremdung* it should be noted that French reaction against US investments did not begin with Servan-Schreiber, who is mentioned by Fieldhouse (1986, p. 17) but can be traced back at least to the end of the 1920s and the books of Hamberg (1929) and Bonnefou-Craponne (1930). Earlier resentment against American corporate investments was expressed in Britain at the beginning of the century (McKenzie, 1901; Thwaite, 1901). In Germany, Gustav Mevissen in 1852 lamented the investment in the Ruhr by French, Belgian and British, including Irish, interests (Kindleberger, 1974 (1984), pp. 206–8).

One further point may be worth making. A fundamental difference between a subsidiary owned by a corporation on the one hand, and cartels and contracts on the other, is that the former is ostensibly a lasting arrangement with no limit set, whereas cartels and contracts are explicitly limited in time. The approach of a limit calling for new arrangements disturbs normal economic incentives. Some contracts are more or less automatically renewed, as for example those in labour negotiations or leases of residential quarters, and some are clearly meant to be unwound on schedule, for example instalment or hire purchase loans. But there is a vast range in between where the approach of the end of a contract produces great uncertainty or distorts normal use. In the 1930s, the European Steel Cartel came close to breaking down with the approach of renewal as each national industry pushed exports to be in position to justify a larger quota in the new contract. John Young of Glasgow advised municipalities planning to expropriate private tramway companies to do so two years before the expiration of the franchise to prevent the operators from running down the companies through neglect of maintenance (McKay, 1976). The Venezuelan government nationalised foreign oil concessions in the 1970s, ten years before they were due to expire, in order to prevent the companies pumping the fields at excessive rates that would have exhausted them. The political advantages of the contract over foreign direct investment recommend them where natural resources are involved provided some means, such as continuous piecemeal renewal, can be found to overcome the disturbance created by periodic major renewals.

Business and economic historians would do well, too, to study the rate of success and failure of joint ventures. My casual observation is that, like alliances, they break up after a few years. In the short run, the enlistment of a local partner may assist the investing corporation in overcoming cultural barriers, defusing a certain amount of xenophobia, acquiring useful information about such idiosyncratic habits such as baksheesh and cheating on taxes. People of good will have advocated joint ventures as a means of moderating the tension between foreign corporations and host countries. The record seems to show, however, that the interests of the two partners rarely coincide for long. The foreign corporation may be interested in long-run profits, the local partner in immediate dividends. The former may more readily tolerate the losses of the start-up period, and be readier than the local investor to add to its investment. Historical analysis of joint ventures is a project that would usefully help to balance the tendency of business historians to study success rather than failure.

The closeness of decisions by business and government

Chandler makes the valid point that foreign direct investment occurs only in oligopolistic industries and that the pattern of such investment differed 'from industry to industry' (1986, p. 51). I would go further and say 'from firm to firm'. Many decisions in the field are so close that two firms in the same industry facing what appear to be similar circumstances will decide to act in different ways. In the discussion at Berne, Stephen Nicholas urged economic historians to tackle the multinational enterprise by gathering masses of statistical data and submitting them to econometric testing. I would counter this advice by pointing out, first, that the data bank assembled some years ago by the Harvard Business School team has gone largely unexploited (Vaupel and Curhan, 1969), suggesting that it is hard to derive useful information from it, and second that information to the effect that firm A has invested abroad while firm B has not implies clear-cut decisions of the go/no-go type, one or zero, whereas actual decisions often wobble in the .55/.45 range. This is attested by diverse paths followed by what appear to be similar companies, by frequent changes of mind by companies, and by frequent shifts of policy regarding foreign direct investment by host countries.

Church describes the decision of General Motors to buy the German automobile company Opel (1986). It might also be noted that both Ford and General Motors turned down an opportunity to buy Citroen in 1919 when it came on the market in need of rebuilding and cash. In the General Motors case the American executives negotiated most of the night and then debated among themselves whether to make an offer or not, deciding against it only just in time to board the morning boat train for the trip back to New York (Wilkins and Hill, 1964, p. 367; Sloan, 1964, p. 317).

Within the same industry, Campbell Soup before the 1960s invested abroad only in Canada, whereas Heinz took its canned goods, including soups, all over the world. Volvo planned an investment in the United States, then withdrew from it, is now reviving the project. Volkswagen first bought the old Studebaker plant in New Jersey, gave it up and abandoned the project, finally converted a railroad repair shop in Altoona, Pennsylvania into an assembly plant for the European model Golf, known in the United States as the Rabbit. In flat glass, St Gobain built a new plant in Tennessee to produce with its new float process, while a few years later Pilkington with a still newer process chose to license it to Pittsburgh Plate Glass for a number of years. When this license finally expired, Pilkington reversed the field to take over the glass subsidiaries of Libby-Owens-Ford and went into production itself. In computers, the German Nixdorf firm undertook production in the United States whereas the Dutch Philips firm, in this line, decided against doing so.

Indecision and changing of minds go on in countries as well. In *American business abroad* (1969, p. 74), I wrote of the ambivalence of the French, quoting the French Ambassador to the United States, Charles Lucet, as saying that French attitudes remained unaltered. It used to be 'No, but...' and remains unchanged as 'Yes, but...'. Similar reversals are noted in the Hjerppe and Ahvenainen essay on Finnish policy (1986). The territorial imperative that leads countries instinctively to limit foreign ownership of natural resources I had first noted in Norwegian legislation going back to 1905. It was directed especially at British ownership of forests, mines and waterfalls, and was inspired by fears of intrusion aroused by the Boer War. In the Finnish case, however, burghers' rights to own land were limited to Finnish nationals as early as 1832, modified in 1851 to extend such rights to Russian nobles. In 1870 an exception was made for sawn timber. Limitations were loosened or tightened – although they remained generally strict – from time to time in accordance with circumstances and need.

Finally with respect to decisions on a firm-by-firm rather than an industry basis, note that this is inescapable in anti-trust matters. To have allowed IBM to buy Machines Bull when it needed an outside partner would have led to monopolisation of the industry, whereas selling it to General Electric, (and later to Honeywell when General Electric backed out) increased the industry's competitiveness. Cases are important, which supports a historical rather than a solely statistical or econometric approach to understanding the phenomenon.

Finally in looking at the papers, I am once more impressed by how political and social factors affecting the multinational corporation are often at war with the economic. This reinforces my belief that the optimum economic area may be the world, whereas the optimum social area is one small enough to give the individual a sense of belonging and identity. There are many economic problems posed by the multinational corporation, including monopoly, market failure, conflicting jurisdictions in taxation, foreign-exchange control and the like. The tension between socio-political and economic factors seems to me to run deeper and to be likely to endure.

REFERENCES

Bonnefou-Craponne, Jean (1930) *La pénétration économique et financière des capitaux américains en Europe* (Paris).
Carlson, Sune (1977) 'Company policies for international expansion: the Swedish experience', in Tamir Agmon and C. P. Kindleberger (eds.), *Multinationals from small countries* (Cambridge, Massachusetts), pp. 49–71.

Chandler, Alfred D. Jr (1986), 'Technological and organizational underpinnings of modern industrial multinational enterprise: the dynamics of competitive advantage' in Alice Teichova, Maurice Lévy-Leboyer and Helga Nussbaum (eds.), *Multinational enterprise in historical perspective* (Cambridge, 1986), pp. 30–54.

Church, Roy (1986), 'The effects of American multinationals on the British motor industry: 1911–83' in Teichova, Lévy-Leboyer and Nussbaum (eds.), pp. 116–30.

Feldman, Gerald D. 'Foreign penetration of German enterprise after the First World War: the problem of Überfremdung', above, pp. 87–110.

Fieldhouse, D. K. (1986), 'The multinational: a critique of concept' in Teichova, Lévy-Leboyer and Nussbaum (eds.), pp. 9–29.

Frankel, Marvin (1957), 'British and American manufacturing productivity: a comparison and interpretation', *University of Illinois Bulletin*, 81.

George, Henry (1886), *Free trade or protection* (New York, reprinted 1980).

Hamberg, Octave (1929), *L'impérialism américaine*

Hirschman, Albert (1958), *The strategy of economic development* (New Haven, Connecticut).

Hohenberg, Paul, M. (1967), *Chemicals in Western Europe, 1850–1914: an economic study of technical change* (Chicago).

Hjerppe, Riitta and Jorma Ahvenainen (1986), 'Foreign enterprise and nationalistic control: the case of Finland since the end of the nineteenth century' in Teichova, Lévy-Leboyer and Nussbaum (eds.), pp. 286–98.

Kindleberger, C. P. (1969), *American business abroad* (New Haven).

Kindleberger, C. P. (1974 (1984)), 'Origins of US direct investment in France' in *Multinational excursions* (Cambridge, Massachusetts, 1984), pp. 118–64.

(1975 (1978)) 'Germany's overtaking of England, 1806–1914', in *Economic response: comparative studies in trade, finance and growth* (Cambridge, Massachusetts), pp. 185–236.

(1985), 'Multinational ownership of shipping activities', *The World Economy* (September), pp. 249–66.

Lanthier, Pierre 'Multinationals and the French electrical industry, 1889–1940', above pp. 143–50.

Leubuschér, Charlotte (1963), *The West African shipping trade, 1909–1959* (Leyden).

Marshall, H., Southard, F. A. and Taylor, K. (1936), *Canadian-American industry* (New Haven).

McKay, John P. (1976), *Tramways and trolleys: the rise of urban transport in Europe* (Princeton).

(1986), 'The House of Rothschild (Paris) as a multinational industrial enterprise: 1875–1914' in Teichova, Lévy-Leboyer and Nussbaum (eds.), pp. 74–86.

McKenzie, Fred A. (1901), *The American invaders: their plans, tactics and progress* (New York).

Nicholas, Stephen (1986), 'The hierarchical division of labour and the growth of British manufacturing multinationals, 1870–1939' in Teichova, Lévy-Leboyer and Nussbaum (eds.), pp. 241–56.

Niehans, Jürg (1977), 'Benefits of multinational firms for a small parent economy: the case of Switzerland' in Tamir Agmon and C. P. Kindleberger, (eds.), *Multinationals from small countries* (Cambridge, Massachusetts), pp. 1–39.

Phelps, D. M. (1936), *Migration of industry to South America* (New York).

Rosenstein-Rodan, Paul N. (1943), 'Problems of industrialization of Eastern and Southeastern Europe', *Economic Journal*, 53 (June-September).

Sloan, Alfred P. Jr (1964), *My years with General Motors* (Garden City, N.Y).

Southard, Frank A. Jr (1931), *American industry in Europe* (Boston).

Thwaite, B. H. (1901), *The American invasion: England's commercial danger* (Wilmington, N.C).

Vaupel, James W. and Joan P. Curhan (1969), *The making of multinational enterprise: a source book of tables based on the study of 187 major US manufacturing corporations* (Boston).

Veblen, Thorstein (1915), *Imperial Germany and the Industrial Revolution* (New York).

Wilkins, Mira and Frank Ernest Hill (1964), *American business abroad: Ford on six continents* (Detroit).

Index of names

Index of firms

243

Index of Subjects

247